DCPL0000340314

MM

Dáil Stars

From Croke Park to Leinster House

D1549835

Conor McMorrow

MENTOR BOOKS

First published in 2010 by
Mentor Books Ltd.,
43 Furze Road
Sandyford Industrial Estate
Dublin 18
Republic of Ireland

Tel: +353 1 295 2112/2   Fax: +353 1 295 2114
e-mail: admin@mentorbooks.ie
www.mentorbooks.ie

A catalogue record for this book is available from the British Library

Copyright © Conor McMorrow

The right of Conor McMorrow to be identified as the author of this work has
been asserted by him in accordance with the Copyright,
Design and Patents Act 1988.

All rights reserved. No parts of this publication may be reproduced, stored in a
retrieval system, or transmitted in any form or by any means electronic,
mechanical, photocopying, recording, or otherwise, without prior written
permission of the publisher.

ISBN: 978-1-906623-58-6

Cover: Mary Byrne
Typesetting and layout: Kathryn O'Sullivan
Editor: Una Whelan

Printed in Ireland by ColourBooks Ltd

Contents

Foreword

ALMOST 90 years after the first meeting of Dáil Eireann in Dublin's Mansion House in 1919, members of the Green Party held a historic meeting at the same venue on 4 June 2007. The members overwhelmingly approved a motion to allow the Greens' six TDs enter government for the first time. It was a momentous decision for a party that had operated on the peripheries of Irish politics for so long.

Some days earlier, after the general election on 24 May, the late Fianna Fáil minister Seamus Brennan got John Gormley's mobile phone number and texted the Green Party leader about the prospect of his party going into government with Fianna Fáil. Eventually the pair spoke on the phone and Gormley began to realise that the offers of negotiation were serious.

When the Green Party ended up in Government Buildings, Seamus Brennan, who was a passionate GAA fan, greeted the party's new ministers with the immortal words: 'You are playing senior hurling now lads.' Brennan ominously added, 'But you are playing with lads who have All-Ireland medals!'

Using the GAA metaphor, Brennan had paid his new government colleagues a considerable compliment. He was using the sporting reference in jest but even a fleeting look through the annals of Dáil and Seanad Éireann shows that Brennan's GAA metaphor rings true; dozens of GAA players have made the leap from playing in Croke Park to the cut and thrust of politics in Leinster House, and further afield in the European Parliament.

Dáil Stars: From Croke Park to Leinster House is an attempt to explore how Ireland's largest sporting organisation has been the launch pad for so many political careers. It is essentially a collection of individual politicians' stories that hopefully, when combined, give a comprehensive picture of the intricate relationship between Irish politics and the GAA.

Jack Lynch's decorated career as a Cork GAA star paved his way to a political career that saw him rise to the office of Taoiseach. The six-time All-Ireland winner is the quintessential Dáil Star. But, as well as prowess on the playing field, the experience of the internal politics of the GAA club or county board has also acted as a training ground for scores of Irish politicians. If prospective politicians can navigate their way through the politics of the GAA, they have a concrete grounding for a career in Leinster House.

During Richard Bruton's failed heave against Fine Gael leader Enda Kenny in June 2010, the Fine Gael parliamentary party held a crunch meeting behind closed doors to decide Kenny's fate. As individual TDs and senators argued for and against Kenny's continuance as leader, Meath East TD Shane McEntee stood up and transformed the scene from a meeting room in the bowels of Leinster House to one akin to a GAA dressing room. A brother of All-Ireland winning footballer Gerry, Shane has trained teams for his local Nobber GAA club and his impassioned speech to the Fine Gael party came straight from the dressing room. With his voice cracking with emotion and tears in his eyes he argued for unity behind Kenny and told his party colleagues that he would 'lie down on that floor and die for you'.

McEntee's speech at a critical moment in the history of Fine Gael contributed to

Kenny's survival. It also showed how politics can arouse levels of passion like those seen in the GAA dressing room.

By exploring the playing and political careers of the GAA's politicians, this book endeavours to probe the nature of their various journeys from Croke Park to Leinster House. Since 1971, All-Star awards have been given to the best player in each of the fifteen positions in hurling and Gaelic football. Echoing those awards this book contains fifteen chapters, each featuring a different politician with a robust GAA pedigree. Politicians have been selected on the Dáil Stars team following consultation with a number of experienced GAA writers and political commentators.

The Dáil Stars players have been chosen on the basis of the positions in which the politicians played during their hurling and football careers. Some players may not feature in the exact position where they played most but each of the six backs, six forwards and two midfielders have been picked as near to their exact position as possible. For example, Fianna Fáil's Seán Flanagan played as a corner-back for much of his playing career with Mayo but he is selected as the full-back on the Dáil Stars team.

The Dáil Stars players have been selected on the basis of a combination of:
- The politician's playing or managerial record/achievements in hurling or football.
- Their contribution to the administrative ranks of the GAA.
- The politician's political record/achievements and length served as a TD.

Although he played little or no GAA, the contribution of Eoin O'Duffy, the first leader of Fine Gael who would later be nicknamed the Irish Mussolini, to the organisation in his native Monaghan and his role as Ulster GAA Secretary in the early part of the last century confirm his GAA credentials and see him selected as goalkeeper in the Dáil Stars team.

The right corner-back is current Fine Gael TD John O'Mahony, who was first elected in 2007. The recently retired Mayo manager won All-Ireland Minor and Under-21 titles with his native county. As a manager he won a breakthrough Connacht title with Leitrim and two All-Ireland titles with Galway.

Coincidentally, the *Dáil Stars* full-back Seán Flanagan hails from the same Ballaghaderreen club as O'Mahony. Flanagan captained Mayo to two of the county's three All-Ireland successes. He served as a Cabinet minister, who famously sought the abolition of the department over which he presided, before completing his political career as an MEP.

Dubbed 'one of the greatest corner-backs of our time' by Taoiseach Brian Cowen in the Dáil chamber in early 2010, Fine Gael TD and Kerry legend Jimmy Deenihan is an automatic choice at left-corner back.

Former Fine Gael TD John Donnellan who featured in Galway's legendary 1960s three-in-a-row team is selected at right half-back and his All-Ireland winning father Mick, who founded the Clann na Talmhan party, is selected at centre half-forward.

Austin Stack, Kerry's 1904 All-Ireland winning captain, revolutionary leader and Cabinet Minister is selected at centre half-back, while John Wilson, twice an All-Ireland winner with Cavan and former Tánaiste, is selected alongside Stack at left half-back.

Mayo's 1936 All-Ireland winning midfielder and Fine Gael TD Henry Kenny, the late father of the party's current leader Enda Kenny, is selected in midfield. And Des Foley, who lifted Sam Maguire for Dublin in 1963 and went on to become a Fianna Fáil TD, completes the midfield pairing.

Although current Fine Gael MEP Seán Kelly is not a member of the Oireachtas, he is selected at right half-forward alongside Mick Donnellan. While not renowned as a player, Kelly's contribution to the GAA's administrative ranks and his role in presiding over the relaxation of Rule 42, the most politically sensitive rule in the GAA rulebook, warrants his inclusion.

Sinn Féin TD Martin Ferris is selected at left half-forward as he won an All-Ireland Under-21 title with Kerry and the story of his early departure from the playing field is intriguing. Ferris was on the fringes of the greatest Kerry team ever in the late 1970s but his involvement in subversive IRA activity saw him quit football for political reasons.

Jack Lynch, the former Fianna Fáil Taoiseach and Cork's six-time All-Ireland winning dual star is selected at right corner-forward. The finest exponent of the way the GAA can launch a successful political career, Lynch is also the *Dáil Stars* team captain.

Dan Spring, former Labour party TD for Kerry North, father of the party's former leader Dick Spring and Kerry's 1940 All-Ireland winning captain, is selected at full-forward.

Roscommon's 1943 and 1944 All-Ireland winning forward, Jack McQuillan, who served as a TD for Clann na Poblachta, the National Progressive Democrats, the Labour party and as an Independent in an extraordinary political career, completes the team at left corner-forward.

As well as the 15 individual chapters on the politicians who make up the *Dáil Stars* team, the book also features a 'Substitutes and Also-Rans' chapter. This chapter looks at some of the other GAA stars who went on to have political careers and the 'also-rans', the GAA stars who unsuccessfully stood for election.

I would like to thank the following people for their help with this book: Dr Fearghal McGarry at Queen's University Belfast, Mickey and Raymond McHugh, Fergal McCarron and his late father Eddie, Jimmy Deenihan TD, Eugene McGee, Dermot Flanagan, Mike Cronin, Donal McAnallen, Mick McCormack, Terry Reilly, John Cunningham in the *Connacht Tribune*, Jim Carney in the *Tuam Herald*, Cllr Colm Keaveney, Ciarán Conlon and colleagues in the Fine Gael press office, Eddie Barrett, John O'Mahony TD, Fintan Lyons, Michael Dermody, Brendan Smith TD and Minister for Agriculture, Philip Hannon, Sheila Reilly in the *Longford Leader*, Kieran Harten, Cllr Shane Reilly, Sinead McGovern formerly of the Fianna Fáil press office, former Tánaiste Dick Spring, Tony Heffernan and colleagues in the Labour Party press office, Ken Foxe, Ali Bracken, Pat Magnier, Enda Kenny TD and Fine Gael leader, Rita Foley, Betty Ward, GV Wright, Daragh O'Brien TD, Senator Martin Brady, Sean Perry, Seán Kelly MEP, Martin Ferris TD, Shaun Tracey, Kaniah Cusack and Seán Mac Brádaigh in the Sinn Féin press office, Finbarr McCarthy, Liam Ó Tuama, TJ Flynn, Tony Conboy in Roscommon, Declan Coyne of Dhá Lon Productions for the copy of his excellent Jack McQuillan radio documentary, Senator Terry Leyden, Angela McQuillan, Colm Keys and Martin Breheny in the *Irish Independent*, Brian Carthy in RTÉ, Cllr Sean McCarthy in Tipperary, Northern Ireland's former Deputy First Minister Seamus Mallon, Alasdair McDonnell MLA, Seamus Kirk TD, the 'voice of the GAA' Micheál Ó Muircheartaigh, Ted Nealon, Dominic Candyman, Pauric Coyle, Miguel Delaney, Ewan MacKenna, Malachy Clerkin, Ger Siggins, Orla Fenelon, Ger Clerkin, Bernard Mallee, Michael Kennedy TD, Clare GAA expert Seamus O'Reilly, Weeshie Fogarty in *Radio Kerry*, Donal Keenan of the *Irish Daily Mail*, Tony Browne Snr in Waterford, Phil Hogan TD, Michael Duffy and Dan Carey of the *Mayo News*, Jack Wall TD, Daniel English and colleagues in the Oireachtas press office, Enda McEvoy, the Gleesons in Tipperary, everyone in the Sean MacDiarmada GAA club, Fergal Quinn, the Murphys of Togan, Sean O'Rourke in RTÉ, Tommie Gorman in RTÉ, the *Off the Ball* crew in Newstalk, the Woods family in Dundalk, Frank McNally in *The Irish Times*, Paddy Fitzsimons and Mick O'Brien in Meath, the Éire Óg crew, Christopher Took and Sean Donnelly for their excellent electionsireland.org website, John Burke of the *Sunday Business Post*, Jonathan Mullin of the *Irish Racing Post*, Colm Dunne, and Liam 'Championship Man' Horan.

I would also like to thank all the political correspondents on the 'prison landing' floor in Molesworth Street, especially Stephen Collins and Déaglán de Bréadún of *The Irish Times*, Paul O'Brien and *The Irish Examiner* crew, Rónán Ó Domhnaill, Micheál Lehane and David McCullagh of RTÉ and Áine Kerr of the *Irish Independent*.

Additional thanks to the staff at the National Archives and the National Library for their courtesy and professionalism.

A special note of gratitude to *Sunday Tribune* political editor Shane Coleman for all his encouragement and for enduring my endless questions, and to my colleague Mick Clifford for his help. To my editor Noirin Hegarty and all my colleagues at the *Sunday Tribune*.

Thanks also to Danny McCarthy at Mentor Books who came up with the original idea for a book about the 'GAA's politicians'; to Treasa O'Mahony at Mentor; and my editor there, Una Whelan for her expert advice and being so easy to work with.

I would like to thank my friends for their support, especially my housemates Shane McGrath (for allowing me to constantly pick his GAA brain), Pauric Marray and Shulagh Callan; and Colm O'Donovan for his help in reading chapters and coming up with suggested improvements.

I would also like to thank my family, especially Marion, Brenda and Kevin McMorrow. And, finally, thanks to Barbara for all her patience and encouragement.

Conor McMorrow
September 2010

For my parents

Marion and Kevin McMorrow,

for giving me a love of the GAA

and a passion for current affairs/politics.

1

Eoin O'Duffy
Goalkeeper

MONAGHAN – FINE GAEL
'The heart and soul of the GAA in Monaghan'

The poet, Patrick Kavanagh, eloquently described how the row had reached fever pitch. His neighbours, the Duffys and the McCabes, were fighting over the ownership rights to a parcel of land between their farms – 'that half a rood of rock, a no-man's-land'.

Kavanagh vividly depicts the scene where he 'heard the Duffys shouting "Damn your soul", And old McCabe, stripped to the waist' in his sonnet 'Epic'.

Towards the end of the sonnet, the Monaghan poet recalls that the agrarian row between the two families happened in 1938, as greater events were unfolding elsewhere: 'That was the year of the Munich bother.'

Kavanagh's reference to the 'Munich bother' draws a tenuous parallel between events in the Third Reich in 1938 and the local row between two farmers. But another one of Monaghan's famous sons had much closer links to the Third Reich – General Eoin O'Duffy.

Leabharlanna Poibli Chathair Bhaile Átha Cliath
Dublin City Public Libraries

O'Duffy invited a Dublin-based Nazi spy to accompany him at an All-Ireland final in 1940, not long after the Munich bother that Kavanagh later alluded to.

During the Second World War O'Duffy was described as 'the representative of the Axis Powers in Ireland' and he appears to have made no effort to conceal his German connections in the years before his death in 1944.

Eduard Hempel was Adolf Hitler's ambassador in Dublin during the war and O'Duffy regularly had dinner with Hempel and his wife Eva. In his eight-year stint as Nazi Germany's Minister to Ireland from 1937 to 1945, Hempel was engaged in espionage activities that saw him send thousands of telegrams and shortwave radio messages to Berlin. These included weather reports and details of German Luftwaffe air raids on Britain. By helping the German forces through his actions, Hempel nearly compromised Ireland's neutrality during the war.

Hempel's colleague in Dublin at the time was Henning Thomsen, an SS officer and diplomat who later became Germany's ambassador to Iceland. Even though Hempel and Thomsen both doubled as Nazi intelligence agents, this did not deter O'Duffy from associating with the two men.

A British military intelligence memo dated September 1940 shows that O'Duffy invited Thomsen to accompany him to the All-Ireland final in 1940, where Kerry defeated Galway by a single point in front of 60,821 spectators.

History has not been kind to O'Duffy and he is often discredited as a *prima donna* who had neurotic, fascist and alcoholic tendencies in his later career.

But it would be wrong to simply remember O'Duffy as the Irishman who invited a Nazi to an All-Ireland final, for he once commanded huge respect in GAA circles.

The long defunct publication, *The Gaelic Athlete* in 1914 described O'Duffy as 'the life of the game, not only in Monaghan, but all over Ulster'. In the same year the *Dundalk Democrat* said: 'A Gael out and out, Mr O'Duffy was the heart and soul of the GAA in Monaghan.'

O'Duffy, who later became one of the most influential public figures in Ireland in the twentieth century, was born in Carrickaduff, near Castleblayney, County Monaghan on 28 January 1890.

Contrary to what some believe, he did not play hurling or football and his involvement in the GAA began off the field when he joined the Monaghan Harps club in Monaghan town after he got his first job as a council surveyor in the town.

His involvement in the administrative ranks of the GAA fashioned the course of his later life. His connections with the organisation began when he became the honorary secretary of Monaghan County Board on 21 September 1912. O'Duffy's organisational prowess was such that he was appointed secretary of the GAA's Ulster provincial council just two months later.

His annual reports as Monaghan County Board secretary dating from 1913 and 1914 are almost as pertinent to the challenges facing the modern day GAA organisation as they were nearly a century ago.

Records show that, in compiling the reports, O'Duffy proposed a series of improvements to the GAA in Monaghan. These included improvements to the county leagues that would reduce the number of delayed games. He also donated his expenses back into the organisation to help offset the county board's deficit.

At Ulster council level, O'Duffy did much to lay the foundations of the modern GAA in the province by overseeing a huge growth in the organisation. The number of GAA clubs in Ulster flourished from just over 30 to more than 110 within a two-year period up to 1914.

He also oversaw his own county win the Ulster hurling and football titles in 1914. This was in no small part due to reforms he introduced for the selection of the county teams, whereby players from weaker clubs were given a fair chance of selection. He attributed Monaghan's dual Ulster successes in 1914 to the sense of unity among the players that had suppressed the 'interior jealousies and dividing lines' within the county.

When O'Duffy resigned as secretary of Monaghan County Board in 1914, he was lauded for his legacy in that role. Two successful county teams had been selected 'without fear or favour'.

He held other positions on the county board but he was by no means an evangelical character within the GAA. For every positive contribution he made, confrontation and roguery were never too far away from his path.

Take the Toal Cup final in Monaghan in 1916 for example. In the definitive biography of O'Duffy, *Eoin O'Duffy: A Self-Made Hero*, Queen's University Belfast historian Fearghal McGarry records O'Duffy's bizarre intervention in that game.

O'Duffy's home team of Clones lost the game to Clontibret. But O'Duffy, still a high-ranking county board official, decided that the referee had prematurely ended the game. He refused to present the cup to the winning Clontibret captain and scheduled a replay to be played at a venue closer to Clones.

McGarry also describes details of a much more serious incident the previous year. Monaghan's neighbours and arch rivals, Cavan, beat them by a single point in the 1915 Ulster final. Monaghan supporters were furious. They complained that the encroachment of spectators onto the pitch had hindered their team's chances. They were further enraged when a Monaghan goal was disallowed by the Cavan umpires.

O'Duffy thought he had a solution. Despite being from Monaghan and as ardent a Monaghan supporter as anyone else present, he demanded that the result be overturned.

O'Duffy's biased request was heard at the next meeting of the GAA's Ulster Council. Cavan denied any wrongdoing on the day of the final but they failed to send a representative to the crucial Ulster Council meeting. Without a Cavan voice in the room, the Ulster Council president Patrick Whelan, who was also head of the Monaghan County Board, heard O'Duffy's request. Not surprisingly, he approved it.

At the time, the GAA's Central Council rarely intervened in the affairs of a particular provincial council. But they could not sit idly by. Such was the scale of O'Duffy's 'stroke' that they later overruled the Ulster body's decision.

The intense GAA rivalry that still exists between Cavan and Monaghan, which share a Dáil electoral constituency, is not as intense as the bitter feeling that existed between the two counties in O'Duffy's era. Two years after the controversial Ulster final, Cavan threatened to leave the Ulster Council on the grounds that the two men behind the 'stroke' – O'Duffy and Whelan – were still wielding so much power on the board.

Throughout his involvement in the GAA, O'Duffy was vehemently opposed to foreign games and he complained in his 1914 annual report as county board secretary that 'the game of the foreigner is promoted to the exclusion of our native pastimes'. His support for the ban on GAA members playing 'foreign sports' was so strong that he withheld an Ulster championship medal from a county player who was caught playing soccer.

After attending a match in Croke Park in November 1917, he was taken to the home of a friend to be introduced to Michael Collins. O'Duffy claims that he joined the Volunteers within an hour of meeting Collins. He recorded how Collins in his 'businesslike yet cheerful manner' said he had heard of O'Duffy's prolific organisation of the GAA in Monaghan, but he also noted that the Volunteers were not so strong in the county.

'When Collins talked of national matters, few young Irishmen could resist the infection of his enthusiasm. The upshot was that I went back to Monaghan a Volunteer and within a short time had recruited virtually every able-bodied member or supporter of the GAA into Volunteer activities,' wrote O'Duffy six years after his meeting with Collins.

O'Duffy's respect for Collins was reciprocated. Collins would later refer to his 1917 recruit as 'the best man by far in Ulster'.

O'Duffy used the GAA as a recruiting ground to great effect and Dan

Hogan, a clerk in Clones train station and celebrated Monaghan county player, would become O'Duffy's right-hand man.

Dan Hogan's brother Michael was a Tipperary footballer who was one of 14 people killed in Croke Park on Bloody Sunday, 21 November 1920. Michael Hogan's name was later given to the Hogan Stand at Croke Park.

In 1918 all unscheduled public gatherings were banned. In Monaghan, GAA matches were broken up while Orange Order parades were tolerated. O'Duffy was outraged at this demonstration of the injustice of British rule.

GAA matches were only allowed to be played after the Royal Irish Constabulary (RIC) had granted a permit. But O'Duffy defied the RIC and refused to apply for a permit for the Armagh-Cavan Ulster final on 7 July.

When the players and supporters arrived at the pitch, they found it occupied by RIC men and British soldiers. O'Duffy was so angry that he had to be restrained from storming the field. This harassment, as O'Duffy viewed it, sparked a national GAA event that will forever be remembered in the annals of the GAA.

Following the RIC and army occupation of the pitch in Cootehill, County Cavan on Ulster Final day, O'Duffy complained of RIC harassment at the GAA county convention the following month. The result was the Ulster Council later endorsed O'Duffy's refusal to apply for permits. It was agreed that the unlicensed matches be played in as many parishes as possible on 4 August.

This event was later endorsed by the GAA's Central Council and over 100,000 Gaels participated in the orchestrated act of defiance that became known as 'Gaelic Sunday'.

Meanwhile, O'Duffy was involved in another incident. Liam Walsh, who was O'Duffy's secretary and acolyte, wrote an unpublished biography of O'Duffy entitled, *General O'Duffy: His life and battles*, and it provides a vivid account of the events of 18 July 1918.

Following the RIC and army harassment at the Ulster final on 7 July, the game was re-fixed for the same Cootehill venue on 18 July. After the match O'Duffy and Hogan, along with around 30 companions, set off for home on bicycles, having cycled from Clones that morning.

As they pedalled along, one of them looked behind to see they were being followed by a group of RIC men, also on bicycles. O'Duffy could not resist the temptation. Knowing that wherever his group went, the RIC were likely to follow, he decided to have a little fun at their escorts' expense.

It was a hot July day. O'Duffy's group were all fit and athletic while the RIC were what O'Duffy called, 'well-fed gentlemen with heavy uniforms and mounted on heavier official machines'.

So instead of taking the direct road home through the village of Newbliss, O'Duffy's group did a circular tour of the area, arriving back at the same place three times. The wild goose chase over the hilly byroads of Monaghan in the sweltering heat exhausted the police who eventually gave up. But they did get their revenge.

Hogan and O'Duffy had used whistles to tell their group to mount and dismount their bicycles on the day. And at 6 a.m. a few days later, the pair were awakened by police and soldiers who arrested them.

They were charged with 'unlawful assembly by leading a procession of cyclists from Clones to Cootehill and back, and blowing whistles as signals for mounting and dismounting'.

The arrests were made because the whistle was seen as a weapon of sorts, for use in drills by Volunteers. O'Duffy feigned shock about his arrest for his use of the whistle and told the RIC with his tongue in cheek that he was using the whistle 'like any cycling club'.

Their trial took place in September where they refused to put up sureties of £25 pounds each, as O'Duffy thought it 'unthinkable' to pay bail. O'Duffy and Hogan were subsequently sentenced to two months in prison in Belfast.

Convict 1089 (O'Duffy) and Convict 1090 (Hogan) were placed in separate cells on D-wing in Crumlin Road Jail Belfast, where well-known personalities such as Ernest Blythe, Austin Stack and Kevin O'Higgins were also political prisoners.

By September 1918, O'Duffy was a brigade officer in the IRA, and his internment that year did nothing to deter his republicanism.

In February 1920 he was involved in the capture of an RIC barracks by the IRA in Ballytrain, County Monaghan. It was the first major event of the War of Independence in the county. O'Duffy led 20 volunteers to Ballytrain, while numerous others blocked the roads around it and cut down telephone wires. After O'Duffy and his men had surrounded the barracks the RIC men inside surrendered and O'Duffy's men robbed their guns. This was the IRA's first capture of an RIC barracks and the pattern of attack used was soon replicated all over the country.

O'Duffy was now a wanted man by the British authorities. But he remained active in the GAA. On 17 March 1920 the Ulster GAA convention was held at Conlon's Hotel in Clones and O'Duffy entered the meeting in disguise as RIC men were waiting outside to arrest him.

He managed to escape before the meeting was adjourned when the RIC raided it. The adjourned meeting was held the following month in Armagh where O'Duffy was arrested. He had attended that meeting without any disguise as he wanted to be arrested. The reason for this was that he wanted to be incarcerated in jail in Belfast again so he could organise a hunger strike. The subsequent hunger strike eventually led to the release of a number of Monaghan prisoners and O'Duffy acolytes.

With his men back home and out of prison, O'Duffy embarked on a campaign of raids on the homes of Unionists in North Monaghan to rob guns. As the 'Troubles' escalated a number of GAA competitions were postponed. The 1921 Ulster final between Derry and Monaghan was one of these fixtures. It was rescheduled for Derry on 22 January 1922.

The Monaghan team had more than playing football on their minds. Three local IRA men were in jail in Derry. The three were under death sentence and due to be hanged so the Monaghan players had decided to use the Ulster final as a decoy. They would travel to Derry to play the game and rescue the three IRA men while they were there.

The team, of which Dan Hogan was captain, were stopped at Dromore,

County Tyrone on their way to Derry. After they were found to be in possession of arms, ten players including Hogan were arrested and imprisoned in Derry jail.

As O'Duffy had recruited most of them to the IRA, he devised a plan for their release. He contacted Michael Collins and proposed his radical strategy. O'Duffy's reprisal involved a sudden swoop on the homes of over a hundred unionists in Fermanagh, Derry and Tyrone.

At 7 p.m. on 7 February, O'Duffy's men started to kidnap unionists. Within 24 hours they had captured over 40 hostages, some of whom were taken by car to Clones. From there they were taken to Trim, County Meath where they were held in the local RIC barracks that had been taken under IRA control.

O'Duffy ordered that they should not be released until Hogan was released. He warned, 'There will be no peace while a number of our people there are held in custody.'

The incident sparked outrage across Northern Ireland with unionist leader James Craig requesting permission to send 5,000 Specials south of the Border to retrieve the hostages. Winston Churchill, the colonial secretary, refused Craig's request for fear of civil war breaking out between North and South. Lloyd George, who had recently signed the Anglo-Irish Treaty with Collins, warned Collins that the kidnappings 'gravely imperil the Treaty'.

Three days after the O'Duffy raids, a spectacular shoot-out took place between the IRA and the A Specials in Clones train station, leaving one IRA officer and four Specials dead. Twenty others were injured in the incident.

A few days later, O'Duffy publicly warned of his 'gravest fears for what may happen'. He claimed that the shoot-out was caused by the continued detention of Hogan.

On 21 February, as the situation threatened to escalate into further bloodshed, the British authorities defused the violence with the release of Hogan in return for the release of the hostages. The capture of the captain of Monaghan's football team had sparked a major diplomatic incident, just weeks after the Treaty was signed.

In May 1921 O'Duffy was elected as a Sinn Féin TD for Monaghan in the second Dáil on the back of a poll-topping 7,298 votes.

After serving as Chief of Staff of the Free State Army during the Civil War, O'Duffy was later appointed commissioner of the new An Garda Síochána force in September 1922. He displayed prolific organisational skills in establishing the new police force and leading their challenge of restoring order to a state that had been lawless since 1919. But he also abused his high-ranking position to the benefit of one of his life's passions – Monaghan GAA. Fearghal McGarry's biography of O'Duffy describes how he had a tendency to transfer the best Gaelic footballers in the gardaí to Monaghan, for obvious reasons.

From his early days of involvement with the GAA in Monaghan, O'Duffy maintained his strong relationship with the organisation and he was treasurer of the GAA's Ulster Council from 1921 to 1934. Holding this honorary position provided him with a seat on the GAA's national ruling body, the Central Council.

Shameless in transferring promising members of the gardaí to Monaghan for football reasons, O'Duffy was also willing to use his influence at national level. In 1927 he represented the GAA in talks with the government that led to the Department of Finance making the GAA exempt from taxation, unlike rugby and soccer, in the 1927 Finance Act.

Following the election of Fianna Fáil in February 1932, Éamon de Valera had O'Duffy removed from his role as Garda Commissioner.

However his influence on Irish sport continued. His impact was immense as he also held positions in the Irish Amateur Handball Association, the National Athletic and Cycling Association and the Irish Olympic Association.

O'Duffy proved himself an outstanding sports coach as well as an administrator and the highlight of his coaching exploits must be when he was made team manager of the Irish Olympic team at the 1932 Olympic Games in Los Angeles.

Funded by a church gate collection, the team travelled by ferry from Cobh to New York before travelling day and night by train through Chicago, Denver, Colorado, and Salt Lake City to Los Angeles.

The Irish team visited the Metro-Goldwyn-Meyer studios in Hollywood, where O'Duffy met film star Maureen O'Sullivan. He was also invited to Beverley Hills to meet Douglas Fairbanks, the host of the first ever Oscar ceremony in 1929, and his wife Mary Pickford, who was known as 'America's Sweetheart'.

On the way to the plush Beverley Hills mansion of one of Hollywood's most famous couples, O'Duffy mistakenly called to the house of another of the film industry's superstars – Charlie Chaplin.

At the opening ceremony of the twentieth Olympic Games, each country's team paraded around the stadium behind a banner bearing the country's name and somebody holding their national flag.

The Irish team of four track-and-field athletes and four boxers insisted on carrying the tricolour and their country being called 'Ireland' and not 'The Irish Free State'. Moments before the ceremony, O'Duffy discovered that the US athletics authorities had arranged for the Irish team to march behind a banner inscribed 'The Irish Free State'. He immediately protested and threatened to withdraw the Irish competitors. He said, 'We refuse to compete as representatives of a truncated Ireland.' O'Duffy got his way; the authorities had evidently pre-empted such an incident as they had another banner inscribed 'Ireland'.

Bob Tisdall won a gold medal for Ireland in the 400 metres hurdle event. Tisdall actually broke the world record with his time of 51.7 seconds but the record was not recognised under the rules at the time because he had hit one of the hurdles. The rules were later changed and Tisdall was presented by the president of the International Olympic Council with a Waterford Crystal rose bowl etched with a picture of him hitting the hurdle.

Tisdall had never run the hurdles before the Olympics and only got into the Irish team after writing a letter to O'Duffy asking if he could be considered for the event.

On the same day that Tisdall won gold, Corkman Dr Pat O'Callaghan achieved an impressive feat. He had been the first man to ensure that the tricolour was raised and that 'Amhrán na bhFiann' was played at the Amsterdam Olympic Games four years earlier in 1928 when he won gold in the hammer-throwing event. He remarkably retained his Olympic title at the Los Angeles games in 1932 – a few hours after Tisdall's success.

From establishing GAA clubs across Ulster to overseeing one of the most successful days in Irish sporting history, O'Duffy had an immense influence on Irish sport.

⑨

The same year as the 1932 Olympic games, the Army Comrades Association (ACA) was founded as a welfare organisation for former members of the Irish Free State Army. The association adopted the role of protecting the political meetings of the pro-Treaty Cumann na nGaedheal party from disruption and interference by the IRA.

Members of the ACA wore blue shirts and black berets and they became known as the Blueshirts. After joining in 1933, it was not long before O'Duffy was promoted to the role of leader of the movement, which was then called The National Guard. An admirer of the Italian leader Benito Mussolini, O'Duffy saw that his organisation adopted symbols of European fascism such as the straight-arm Roman salute.

Replicating the recruiting ability he used to garner Volunteers from the GAA, the ranks of the Blueshirts swelled under O'Duffy, especially in County Monaghan.

In August 1933 a 'March on Dublin', imitating Mussolini's March on Rome, was planned by the Blueshirts to commemorate Arthur Griffith and Michael Collins. De Valera banned the march due to fears of a *coup d'état*.

But de Valera's ban did not deter O'Duffy who by now was nicknamed the Irish Mussolini. He held rallies throughout Ireland, with one of the largest taking place in Monaghan town on 20 August 1933.

The Blueshirts were later renamed The Young Ireland Association to circumvent a ban placed on the organisation by de Valera, making it illegal.

O'Duffy's involvement in a radical movement like the Blueshirts saw him create a lot of enemies within the ranks of the GAA. He drifted away from the organisation. His official ties were broken at the Ulster GAA convention in February 1934, when he was voted out of the role of treasurer on the Ulster Council.

The Fine Gael party was born in September 1933 following a merger of Cumann na nGaedheal, the Centre Party and the Blueshirt movement.

Even though he was not a TD, O'Duffy became the first leader of the party with WT Cosgrave serving as the party's parliamentary leader. Although he was an impeccable military leader, he was a weak political leader. His temperament was not suited to politics and he resigned suddenly from Fine Gael on 18 September 1934.

O'Duffy's short stint as president of Fine Gael was disastrous as it destroyed his credibility and reputation. Motivated by egotism and megalomania, O'Duffy's rhetorical speeches caused violence and rioting. He was a source of embarrassment to the party. Key figures in Fine Gael such as James Dillon and Ned Cronin were instrumental in forcing his resignation. History has not been kind to him as he is still looked upon with disdain.

After leaving Fine Gael, McGarry notes that O'Duffy's resignation 'left him free to follow his instincts towards undisguised fascism'. In June 1935 O'Duffy launched a new political party which was unashamedly fascist – the National Corporate Party. This party had no mandate or support but O'Duffy used it to portray himself as the leader of Irish fascism in the eyes of European fascists.

In 1936 O'Duffy rose to international prominence as an ally of General Franco in the Spanish Civil War. O'Duffy later wrote a memoir entitled *Crusade in Spain* about the travails of his Irish Brigade in Spain.

The lyrics of Christy Moore's song 'Viva la Quince Brigada' describes how O'Duffy's men set off for Spain with the blessing of the Catholic church in Ireland:

Many Irishmen heard the call of Franco
Joined Hitler and Mussolini too
Propaganda from the pulpit and newspapers
Helped O'Duffy to enlist his crew.
The call came from Maynooth, 'support the fascists'
The men of cloth had failed yet again
When the Bishops blessed the Blueshirts in Dun Laoghaire
As they sailed beneath the swastika to Spain.

When O'Duffy's men landed in Spain they saw little fighting. In fact the Irish Brigade proved themselves inadequate men of violence. After killing more of their own side than the enemy, and getting embroiled in a number of drunken sprees, they were sent home by Franco in 1936.

After the self-made 'Irish Mussolini' was sent home disgraced from Spain he started drinking heavily and his life went into terminal decline.

With the outbreak of World War II, O'Duffy was expected in some quarters to become a player in the world of European fascism but this did not materialise. He drifted into a political and personal wilderness at his Dublin home and he was regarded as a failure. On 13 November 1944, after a series of treatments for alcohol poisoning and bouts of bad health, O'Duffy died at the age of 54.

During these years of decline O'Duffy maintained links with Nazis in Ireland such as Eduard Hempel and Henning Thomsen. And so we see him, shortly before his death, inviting the SS officer Thomsen to the All-Ireland final in 1940. They may have been two inconsequential figures in the middle of the 60,821 spectators who watched Kerry beat Galway on that day but O'Duffy left a legacy in the GAA and Irish sport that should never be forgotten.

John O'Mahony
Right Corner-Back

MAYO – FINE GAEL

'The greatest pleasure in life is doing what people say you cannot do.'

It's Kildare 1–5 to Galway's 0–5 when referee John Bannon blows the whistle to signal half-time in the 1998 All-Ireland football final. After opening the game brilliantly, Galway have not scored in ten minutes. Kildare are in the ascendancy.

During the half-time analysis on RTÉ television, former Mayo and Donegal star Martin Carney talks up the Lilywhites' chances. His co-analyst Pat Spillane says, 'Kildare are totally dominating.'

Deep in the bowels of Croke Park, the Galway squad is in the dressing room. Steamy sweat rises from the fifteen men who have played the first 35 minutes. They sit down, sipping water bottles and listening to their manager.

John O'Mahony is dressed in a maroon top with the word 'Bainisteoir' emblazoned in white print across the back of it. He stands in the dressing room with his left hand out. He keeps circling the room, pointing the index finger of his outstretched hand at the players as he moves slowly around. He looks passionately into the eyes of each of his players as he talks to them.

He shouts, 'There is going to come a time after ten or fifteen minutes when it's there for whoever wants it.

'Now I know that Galway want it. I know that, deep down, each one of you know that you deserve it, but you have got to go and take it by the jugular at that stage.

'And remember they will be coming in waves at you. But remember,' his voice continues to rise, 'you have stopped them more than any team has stopped them this year already in the first half. And ye haven't played well at all. Now do we fucking want it, really, really want it? Now's the time. Let's go for it!'

O'Mahony has left the hairs standing on the back of the necks of every member of the Galway squad.

He takes the 15 players who will start the second half into an adjoining room. In that room, used for pre-match warm-ups, the 15 men get into a huddle with O'Mahony in the centre. He talks to them again before they all give a collective roar and head for the pitch.

Their time has come. It is time to go out and win Galway's first All-Ireland since 1966. Thirty-five minutes later they have done it. The scoreboard reads: Gaillimh 1–14, Cill Dara 1–10.

O'Mahony has immortally etched his name into the annals of Galway GAA history. But it has been a long time coming.

A native of Kilmovee, County Mayo, O'Mahony played football for the nearby Ballaghaderreen club. He won a number of underage honours before breaking into the Mayo county minor team in the early 1970s.

He is remembered as a dogged right corner-back. He won an All-Ireland Minor title with Mayo in 1971 and his second All-Ireland title at under-21 level three years later. As well as winning the All-Ireland titles in 1971 and 1974, Mayo were runners-up in the 1973 Under-21 final when they were beaten by Kerry.

Mayo won the National Football League in 1970 and the successes of the minor and under-21 teams suggested that O'Mahony was one of a privileged group of players with a bright future ahead of them.

O'Mahony recalls, 'That was the Kerry team that went on to win all those All-Irelands, so there was reason to be optimistic about the future of Mayo football.

'We lost narrowly to Kerry in 1973 in that All-Ireland final in Ennis. That team contained Jimmy Deenihan and I was actually marking Martin Ferris, who is now a Sinn Féin TD.

'It was Micheál Ó Muircheartaigh who reminded me a few years ago that I was marking him [Martin Ferris] in the final. We, Ferris and myself, are actually sitting about five seats away from each other in the Dáil now so it is remarkable what happened. It really is a small world in many respects.'

After the Under-21 win over Antrim in 1974, Mayo had serious ambitions to go on and win the Sam Maguire Cup for the first time since Seán Flanagan lifted it for the county in 1951. But the promise of the early 1970s never materialised.

O'Mahony remembers, 'The 1970s was a very barren time for Mayo. It was one of the few decades where we didn't even win a Connacht title.'

He was on the senior team when minnows Sligo beat Mayo in the 1975 Connacht final.

He recalls, 'That was the last time I played in the championship. It was seen as sacrilege, almost, to lose to Sligo and the team was broken up after that. So I was a retired senior county footballer at 23 years of age.'

As the door of inter-county football slammed behind him, O'Mahony's managerial career began.

Taking up a job as a geography teacher at St Nathy's College in Ballaghaderreen, County Roscommon, where he had been a pupil, the young teacher started to coach school football teams.

The fledgling manager took control of the Mayo under-21 team when he was just 30 and by the autumn of 1987 he was appointed to the senior team role.

'We won two Connacht Championships back to back in 1988 and 1989 which had not been done for over 30 years. Then we got to the All-Ireland final in 1989. The rollercoaster of management really took off after that, in the sense that I would have always maintained that I was constructively dismissed in 1991.

'I felt at the time that I should have been given longer in the role. We had reached the All-Ireland in 1989 and that team had come to the end of its development stage. But we had started a new team. It was felt that a fresh voice was needed and that is what happened.'

O'Mahony says he was very hurt by the way the Mayo County Board ousted him from the job in 1991 and he took a year out of management after that.

He says, 'I had an option at that stage to start whingeing about what happened or continue my managerial career – and Leitrim gave me the opportunity.'

Leitrim were the whipping boys of Connacht GAA. With a population that would easily fit into one of the stands in Croke Park, they had a tiny pool of talent to pick from and they had not won a Connacht title since 1927.

But there were some green shoots of hope. The county won the Connacht Under-21 title in 1991 and there was a real sense of optimism growing when the Leitrim County Board invited O'Mahony to become their new manager in the autumn of 1992.

O'Mahony recalls, 'At the time Leitrim were going well. They had played Roscommon for two or three years in the championship and they were only losing by a point or two.

'What Tony McGowan, their county board chairman at the time, saw in me was that I had won Connacht titles. Winning a Connacht Championship would have been as good as winning an All-Ireland for them at the time.'

When O'Mahony could see that the county board was serious about Leitrim going places, he asked to meet some of the players as well. He soon discovered that they were even more driven.

It was not the norm at the time for managers to leave their own county to manage elsewhere – and O'Mahony was initially reluctant to be one of the first.

He asked the Leitrim County Board if they had anyone else in mind for the job. They said that All-Ireland winning manager and journalist Eugene McGee and former Fermanagh player Peter McGinnity were in the shake-up.

'I told them if they had somebody else in mind, "Give it to them". He [McGowan] told me the other two were in the mix but he was back two days later to say that the job was mine. I never found out if I got it after they had turned it down,' he laughs.

Once O'Mahony was convinced of the Leitrim players' determination to make a breakthrough, he started to enjoy the challenge.

'I really enjoyed it because I was in a situation where people said it would be an impossible thing to do. I have a little saying in my office at home: "The greatest pleasure in life is doing what people say you cannot do." I have it on a plaque in the office.'

Five years after taking up his first senior inter-county management post with Mayo, O'Mahony's techniques were ahead of their time. He was one of the first GAA managers to use video analysis of opponents' games. He also utilised his own methods of sports psychology to great effect.

He explains, 'When I started to mentally develop the Leitrim team, I got together a montage of newspaper headlines. These were headlines from Leitrim's games in the Connacht Championship where they had been well beaten.

'I put them together on the wall and got the players to confront the perception that was out there about Leitrim being no-hopers. Then I asked them what they would like the headlines to be. I got the players to visualise what the headlines would be like and I worked to bring them through that process.'

In the middle of the montage of dreary headlines describing Leitrim's defeats, O'Mahony had his phrase, 'The greatest pleasure in life is doing what people say you cannot do.'

He remembers, 'Eventually they were able to produce their own headlines in the sense that they were miracle workers and competing with the best. I confronted them with the task of doing things that people said they couldn't do and I enjoyed that.'

Leitrim beat Roscommon by a point and Galway by a point after a replay before they met Mayo in the 1994 Connacht final.

O'Mahony recalls, 'There were 25,000 people living in Leitrim. That is the size of a few housing estates in some of the bigger urban areas in other counties. The message that I kept on telling those guys was that they had to do everything better than anyone else at the time – and in fairness they did.'

Leitrim ended their 67-year famine on a scoreline of Leitrim 0–12, Mayo 2–4.

'It was fantastic to win that final. We beat Mayo in the Connacht final. That was hard for me. It is always a traumatic thing to beat your own county.

'But it was amazing because there were 30,000 people at the match. About 25,000 of them were from Leitrim. The Mayo people did not travel in big numbers to the match in Roscommon as they would have assumed that they were going to be playing in an All-Ireland semi-final.

'I must say, at the end of the game, the Mayo supporters were actually happy for Leitrim. Leitrim were a universal underdog and the country rejoiced in their win.

'Mayo supporters were very magnanimous. I remember getting home in the early hours of the morning and getting 40 or 50 messages of goodwill and congratulations. They were mainly from Mayo GAA supporters – so that was very gratifying.'

Twice in O'Mahony's tenure as Leitrim manager, his team beat the most successful football county in the west – Galway.

As is tradition in the GAA, the winning manager goes into the losing team's dressing room after championship games as a sporting gesture – to offer his best wishes to the dejected team.

'Leitrim had beaten them in 1993 and 1994 and I had been in the Galway dressing room and had a look around at the players. I was saying to myself what if these lads could implement what the Leitrim boys had done, given the pool of talent that Galway had,' says O'Mahony.

After the 1996 championship he stepped down as Leitrim manager and he jumped at the opportunity to manage Galway when a number of GAA clubs in the county asked him to take on the role.

He explains, 'I wasn't required in Mayo as they had contested the 1996 All-Ireland. It turned out that they contested the 1997 All-Ireland as well, and John Maughan was manager so there was no question of Mayo coming back looking for me.

'I had enjoyed the management gig and when the opportunity came to manage Galway, I jumped at it.

'Some people in Mayo saw that differently to the time when I took the Leitrim job. People would have said, "Well he won't do much damage there [in Leitrim]." But Galway was different as they were the main Connacht rivals to Mayo.

'But I didn't take the Galway job to get back at Mayo in any sense. It was because I wanted to further my own managerial career.'

Not only did O'Mahony further his own managerial career, he led Galway to their first All-Ireland since 1966.

In a new departure for the GAA that came some years before the global phenomenon of reality television, Galway's substitute goalkeeper and documentary-maker Pat Comer, captured every moment of Galway's journey in a fly-on-the-wall documentary called *A Year 'til Sunday*.

That landmark documentary gave a behind-the-scenes insight into the Galway camp that included O'Mahony's phenomenal half-time team talk, detailed earlier, during the All-Ireland final.

So was this passionate talk standard fare from O'Mahony?

He smiles, 'That would be typical. You tap into the pulse or the psyche of whatever team or county you have. That speech would not be typical of modern management as the art of management has changed a lot over the years.

'The fire and brimstone that would have been there 20 years ago is gone and now it is much calmer and more scientific, so there has been a transition period since then.

'You are always evolving. There are times when you want to bring a sense of emotion to what you say. You want to evoke the emotions but you want to encourage calmness because you want the energies to be used on the field rather than in the dressing room.

'The nature of the GAA over the years is that the emotions are evoked as well and that was part of that.'

Galway's 1998 All-Ireland win was no flash in the pan victory. O'Mahony's team drew the 2000 final with Kerry on a scoreline of 0–14 each. Kerry won the reply by four points.

Galway got back to the final again the following year and demolished Meath, on a scoreline of Galway 0–17 to Meath's 0–8, in a game that saw Pádraig Joyce score a personal tally of ten points.

Looking back on his two All-Ireland successes with Galway, O'Mahony says, 'The Galway years amounted to elation and euphoria in 1998, regret in 2000 when we lost the replay to Kerry, and great satisfaction in 2001 when we beat Meath. If you include the All-Ireland draw and replay of 2000, Galway had played in four All-Irelands in that period and we were right up there.

'The pleasing thing about 1998 and 2001 was that they were All-Irelands that were won using attacking-style football. Kildare in 1998 and Meath in 2001 contributed to allowing that type of football and competing in the game in a very positive way as well.'

O'Mahony left the Galway job in 2004 with two All-Irelands under his belt and returned to club management.

He was coaching two clubs in 2007, St Brigid's club in Kiltoom, County Roscommon and his home club of Ballaghaderreen, when he was elected to Dáil

Éireann as a Fine Gael TD for Mayo.

So did he fall into politics on the back of the GAA?

He explains, 'Traditionally in families, particularly in rural Ireland, the father or head of the house would almost always dictate the politics. My father was very much a Fine Gael person. He was from Dreenagh in West Cork, close to Béal na Bláth and he would have been steeped in the Fine Gael tradition.

'As a youngster growing up I was sucked into that way of thinking. James Dillon was the leader of Fine Gael and living in Ballaghaderreen when I was growing up.

'I remember going into Ballaghaderreen for election rallies when James Dillon would be speaking from the back of the lorry as leader of Fine Gael. He was a great orator, so I remember that.

'My father was not a member of a branch or anything but he was known as a Fine Gael supporter. He would not have gone door-to-door but because he had a travelling shop he would have been unofficially canvassing anyway.'

He adds, 'Then as I grew older I bought into the policies and the ethos of Fine Gael.'

Around the time O'Mahony's managerial career started, when he began teaching in St Nathy's College in Ballaghaderreen, he was also PRO for the local Fine Gael organisation. His involvement in the party did not develop much at this point as he was so preoccupied on the GAA front.

'There was always the interest in politics. I always watched programmes like *Today Tonight* and *Prime Time*. So even though politics was at arms' length, I always had an interest,' he says.

The next time politics really came onto O'Mahony's radar was in 1999. There was speculation that sitting Fine Gael MEP for the Connacht-Ulster constituency, Joe McCartin, was going to retire from politics after his next five-year stint in Brussels ended in 2004. So O'Mahony was approached by the party to see if he would allow his name to be added to the party ticket. Fine Gael planned to blood O'Mahony as McCartin's running mate in 1999 with a view to him becoming an MEP five years later.

O'Mahony adds, 'I would have thought about it but at the time I was managing Galway and we were just after winning the All-Ireland.

'Maybe it was in that context that I was asked. The amazing thing about politics is that parties know your politics maybe better than yourself so I was surprised to have been approached.

'As we were just after winning an All-Ireland, I didn't want to be seen as a kind of glory hunter going into politics on the back of the football success in 1998. That would have been the last thing I wanted.

'The leader of Fine Gael, John Bruton, contacted me at the time so it was a serious offer. I would imagine it was with the view, maybe not to have been elected on that occasion because Joe McCartin was the sitting MEP, but they probably wanted me to put down my name and have it there for the future.

'Effectively I turned that down but maybe that reawakened my own interest for the future.'

The next time O'Mahony heard from Fine Gael was the offer to run in Mayo in the 2007 general election.

Over a year out from the election there was a sense of excitement in Mayo at the prospect of the county having its own Taoiseach. Bertie Ahern had won two elections but surely Enda Kenny was going to win the 2007 battle.

Having left the Galway job in 2004, O'Mahony had established himself as a GAA analyst on RTÉ's *The Sunday Game* programme. He was still teaching in St Nathy's and was juggling his roles with the two football clubs in Roscommon and Mayo at the same time.

But Fine Gael had real ambitions of winning three Dáil seats in the five-seat Mayo constituency. Jim Higgins had moved on to Europe so they approached O'Mahony again.

'People from party headquarters and Jim Higgins were sent to ask me in 2006,' he recalls.

'I didn't actively look for it and I was surprised that people were looking for me to run. But it got me thinking. At that stage I had been a teacher for 31 years. While I was enjoyed the teaching, I realised all things were on the table and I suppose I was at a juncture in my life where I had freedom from inter-county management. I had turned it down in 1999 so I thought that if I turned Fine Gael down again, you can't expect to get the opportunity again.'

O'Mahony was afraid that he would be perceived as a 'parachute candidate'.

He says, 'Most of the jobs in my life, including all the management jobs I got, I have been asked to do them. I would not have gone canvassing looking for management jobs and it was the same in politics. I wanted to be sure that I wasn't jumping the queue on councillors who might have ambitions.

'That was a big consideration of mine. I initially felt interested as long as there was a smooth passage into it. I didn't want to cause a world war over it.'

He did not rush into the decision. But after much discussion with his wife Gerardine and their five daughters, O'Mahony's name was added to the party ticket.

Having been selected at the Fine Gael selection convention in June 2006, O'Mahony spent the next few months knocking on doors, introducing himself and letting people know that he was standing in the following year's election.

He recalls, 'I just wanted the signal to go out that I was serious about standing for election. Then I opened an office in Claremorris towards the end of the year.'

He adds, 'The campaign was an amazing rollercoaster once I decided to put my name in the hat.

'When Fine Gael asked me to go, I was told that there were private opinion polls done which showed Fine Gael doing well and I was chosen because I had a high profile.

'So it was a shock to the system when the results of a few opinion polls came out. I remember one morning I was going out for a training session with one of the clubs, Ballaghaderreen or St Brigid's, and the *Mail on Sunday* had done an opinion poll and I was zilch in that poll. Zero per cent – I'll never forget it!

'I remember ringing Jim Higgins and saying: "What the frig have you got me into here?" But something like that encourages you. The bigger the challenge, the bigger the opportunity.'

Getting zero per cent in an opinion poll was a rude awakening for the rookie campaigner but O'Mahony showed resilience.

'Once I spoke with Enda Kenny and eventually allowed myself to go forward, I was going to leave no stone unturned. So when that opinion poll came out I was not going to walk off. If anything, something like that copper-fastens your determination.

'There was another opinion poll in the *Western People*, well into the campaign as we were canvassing, which showed me at only 4%. I felt the poll did not reflect what we were sensing on the ground.

'I remember the evening that poll came out. I got a call to say what the results were. I was actually out canvassing in the Hollymount area of Mayo when I got the word.

'Again, it was a bit of a downer as I thought that we would be up at around 6 or 7%. So it was a slow burner. Matt Gill, a member of the party, was with me and we were due to finish up canvassing that evening at 6 p.m. So I said we would do another hour, and that kind of epitomised my attitude. The polls made me more determined to work harder and prove them wrong.'

By the time the election came around, O'Mahony had been reinstated as Mayo manager. His notoriety in GAA circles may have helped his selection as an election candidate. But the events of election week 2007 would suggest that O'Mahony's electoral prospects were not index-linked to Mayo's success on the football field.

He recalls, 'There was a big championship match on the Sunday before the election. Mayo played Galway. A continuous feature of the election was that people were linking whether I would be elected to success on the field.

'My ambition was to convince people that I wanted to be a candidate and a public representative based on what I could do for them in politics. People inevitably were linking them but I didn't want it that way and I didn't see it that way.

'Over the years it has been linked but when I look back on it now I was glad that the match was the week before the election. People had to make a decision after the match if they wanted to back me or not.'

Less than a week before polling day, Mayo lost the Connacht Championship match to Galway in Pearse Stadium by seven points.

O'Mahony says, 'It is devastating when you lose a championship match, particularly against Galway, who are our biggest rivals.

'I knew it was going to be a crucial four or five days then ahead of the election so there was no opportunity to wallow in the defeat and put the head down. I had to get up and at it.'

Despite the devastation of the defeat, O'Mahony had to attend a political function on the evening of the game. Worse still, he had to go out knocking on doors in search of votes the following morning in a GAA-mad county.

'It was devastating to lose the match but it was better when I look back that the election was not the Thursday beforehand. If I had been elected and then went on to lose the match people might draw a link. They cannot do that given that we lost the match and I was elected afterwards.

'People had to make the decision and they backed me. When I was knocking on doors, I was able to use football as an introduction point. But I wanted the conversation to be about politics and be seen as a political candidate.

'Inevitably, and maybe it is one of the reasons for the low opinion polls at the beginning, people saw me as the Mayo manager going for election rather than the Fine Gael candidate going for election. That was the challenge – for me to turn that around.'

O'Mahony was elected on the eighth count on the back of 6,869 first-preference votes. Poll-topper Enda Kenny and Michael Ring took the other two Fine Gael seats in the five-seat constituency.

As a TD, O'Mahony believes that GAA management has given him a good grounding for politics.

His first political ambition was to get elected. After achieving that he says that he wants to bring his qualities to politics.

He explains, 'I have a sense of integrity, a sense of hard work, methodical planning of what I do. As a manager of a team as well, I have to have meticulous planning to keep the two things going because the one thing I don't want to happen is for one thing to be neglected for the other.

'Whereas people would say football is going to elect you, I never saw it that way. I see it as a double-edged sword. I have been involved in inter-county management since 1983 at underage level so I know that people think you are fantastic if you win an All-Ireland. But if you lose a first-round championship match you are the worst in the world – so it is a double-edged sword.

'The vital thing is that people see you for how you perform, so I tried to get my feet under the table as quickly as possible in the political scene.

'I wanted to do that and become a team player. The contribution I make in the party is that I have an expert knowledge in education and sport. If there were any opportunities within the party that would allow me to express that potential and expertise that is what I want to do. I am on the education committee and I am the Fine Gael spokesperson on sport.'

As well as holding his Oireachtas and Mayo management roles up to 28 June 2010, O'Mahony has managed the Connacht Railway Cup team since the early 2000s up to the present when the future of the competition is in doubt.

His critics might say that by managing this team, his tentacles are spread across five different GAA communities and this helps him maintain a high profile across Connacht, should he ever stand for the European elections. But the Railway Cup competition is no longer held in the same regard as it once was and it is hard to realistically quantify any political benefits O'Mahony gets from this role.

'People from opposition parties say that I am using my management of the Connacht Railway Cup team to keep my options open. I wouldn't see it that way. I was involved in management and football long before I ever got involved in politics.

'I don't think that genuine GAA people would ever question that. I have been managing Connacht since the early 2000s and it is not a glamour role. It is not a hugely onerous task; you only meet up for training once or twice for the game. I see it as a privilege to do it but I wouldn't keep it going for that reason.'

So does he have one eye set on the European Parliament?

He replies, 'Maybe down the line but it is not something that I am actively pursuing. Whether that challenge will ever be put to me, I don't know.'

In June 2010, after Richard Bruton staged a leadership challenge against Fine Gael leader Enda Kenny, the nation held its breath as the party's TDs and senators gathered in a room in the bowels of Leinster House for a confidence vote in Kenny as leader. Hundreds of journalists waited outside on the Leinster House plinth for news of the result. Inside the building, a small group of Fine Gael councillors from Mayo paced up and down outside the door of the room where the crunch vote was taking place.

O'Mahony went in and out of the room to inform them about how the meeting was progressing. Then news filtered through that the vote was taking place. A few minutes later the door opened and O'Mahony emerged from the room. He had tears in his eyes. He was almost stumbling as he walked. Then he clenched his fists and held them up in the air as he looked at his Fine Gael colleagues from Mayo and said, 'He did it. Enda won it.'

Kenny had survived a leadership heave and O'Mahony was ecstatic. The political victory in Leinster House echoed scenes from Croke Park after a GAA match as one councillor took it upon himself to run up the stairs in Leinster House and go outside shouting 'Up Mayo!' to the awaiting crowd.

John O'Mahony is not the first member of Ballaghaderreen GAA club to become a TD, as O'Mahony has followed in the footsteps of two-time Mayo All-Ireland winning captain, Seán Flanagan.

Flanagan was a Fianna Fáil TD and government minister and served in the Dáil from 1951 to 1973. His son Dermot played for Mayo under O'Mahony and captained them to win the Connacht title in 1988.

Seán Flanagan captained Mayo to their last All-Ireland Senior title in 1951 and he was elected to the Dáil in the same year. He pursued his political career after his football days ended, whereas O'Mahony had an immense workload in serving as a TD and managing the Mayo team at the same time until he resigned following Mayo's shock championship 2010 exit after defeats by Sligo and Longford.

Before then an average week in the life of Deputy John O'Mahony was hectic. What other inter-county GAA manager would find themselves at 18 funerals in the course of a weekend?

He used to spend all day on Monday between his constituency office in Claremorris and various meetings and appointments in various parts of Mayo. Late on Monday night, usually after a meeting, or early on Tuesday morning he would drive to Dublin.

After spending the day in Leinster House, he would meet up with the seven or eight members of the Mayo football panel who were working or studying in Dublin. It is too far to travel back to Mayo for training on a Tuesday so the Dublin group train together while the bulk of the panel train in Mayo.

Then on Wednesdays and Thursdays, O'Mahony divided his time between his Leinster House office, various meetings and the Dáil chamber before departing for Mayo on Thursday evening to hold training for the county panel in Castlebar.

When training was over O'Mahony would, more often than not, have to head to a meeting of the local party organisation or of a community group who wanted to air a particular concern with their local TD.

He holds his constituency clinics on Fridays and had county training on a Saturday morning ahead of a game on a Sunday.

He adds, 'As a rural TD, funerals are a big part of it. The weekend before last – that includes the Friday, the Saturday and the Sunday evening – I was at something like 18 funerals.

'My wife Gerardine represents me at some funerals when I am in Dublin on Tuesday, Wednesday and Thursday.

One of John O'Mahony's All-Ireland winning Galway stars from 1998 and 2001, Kevin Walsh, was the Sligo manager who guided the Yeats' County to beat O'Mahony's Mayo in the 2010 Connacht Championship. When Sligo beat Mayo in the Connacht final 35 years earlier in 1975, O'Mahony was playing for Mayo. That defeat prompted his retirement from senior county football at the age of 23.

The 2010 defeat to Sligo did not quite end O'Mahony's managerial career but Mayo's shock All-Ireland qualifier defeat at the hands of Longford soon afterwards saw him resign as Mayo manager immediately after his team's abject display.

His first three years in public life as a TD overlapped with Mayo management. But O'Mahony refutes the view that his management suffered because of his political career and says, 'That would be the kind of personal thing that's very hurtful because I gave this job as much as I gave Galway or Leitrim or Mayo in the past.'

So, since O'Mahony's second term as Mayo manager did not yield an elusive All-Ireland title, has his legacy been damaged?

'My legacy as a manager is for others to decide. I've been lucky enough to be involved in winning five or six All-Irelands, 14 or 15 Connacht titles. I have been through it all. If people choose to think that my legacy is damaged in some way, that's fine. I have no problem at all.'

Mayo have yet to break their All-Ireland final day voodoo. The famine continues as they have not won Sam Maguire since 1951. Back in 1998, O'Mahony told his Galway players at half-time in the All-Ireland final, 'There is going to be a time after ten or fifteen minutes when it's there for whoever wants it.'

He may not be the Mayo manager any more, but Mayo GAA is part of his DNA. When the time comes again in an All-Ireland final that the Sam Maguire is there for whoever wants it, there will be few people there who will want to see a Mayo team seize that opportunity more than 'Johnno'.

Seán Flanagan
Full-Back

MAYO – FIANNA FÁIL
Arsenal, The Ashes and the original Roy Keane

Mayo have won three All-Ireland titles in GAA history. Seán Flanagan captained them to lift Sam Maguire on two of those three occasions. Flanagan also led a colourful political career where he was a government minister and developed his own brand of 'Fianna Flanagan' politics.

But there was much more to him. He was a man of vision. As a young boy he was listening to the Ashes cricket series on the crackly old 'wireless', at a time when cricket was alien to most Irish people. In later years he would bring his children to watch Ian Botham play.

In the 1950s he took his teammates from the Mayo backline to London. Despite the GAA's ban on members playing 'foreign' sports, Flanagan saw the merits of learning from other sports and took the Mayo backs to Highbury to watch Arsenal's legendary defence play.

In politics he was an ecumenist to his fingertips. He befriended Ian Paisley at a time when Paisley was one of the most detested people by nationalists in Ireland. And he paid Tom Enright's wages as Enright embarked on a general election campaign to win a Dáil seat for the enemy, Fine Gael.

Seán Flanagan was a remarkable figure.

The nation was shocked when Roy Keane departed the Irish squad ahead of the 2002 World Cup. But Keane was not the first Irishman to walk out on his team after being frustrated by a lack of organisation, adequate facilities and proper equipment.

GAA aficionados might argue that Mayo's Seán Flanagan was the original Roy Keane. A lot of what Flanagan did in the mid-1940s was akin to the actions of Keane in a different code, in a different era, some 55 years later in Saipan.

As well as his frustration with the way the Mayo team was being treated by the county board, Flanagan was like Keane in other ways: Flanagan demanded the highest standards of physical and mental preparation of himself and his teammates, he refused to be second best and he had an ability to articulate that to his teammates as he led by example. And the results speak for themselves.

Seán Flanagan was a product of that great football nursery St Jarlath's College in Tuam, where he captained their senior team in 1939, in the last year on a run of eight successive Connacht Colleges' titles. After playing minor football for Mayo in 1939 and 1940, he burst onto the senior team in the mid-1940s. Even as a younger member of the team, Flanagan immediately stood out as a unique character on the Mayo scene.

One of his teammates during that era, the late Eamon Mongey, often made the point that even though Mayo had a good crop of players at the time, they would not have been nearly as successful without Flanagan.

'He was known as being somebody who had an unquenching commitment and a refusal to accept second best,' says Dermot Flanagan, his son, who also played for Mayo and is now a successful senior counsel.

Flanagan's refusal to accept second best was shown in 1947 when he resigned from the team. After being encouraged by teammates to return, he and four other Dublin-based Mayo players – Padraic Carney, Liam Hastings, Tom Langan and Eamon Mongey – wrote to the Mayo County Board to make a complaint on 5 November 1947.

Mayo had just drawn a tournament match with the Kerry team which had been beaten a few weeks earlier by Cavan in the famous Polo Grounds final in New York. Kerry had a near full-strength team, while Mayo had travelled to Kerry without a full team of 15 players. A man who had driven some of the players from Dublin and the county secretary, Finn Mongey, had to tog out to make up the numbers.

Enough was enough. Led by Flanagan, the Dublin-based players wrote a lengthy letter of protest to the county board.

He included the lines: 'We ask you to put aside petty jealousies and favouritism, to get together, stay together and pull together, to pick a team, not of "historic" players nor of "friendly" or "kindred" players, but a team made up of the best 15 players available. We know you can do it – we not only ask you but we demand that you do this and do it here and now.'

That letter was a landmark in the history of Mayo football. 1947 was the start of an amazing journey for Flanagan and his team.

His son recalls, 'My father was a deeply analytical guy. He believed that you won football matches by looking at the matter in an objective way. My understanding is that he wrote to the county board to say, "If you don't interfere with us, if you give us the opportunity, we will win the All-Ireland." Sometimes these things in folklore can be described as defiance. What happened was, my father and a number of others wrote a letter and outlined that if they were left alone to do their job the right way, they believed they could deliver an All-Ireland for Mayo.'

While Flanagan's attitude to Gaelic football was like Roy Keane's attitude to soccer, the story of Flanagan and the Blackthorn boots has an uncanny resemblance to Keane's Saipan debacle in 2002.

Dermot Flanagan explains, 'My father went around one day and found that the players' boots had no studs and he realised that they couldn't afford new boots. Blackthorn was the top boot-maker at the time so he ordered 20 or 22 pairs of boots and directed Blackthorn to send the bill to the county board. The county board was outraged that a player would take that upon himself. But that shows you that he wasn't prepared to put something like the absence of proper equipment in the way of success.'

Flanagan did not stop at insisting Mayo had proper boots. When the famous Paddy Prendergast, who was the full-back on the team alongside Flanagan, played his first game for Mayo he had a baptism of fire. So Flanagan spent two hours with him afterwards in a restaurant introducing him to, what Flanagan thought, were the correct elements of defensive play.

'They were a team that analysed their game and they used to write to one another. If a player underperformed on a Sunday, he could expect to get a couple of letters from his teammates within the week, pointing out that his game was not up to scratch,' says Dermot. 'It was all about setting standards and sticking to them. He brought the Mayo backs to watch Arsenal playing in the 1950s. Arsenal had the best defensive team at that time and he wanted to show the Mayo defence how another defensive discipline did their stuff. That was the kind of man he was.'

Arsenal beat Liverpool 2–0 in the 1950 FA Cup Final in a game that has long been remembered for the defensive displays of Joe Mercer and Alex Forbes. Flanagan heard about Arsenal's defensive qualities and he wanted Mayo to learn from them.

The Mayo team that Flanagan played on in the late 1940s and early 1950s was exceptionally talented. Flanagan, at corner-back, and Tom Langan, at full-forward, were both named on the GAA's Team of the Millennium. They also had players like Eamon Mongey, Padraic Carney, John Forde, John McAndrew, Seán and Mick Mulderrig, and Mick Flanagan.

Dermot Flanagan says, 'In their own right this was a great team. This team was compared to the Dublin team of the 1970s. The reason why is that a significant number of them went on to be highly successful in their lives, beyond football. These people had an intellect and a desire to succeed.'

It has long been noted how the Dublin team of the 1970s went on to have successful careers in various professions. The Mayo team of the 1950s were similar. For example, Eamon Mongey went on to be a Supreme Court registrar, Padraic Carney, known as 'the flying doctor', was an eminent surgeon in the United States while others became lawyers, doctors, gardaí and bankers.

Dermot Flanagan also recalls, 'They also had another attribute. Times were very bad in Mayo at that time and that group of players saw that the success of the team would lift spirits in the county.

'There was a TV programme some years ago called the *Bonfires over Bohola* where some of the players were interviewed. In the 1950s these players understood that success on the field of play was something that would lift Mayo as well.

'They were very fortunate and there is no doubt that, while my father had challenges in later life, in his 20s and 30s he was a man of enormous determination.'

At the time, the captain of the Mayo team was chosen from the ranks of the club that had won the previous year's county championship. Under this rule Flanagan was not entitled to be captain, but his teammates thought so much of his leadership abilities that they lobbied for the rules to be bent in Flanagan's favour.

Dermot laughs, 'There was some form of gerrymandering, as you might say in the political sense, to get him in. Sometimes you only know the true worth of somebody when they are made captain. If you think of Roy Keane – sometimes when people are made captain, it trebles their presence. It brought out the best in my father and that is not to say that people did not disagree with him internally.

'There may have been personality differences with strong-willed people but whenever I saw that team come together later in life, as they did on many occasions, there was a great bond between them all. I think that most of them realised what my father did.'

Two years after writing the controversial letter to the county board and Flanagan duping the board into paying for new football boots for the team, the rewards were evident. After losing the 1948 All-Ireland final to Cavan, Mayo won the League title in 1949.

The following year they beat Louth in the All-Ireland final to claim the Sam Maguire for the second time ever. The banner headline in that week's edition of the *Western People* newspaper read: 'Mayo are All-Ireland Champions as 14 years of waiting ends in triumph'. The match report said, 'Seán Flanagan played more than a captain's part in the winning of that All-Ireland. In the first quarter, with John McAndrew still suffering from an early blow that paralysed his arm, Flanagan had two positions to hold.'

There had been a 14-year gap between Mayo's first and second All-Ireland titles. Flanagan and his team were not willing to wait as long for their second, and they returned to Croke Park to play Meath in the 1951 All-Ireland final.

For some reason or other, the Meath team had to walk through the Mayo dressing room to get onto the field in Croke Park to play that final. Flanagan immediately seized on the opportunity to use this to Mayo's advantage.

His son Dermot explains, 'He instructed all the team that under no circumstances were any of them to acknowledge or make eye contact with any of the Meath team as they went through the dressing room.'

Flanagan wanted his team to keep focused on the ultimate goal and psyche out the opposition at the same time. And it worked. The final score was Mayo 2–8 to Meath's 0–9.

Mayo won another League title in 1954 with the same group of players, and after they suffered defeat at the hands of Dublin in the 1955 All-Ireland semi-final, it was more or less the end of the line for that team.

Flanagan did not retain the Mayo captaincy throughout his playing career. Dermot remembers, 'He was personally very upset when he was relieved of the captaincy. That was done without him having any say, and the view I formed was that people thought he got too big for his boots and that was a shame.'

Even though he was the best-known Gaelic footballer of his generation in Mayo, Flanagan's sporting interest did not stop at GAA. The fact that he took the Mayo backs to see Arsenal play in the early 1950s stands testament to that. But his interest stretched beyond football.

Dermot claims, 'He deplored the ban. He was a lover of all sport. As a ten-year-old he used to listen to the Ashes series. When he was challenged about listening to cricket matches in the 1930s he had to put on a kind of a nationalistic front and say that it was only because England were being beaten, which pleased everybody – but he really deplored the ban. He had a passion for cricket. We used to go to England to watch Ian Botham playing.

'He used to go to rugby matches in the 1950s to watch Jack Kyle and the boys. He used to go to Lansdowne Road with an Irish scarf wrapped around his neck.'

When Flanagan finished playing for Mayo he had won five Connacht titles and two All-Ireland titles. Dermot says, 'He had five daughters and he gave his five Connacht medals to his daughters. He had two All-Ireland medals and he gave those to his two sons.'

As well as the honour of winning so many medals as a Mayo footballer, Flanagan held another distinction. After captaining Mayo to their 1950 All-Ireland title in September of that year, he was elected to the Dáil the following May. So he was actually a sitting Dáil deputy when he lifted Sam Maguire for the second time in 1951.

So, like many other GAA stars before and after him, did Flanagan gain a Dáil seat on the back of his reputation and fame as a player?

His son Dermot refutes this and claims, 'I don't believe he won his Dáil seat solely on the back of the first All-Ireland win. My understanding is that my father was first and foremost a politician. He was also a qualified solicitor; he had a first class honours degree and he also won the gold medal for oratory as a student in the Law Society, so he was always very gifted in terms of speaking. He was always interested in politics. Our background would have been Fianna Fáil/republican.'

Flanagan was elected as a TD for the old Mayo South constituency in 1951. He got the fourth seat with 3,887 first-preference votes.

Dermot remembers how his father served a lengthy 14 year 'apprenticeship' before he was promoted to the role of parliamentary secretary in 1965. It is understood that Flanagan was offered the Justice ministry in 1961 but he turned it down.

Dermot suggests, 'The reasons for declining that role may have been to do with the fact that he had six young kids and another on the way. He was also a practising solicitor and that was paying the bills. There may have been an economic reason why he held off.'

Seán Lemass, who was Taoiseach from 1959 to 1966, held Flanagan in high regard and, after appointing him parliamentary secretary in 1965, he appointed him Minister for Health the following year. Flanagan moved his family to Dublin around this time.

After being appointed to a ministry regarded as second only to an economic portfolio, Flanagan appeared to be on course for a lengthy career at the Cabinet table. But this never materialised.

As well as being GAA rivals, Flanagan and Lemass's successor as leader of Fianna Fáil, Jack Lynch, were political rivals within the same party.

Dermot says, 'They would not have seen eye to eye and my father was politically demoted in 1969 by Lynch. My father had supported Charlie Haughey in his leadership race with George Colley after Lemass resigned in 1966. In the end Lynch entered the race as a compromise candidate and won it.'

When Lynch took charge he banished Flanagan to the role of Minister for Lands in July 1969. Flanagan's reaction to this appointment was truly remarkable. He reacted in a way that had never been seen in Irish politics before, and probably never will be again. He recommended that the government department, that he had just been appointed to take charge of, should be scrapped.

'It was the most unusual political move ever. Most politicians are into self-preservation but that is an example of my father,' laughs Dermot.

'The Land Commission had done its job and he said, "What's the point in this ministry?" You can see the big-picture guy he was. He was quite different in some respects.'

By the early 1970s Flanagan was deeply frustrated with domestic politics, and Dermot recalls, 'By that stage it was clear that he wasn't a favoured son of Jack Lynch anyway.'

But falling out of favour with Lynch added to his sense of disenchantment with the Oireachtas. Europe beckoned.

Dermot explains, 'Certain elements of politics frustrated him as he always saw a bigger picture and to that extent his ten years in Europe were probably his happiest years politically.'

From the day he was first elected in 1951, Flanagan displayed an interest in Europe and he got involved in the Council of Europe.

'He had a vision of Ireland punching above its weight as part of the wider European Community. He was always a bigger-picture person. Anyone who knew him would know that sometimes day-to-day politics frustrated him and he found some parts of politics unnecessarily tedious.'

Flanagan really struggled to hold his Dáil seat in the 1973 general election and his son Dermot remarks, 'There were certain personal challenges for him at the time.' The Fine Gael-Labour coalition, led by Liam Cosgrave, came into power in March 1973 and Flanagan abhorred his time on the opposition back benches before he lost his seat in the 1977 general election.

One of Flanagan's close friends, Tom Earley, was the secretary general of the Fianna Fáil group in Europe in the 1970s. Earley astutely recognised that Flanagan would be better suited to the European Parliament and told him, 'Europe awaits you.'

So Flanagan contested the first direct elections to Europe in 1979 and won a seat in the Connacht-Ulster constituency. Neil Blaney topped the poll with over 80,000 votes, Fine Gael's Joe McCartin was elected with 47,000 votes and Flanagan garnered over 38,500 votes. He spent ten years as an MEP and his son believes that these were 'intellectually, some of the happiest years of his life.' Flanagan enjoyed working with people from across party lines. He had the attitude that when Irish MEPs were in Brussels they had to work together for Ireland. When he came home he engaged in rabble-rousing and party politics but in Brussels he developed close friendships with political adversaries such as Fine Gael's Mark Clinton and Labour's Liam Kavanagh.

Shortly after his arrival in Brussels, Flanagan was one of the MEPs appointed to an ad hoc committee formed to help disadvantaged island communities in Europe. The committee included Irish MEPs, encompassing those from the North, who were trying to advance the cause of Rathlin Island, off the coast of Antrim, and Tory Island, off Donegal.

'My father went up to Ian Paisley to introduce himself as one of the new committee,' recounted Dermot, 'and Paisley replied, "You Papish fiend".

'So dad left him for a while, before returning to ask, "Do you know the Doherty family in Wellington Place in Belfast?" Paisley replied, "Yes, the Dohertys, the tea merchants. I know them."'

Flanagan replied that he was married to their daughter and then walked off. A few minutes later, when Paisley realised there was a connection with Northern Ireland, he came over to Flanagan and apologised. The pair enjoyed a healthy working relationship after that.

Dermot Flanagan recalls, 'In the 1980s Charlie Haughey became Taoiseach and there was a lot of turbulence in Fianna Fáil. When Fianna Fáil got back in on one of those elections, my older brother said to my father, "Well, you know Theo (that is my father's nickname from his football days), if you were still a TD you might be in government now", but my father said that he felt he was better off out of it.

'My father was greatly disheartened by the level of strife within the party. He was a team player and I don't think he chose to be as politically ruthless as he might have been.'

Flanagan's family like to remember him for all the decent things he did for people.

'He was a man of great humanity. Despite any faults he may have had, people remember him as a man who did not lose his common touch,' claims Dermot.

Mary Hanafin, the Minister for Tourism, Culture and Sport, is one of those people.

Dermot explains, 'The current Minister, Mary Hanafin, reminded me that when she was a teenager she went to Brussels on one of these information trips. He brought her out to dinner and gave her a bottle of perfume on her way home and she never forgot that.'

As well as impressing people like Hanafin with his kindness, Flanagan caused a major wave of excitement across unemployment-hit Ireland on Wednesday, 28 March 1984.

'MEP claims £500m US projects planned' read the headline on the front page of *The Irish Times* that morning. Flanagan had called a press conference in Strasbourg the previous night to announce plans by a US company to invest £500m in projects in Ireland.

The investment in projects in the north Mayo bogland, the Scariff Chipboard plant in Clare, and Clondalkin Paper Mills in Dublin was set to create a major jobs bonanza. He told the press conference, which included the European correspondents of the Irish newpapers, that a company called AGM Holdings of Maryland in the USA had already bought 5,500 acres of north Mayo bogland. The company was going to use this land as part of an extensive scheme to produce peat pellets for commercial, industrial and domestic use.

Flanagan's impromptu announcement created some controversy at the time as the Industrial Development Authority (IDA) publicly said that they were not aware of the £500m investment until he broke the news. Flanagan's critics claimed that the announcement was an election stunt, as his seat in Europe was under threat in the forthcoming Euro elections. But in the days after the announcement, Flanagan claimed that journalists had picked him up wrong as he had told them that the company behind the investment was based in France. A former Hungarian resistance fighter called Dr Sandor Mihali was behind the initiative, according to Flanagan.

Looking back on the announcement, his son Dermot explains, 'There was a Hungarian guy in his late 60s or early 70s, called Mihali, who had been a former resistance fighter in the Second World War. He was an alleged industrialist and he came to my father to say that he was interested in setting up a number of large industries in Ireland for the production of peat pellets.

'He approached my father as an MEP on the basis that if he was investing all this money then Europe would match his investment pound for pound.

'I remember my father had certain doubts as this guy was a larger than life sort of character. But then again he was an investor with a proposal to invest in Ireland so my father thought he was advancing the cause of this potential investment.

'I saw that my father had certain doubts about it but I also recall seeing the fax where Mihali had indicated to my father that the first tranche of funds would be in place by a certain date.'

Mihali made a number of presentations about the project. He was supposed to be a wealthy industrialist and his reputed past as a Hungarian resistance fighter gave him more credence, with a whiff of sulphur.

A Mullingar businessman called John Duff, owner of a company called Gaelic Liquid Peat, emerged as the conduit between Mihali's company and Ireland. Duff proclaimed to be the investor's representative in Ireland and claimed to *The Irish Times* on 29 March 1984 that the £500m would be invested in Ireland over 15 years.

Dermot Flanagan says, 'As I understand it, my father was to be the one who would advance the cause for getting appropriate subsidies and grant aid for this guy on the basis that he delivered the projects. It would have been amazing had it ever come to pass. It was really a question of waiting on this guy [Mihali] to deliver on his proposal. But ultimately it never came to pass.

'From my father's point of view, it would have been an amazing investment for the country at that time but equally, it was very disappointing that Mihali never followed up on any of this.'

Despite the collapse of the Mihali plan, the fact that Flanagan had made such a seismic announcement cannot have done his election prospects any harm as he faced into the European elections in mid-June 1984.

That election posed a mammoth political battle for Flanagan, as tough as anything he had experienced in Croke Park over 30 years earlier. And he rose to the challenge: 1984 saw the birth of a new phenomenon in Irish politics – 'Fianna Flanagan'.

Before the campaign started, Flanagan's close friend Tom Earley found himself at loggerheads with Fianna Fáil party headquarters in Mount Street. Charlie Haughey wanted to cut the funding that was allocated to the Fianna Fáil group in Europe and Earley, the party's secretary general in Europe, had resisted Haughey's move.

'After that, the knives were out for Tom Earley and my father helped him to survive at that time,' says Dermot.

'So my father certainly was not the favoured candidate in 1984. In fact he had no support from Mount Street, on the basis that he was 64 years old. They thought he was going to lose his seat and he was a has-been.'

Ray MacSharry was Fianna Fáil's favoured candidate. Before the election, Flanagan was written off by political pundits who predicted MacSharry would win the Fianna Fáil seat, Joe McCartin would take the Fine Gael seat and the Independent Fianna Fáil candidate Neil Blaney would hoover up the republican vote to take the third and final seat.

But Flanagan and his family had other plans as Dermot, who was his father's personal director of elections, explains: 'We ran a tremendous personal campaign. It was a Mayo campaign. It was a "Fianna Flanagan" campaign.

'All I can say is that the Monday night before polling day on Thursday, RTÉ were showing GAA victories from the past and the Mayo team of 1950 and 1951 was featured. We never asked and they never told us but my father must have had some nice friends in RTÉ.

'Six weeks before that, he managed to get on *The Late Late Show*. He was quite a good fiddle player and some politicians were brought on by Gay Byrne to play music.'

In the weeks before polling day in June 1984, Flanagan walked the roads of Mayo like it was 1948 all over again.

'People like Bobby Molloy was a big supporter of his in Galway and that was a big help but the bottom line is that he beat Blaney by 1,500 votes on the back of a vote from the people of Mayo,' says Dermot.

'In 1979 he was the leading Fianna Fáil candidate and he was expected to take a seat, but in 1984 he was in the winter of his career. But I saw for three months fantastic battling qualities there and I think that even Ray MacSharry marvelled at his stamina. He displayed those fighting qualities that had made him indomitable in his 20s and 30s.

'He beat Neil Blaney who came down from 70,000-plus votes to 37,000 and my father got 38,500. Interestingly, he got 20,000 votes in Mayo, which meant a third of the votes were not Fianna Fáil votes. It was a "Fianna Flanagan" vote.'

Despite growing up in Dublin, where Flanagan had moved his family in the late 1960s, Dermot Flanagan came back and played for Mayo minors as a teenager. He later broke into the senior team and became one of the county's longest playing servants. While Seán Flanagan won two All-Irelands, Dermot lost finals in 1989, 1996 and 1997. These defeats, especially the 1996 loss, are still a source of much heartache for the prominent senior counsel who was very close to his father.

'He was a guy I enjoyed. I was very close to him because of the football. We were very close,' recalls Dermot.

'But once in my life I asked him about the Arms Crisis and he responded to me that as a Cabinet member he was bound by Cabinet confidentiality and he refused to talk about it. He never talked about it to the family.'

As well as having immense loyalty to the Cabinet, Flanagan was one of those politicians who was held in high regard by his political adversaries. The story of Flanagan helping to launch Fine Gael TD Tom Enright's political career confirms this.

Enright, whose daughter Olwyn is now a Fine Gael TD for Laois-Offaly, was a solicitor. Early in his career, Tom Enright ran Seán Flanagan's legal practice in Ballaghaderreen, County Roscommon for a couple of years after Flanagan was appointed Minister for Health.

'Tom ran my father's practice from 1967 until 1969, when he informed my father that he wanted to go back home to Laois to run as a Fine Gael election candidate,' says Dermot.

'My father gave him three weeks off, paid leave, to go home to fight the election. The fact that he was going to run for Fine Gael was not an issue. And in the months before Tom retired in 2002 I joined him in the Dáil for dinner and he recalled my father doing that for him.'

'You could write a bible with stories about Flanagan', is how a Ballaghaderreen man described one of the greatest characters in Irish politics in the last 50 years. But despite all his sporting and political achievements, Flanagan was a tortured soul in some respects.

Dermot recalls, 'By the end of his career he was the father figure in the Fianna Fáil party. So he had an amazing career by everybody else's standards. By his own, I think that he reflected on his under-achievements. While others remember the greatness of his achievements, I think that sometimes he was probably his own harshest critic.'

Like many successful sports stars, Flanagan had such high standards that he spent a lot of time in later life, prior to his death in 1993, talking about 'the ones that got away', games such as the lost 1948 All-Ireland final.

As well as regretting sports defeats, Flanagan also had some regrets about not always achieving his political goals.

'I would have regrets about that too as, sometimes, I feel that he didn't realise what he had achieved in life. He was always striving maybe to be a super-human figure and sometimes being good is good enough. Sometimes he should have given himself a pat on the back and realised how much he did achieve in life,' claims Dermot.

'I have come in later life to realise that there were huge expectations on his shoulders from the moment he lifted Sam Maguire in 1950 and 1951. Even in politics there were huge expectations on his shoulders from the people of Mayo, naturally, because they thought of him as somebody who could deliver for them. But I am not sure it was as easy in politics to deliver as it was when you were in charge of the Mayo team. I think he had more control over his destiny when he was captain of the Mayo team.

'I am not sure that politics gave him the chance to fulfil his destiny because politics is so adversarial and there are so many other people who want the same thing.

'The statistics still show his achievements. Mayo has only won Sam Maguire three times and he was the captain twice. On reflection, if I was speaking to him now, having concluded my own playing career and knowing how hard I tried, I would tell him that his achievements were almost unbelievable because we have failed to win it since.

'There are so many challenges in Mayo and he overcame all the obstacles and to me that speaks volumes. While he may have disagreed with people, people may have felt he was arrogant or aloof, but he got rid of all that stuff and rose above all that.'

Dermot adds, 'He was named on the Team of the Century in 1984 so during his lifetime he got that honour. Equally, it is a measure of his stature that 15 years later he made the Team of the Millennium. It is an enduring thing about him that his greatness has not been diminished through the passage of time. Unfortunately, that is partly because Mayo have not won an All-Ireland since.

'When all is said and done, in Irish culture he is remembered more as the Mayo captain than the government minister who spent 38 years in politics, 27 as a TD, 11 as an MEP.'

Jimmy Deenihan
Left Corner-Back

A Fine Gael TD should never look a gift horse in the mouth. Especially if said gift horse is a Fianna Fáil Taoiseach paying him a compliment across the floor of the Dáil chamber. It is a rare and extraordinary occurrence, but it did happen on 3 March 2010.

During a routine Dáil debate, Fine Gael TD Jimmy Deenihan asked Taoiseach Brian Cowen a question. The quick-witted Cowen had a grin on his face as he quipped, 'I would be one of the last to try to rotate around one of the great corner-backs of our time.'

Despite being polar opposites on the political spectrum, even Cowen could not hide his admiration for Deenihan. Few can disagree; Deenihan was one of the great corner-backs of our time.

So what did it mean to the Fine Gael TD to have such an honour bestowed on him by the Fianna Fáil Taoiseach? Deenihan joked, 'The Taoiseach is obviously a very good judge of football! Obviously it was in jest but you have to take a compliment when you get one – especially from Mr Cowen.'

The same Fine Gael supporters who must have been amused to hear Cowen compliment a GAA star within their ranks, must still wince when stories of former Taoiseach Garret Fitzgerald's GAA knowledge are recounted.

Three years after captaining Offaly to their first ever All-Ireland hurling title in 1981, Pádraig Horan stood for political office. The death of Fianna Fáil TD Ber Cowen had precipitated a by-election in Laois-Offaly and Horan had been chosen as the Fine Gael candidate to contest the vacant Dáil seat.

As well as leading Offaly to its breakthrough in hurling, Horan had the political credentials to go with it: he had been involved in Fine Gael since his college days, he had served as chairman and secretary of his local branch and as constituency organiser.

The local GAA hero with the political nous polled 18,173 first-preference votes on 14 June 1984. But he was no match for the Fianna Fáil candidate who garnered a massive 26,022 first preferences. Brian Cowen, the son of the late Ber, had arrived on the national political stage.

Horan left the political scene and went on to win another All-Ireland with the Faithful County while Cowen would remain in politics and later become Taoiseach.

During that by-election, Horan began his campaign in the Laois end of the constituency at Ballyfin College. Taoiseach Garret Fitzgerald was there to launch it. While nobody can ever doubt the dyed-in-the-wool GAA credentials of Taoisigh such as Brian Cowen and Jack Lynch, Garret Fitzgerald was by no means a GAA aficionado. Standing at Ballyfin College, he did not even know what his candidate, Horan, looked like. After waiting for a few minutes, he wondered out loud, 'where the bloody candidate was'. Horan sheepishly replied to his party leader, 'That's me!'

Over a year after losing the by-election to Brian Cowen, Horan had returned to inter-county hurling and won an All-Star on the back of some heroic performances along the way to Offaly winning their second All-Ireland.

As the Offaly players came up the steps of the Hogan Stand to lift the Liam McCarthy Cup, Fitzgerald still failed to recognise Horan. Spotting Fitzgerald's flaw in failing to recognise his own by-election candidate from the previous year, one Charles J Haughey emerged from his seat a row or two behind Fitzgerald to shake Horan's hand.

If the story of their party leader getting outfoxed by Haughey on the steps of Croke Park is something that Fine Gael supporters do not like to hear, then the story of Garret and the teddy bear is much worse. Fine Gaelers must blush to this day when they hear it.

The story goes that Fine Gael was in the middle of a general election battle in the 1980s and party leader Garret Fitzgerald was on the canvass trail in Cork. When he was presented with a large teddy bear decked out in red and white colours, Garret smiled at the donor and genially asked why the teddy was wearing the red and white colours!

Anything Fitzgerald may have done to damage Fine Gael's kudos in GAA circles in the early 1980s was certainly overturned with the arrival of Kerry legend Deenihan to the party ranks in 1982.

Deenihan's first GAA memory is of listening to the 1958 All-Ireland final between Kerry and Derry on the radio. Hearing the commentary on Mick O'Connell's and Jim McKeever's spectacular performances on the day, the young Deenihan dreamed of one day playing for Kerry in Croke Park.

After a number of underage successes with his club Finuge, Deenihan broke into the Kerry minor team and he played at corner-back on the team that lost out to Galway in the 1970 All-Ireland Minor final replay.

After finishing school he went to St Mary's College in Strawberry Hill, London, to study to become a PE teacher. Here he learned from a number of world-class coaches who had trained teams such as the British Olympics gymnastics team and Chelsea underage soccer teams.

He says, 'We did a lot of power and speed endurance and that really benefited my football career.'

The beginning of Deenihan's football odyssey was far from ideal. After losing the Minor All-Ireland in 1970, he lost the Under-21 final in 1972 before his team finally made a breakthrough and won the 1973 Under-21 title.

'Some of us on that team had suffered heavy defeats so there was a question mark over our ability to be successful Kerry players. That's why 1973 was very important for us as that was really the launching pad for that great Kerry team,' he adds.

Deenihan won his first Senior All-Ireland in 1975 and he recalls how their manager Mick O'Dwyer told them on the night of that win that they were good enough to go and win half a dozen All-Irelands.

'I think we might have believed him too much,' says Deenihan, who played in Kerry's defeats to Dublin in 1976 and 1977.

'But I think that after those defeats we became a very mature team. At that stage we knew the difference between winning and losing.'

Throughout Kerry's golden period in the late 1970s and 1980s, Deenihan and O'Dwyer became close friends. They roomed together on team trips to the US and Deenihan attests to understanding O'Dwyer more than most. The pair are still close friends.

'Micko inherited a very strong, enthusiastic and well-motivated panel of players by virtue of the fact that we had lost All-Ireland Minor and Under-21 finals. We knew what it was like to lose and that drove our ambitions to win,' he claims.

Mick O'Dwyer had about 18 years playing experience under his belt when he became Kerry manager so he had a thorough knowledge of the game. If the Kerry team were training in Killarney at 7.30 p.m., O'Dwyer would arrive at the pitch at 6.30 p.m. to have the pitch set up for training.

Deenihan remembers that the football was always the most important piece of equipment in any O'Dwyer training session. Micko had his own very specific training methods and not a second of the hour and ten minutes long training session was wasted.

Deenihan recalls, 'He would rarely lift his voice. He would only stop play occasionally to correct a mistake. Generally he let the play flow and as a result we developed an understanding as players rather than Micko imposing that understanding on us. People got to know each other so well that they just knew what was in each other's minds when we had the ball. That is why we were so good at supporting each other, running off the ball and making space for each other.'

After being beaten by Dublin in the 1976 All-Ireland final and the 1977 semi-final, Kerry were ready for success in 1978. They hammered Dublin on a score-line of Kerry 5–11 to Dublin's 0–9. The following year, Kerry beat Dublin again and their win over Roscommon in the 1980 final marked a Kerry three-in-a-row.

Deenihan collected his seventh consecutive Munster Championship medal in 1981, and 21 September the same year left Deenihan with his best memory from his playing days.

'The first All-Ireland is always a big one so winning that in 1975 was a great day. But my greatest memory was captaining the Kerry team in 1981. It is a major badge of honour in Kerry to be captain of the football team.'

When the final whistle blew, the scoreboard read: Kerry 1–12 Offaly 0–8. Deenihan recalls being very affected by the occasion that he had dreamed of all his life.

'I found it a strange sensation to stand in the Hogan Stand and lift Sam Maguire. I know how important football is to people in Kerry and to my father in particular. He always boasted that he never missed an All-Ireland from 1924 until the time he died in 1974. He was a religious man but the two great elements of his life were Gaelic football and Michael Collins. That is all he ever spoke about,' laughs Deenihan.

'I was only 10 or 11 when I first played football with Finuge as a juvenile. The first touch of the ball I got, I got a goal and I just remember the reaction of my father. He was so excited that his son had arrived.

'So all of those emotions come together when you are up there to lift Sam Maguire. My dad died seven years before it, but my mother was there and he was certainly there in spirit.'

Deenihan played as a back in six All-Ireland finals for Kerry and, astonishingly, he only ever conceded one point in the six finals. Even more astonishing is the fact that conceding that one point still rankles with Deenihan – nearly 30 years later.

With a wry grin on his face, he says, 'There is a mistake made in some GAA books. Some people say that I conceded two points in the six finals so I would like to clarify that. There was just one. Another defender called for that ball and I stood back, foolishly, and Offaly's Brendan Lowry nipped in and put the ball over the bar.

'It was my fault as I should not have hesitated. He who hesitates is lost. I heard a call and momentarily hesitated. Brendan Lowry was a very good player, very skilful and very resilient. We enjoyed a couple of really hard battles.'

Brendan Lowry, who is the father of the professional golfer Shane Lowry, was on his way to the Listowel races in 1981 with his brother and Offaly teammate Sean, when they decided to call in to Deenihan's GAA club, Finuge, where the Kerry team were enjoying a homecoming celebration.

'To have that magnanimity to come to the celebrations when the cup came to Finuge was a great gesture. The Lowrys were fine individuals,' says Deenihan.

As Deenihan and a number of his teammates stood on the back of a trailer in Finuge with the Sam Maguire, they spotted the Lowrys. Sean Lowry was pulled from the crowd and brought up onto the trailer.

He touched Sam Maguire, smiled and said, 'It'll be back in Offaly next year!'

Nobody else in Finuge believed Lowry that night, but Offaly had designs on stopping Kerry winning the five-in-a-row, even at that early stage.

Deenihan went on to captain Kerry to the National League title in early 1982, and after that it was time to get down to the serious business of training for Kerry's five-in-a-row.

The week after the League final, Mick O'Dwyer had his team back in Fitzgerald Stadium in Killarney for training. The session had more or less ended when O'Dwyer called for the last attack in a training game of 'backs and forwards'.

O'Dwyer always liked to end his sessions on a high note for his forwards, preferably with one of them outwitting one of the backs and getting a score. After what was supposed to be the last attack broke down, O'Dwyer called for another one. He told his players that they were going to have one extra attack, when disaster happened.

The ball broke between Deenihan and corner-forward John Egan. Deenihan recalls how he was a little behind Egan so he put his foot in to knock the ball away.

'Our legs just got entangled together. My leg got caught in the ground and we fell in the opposite direction. I broke my leg in three places. The sound of the broken bone could be heard in every part of the stadium,' recalls Deenihan.

The sound of Deenihan's breaking leg echoing through the empty Fitzgerald Stadium marked a major blow to Kerry's chances of winning five-in-a-row. But Deenihan refused to give in and did everything possible to get back to full fitness for the third Sunday in September.

'I tried everything to get back for the All-Ireland. I convinced the surgeon that my leg felt great even though I was in pain and I got him to take the plaster off,' he says.

After that he walked Ballybunion Strand every morning at dawn, in the hope that the salt water would aid his recovery. He swam daily in a pool in Killarney and did weights training in Tralee.

He also read a lot of books and took inspiration from the story of Rocky Bleier. Bleier played American football for the Pittsburgh Steelers in 1969 before he was drafted for service with the US army in Vietnam. That August he was caught in an ambush that left him with rifle wounds in his left leg and shrapnel from a grenade embedded in his right leg.

Bleier, amazingly, returned to America and took it upon himself to rebuild himself. By 1980 he had regained his place with the Pittsburgh Steelers. If Rocky Bleier could do it, so could Jimmy Deenihan. By the time the All-Ireland final came around, Deenihan was back running and he was able to kick a ball.

'I suppose I just wanted to be part of it. After being part of it for seven years and having won so many All-Irelands, I wanted to be part of the team and the atmosphere of training for five-in-a-row,' he claims.

O'Dwyer knew that Deenihan was not fit to play in a game of such magnitude so soon after his leg break, so he left Deenihan on the substitutes' bench for the final. He promised Deenihan that if Kerry were winning by a decent margin, he would give him five minutes game time at the end.

'We were not complacent. We had trained very hard but Offaly had given us a very close run the previous year. Their manager, Eugene McGee, knew that there was very little between the two teams going into the game.

'They had great players like Matt Connor and his brothers and right through the team. They had one of the best ever goalkeepers in Martin Furlong, and McGee knew that. They had the ability and the capacity and McGee knew that because he had trained some of the Kerry players in UCD. He was underestimated and under-rated and he knew everything that was to be known about that Kerry team and he made it his business to find out everything about that team.'

The 1982 All-Ireland football final was one of the most memorable games ever played in Croke Park. Kerry had won the previous four All-Irelands. They were on the cusp of immortality: five-in-a-row. The T-shirts had been printed and the songs written. Kerry had led for most of the game.

By the sixty-ninth minute Kerry had scored 17 points. Offaly were behind on 15. Then it happened.

Offaly's Richie Connor passed the ball to Liam O'Connor who took a few strides before he launched a high kick in towards his forwards. RTÉ commentator

Michael O'Hehir called it 'the high, lobbing, dropping ball'.

Wearing the number 20 jersey, Offaly's Seamus Darby, who had just come onto the field, was standing on the edge of the square right behind Kerry's Tommy Doyle when the ball dropped into his hands. Darby turned and shot the ball past Charlie Nelligan into the Kerry goal. He had all but buried Kerry's five-in-a-row hopes.

Deenihan was in the Kerry dugout when the ball hit the net. Ever since that goal there has been debate over whether Darby pushed Doyle in the back before he gained possession and took his shot.

Deenihan says, 'It was a nudge more so than a push. It would have been very hard for the referee where he was positioned to have noticed that nudge because he was positioned out the field. It happened so quick that it would have been difficult for him, unless he was on the spot to see it.

'The great thing about his goal was the strike. It was one of the greatest ever strikes of a ball in Croke Park. First of all because of the skill he displayed in putting the ball in over Charlie Nelligan which wasn't an easy thing to do. Secondly, putting the ball in between his hands and the crossbar took a lot of skill.

'People remember the nudge but they don't remember the strike. I think that the strike and its historical importance in depriving Kerry of five-in-a-row should be remembered more.

'If we had won that All-Ireland there would never have been any dispute about who were the greatest team ever. The goal was a traumatic experience for us as it came so late in the match. Had it come a bit earlier, we would have been prepared for it. People were in shock after the game.'

Former GAA president Seán Kelly likens the way the Kerry supporters came out to show their appreciation during the team's homecoming to any Irish funeral.

Asked why that great team rarely get together as a group nowadays, Deenihan explains, 'Kerry football is like a conveyor belt. There have been a number of teams that have won All-Irelands so we were not just one group of players in isolation.

'There would still be a bond but we would not be meeting up too often. There was never an effort made to keep that group together. It is very difficult to do that.

'People have spoken about how the Dublin team of the same era had such camaraderie after that period. They stayed together but I think they had totally different circumstances, geographically and otherwise.

'I meet Eoin Liston, Ogie Moran, John O'Keeffe, Sean Walsh and Mikey Sheehy socially and through work on a regular basis. There is no annual event where we all get together. That is not how Kerry football works. It is not one identifiable group. It is a conveyor belt. You are just part of the whole movement that is Kerry football when you play with Kerry.'

He adds, 'The most important thing for any team is to be a unit on the field rather than off the field.'

In August 1999 the omission of seven-time All-Ireland winning Kerry player Jack O'Shea from the GAA's Team of the Millennium became a major talking point. Mayo's Seán Flanagan, a two-time All-Ireland winner, and Galway's Enda Colleran, a three-time winner, were the two corner-backs on that team.

So how did Deenihan feel about his own omission? He insists, 'I was never really into that recognition but if you compare my record with both of theirs [Enda Colleran and Seán Flanagan] I would have won more All-Irelands. Also, I haven't analysed who scored off them at that time but the primary function of a corner-back is to prevent his man scoring. I only conceded a point in six finals.

'Looking at the two corner-backs, I don't begrudge it to either of them as they were two great individuals, but I would say that if somebody was picking a team to maybe win an All-Ireland, I would be in the shake-up.

'The good thing about it is that Kerry picked a team of the millennium and I was on that. That was the important one.'

In November 1982, two months after Kerry's defeat to Offaly in the All-Ireland final, the minority Fianna Fáil government that had been in power since the previous February, fell, sparking a general election.

Deenihan had taught PE in Tarbert, County Kerry since 1975. He was enjoying it and his passion for sport had led him to pursue a post-graduate degree at Berkeley University in California. Using contacts he had built up during trips to the US with the Kerry team, he had made arrangements to go to the prestigious San Francisco university.

When the election was called, the former Kerry captain was approached by Fine Gael to see if he would contest the party's nomination to run.

He says, 'The GAA is the only reason I am a politician. It was the only reason I was asked to run for politics. I came from a strong Fine Gael background but I had never gone to a political meeting in my life. And it wasn't at all my ambition to be a politician.

'The only reason Fine Gael asked me to run for politics was because I was captain of the Kerry team in 1981. I had a big profile and there was name recognition. While I did come from a Fine Gael background, it wasn't because of any political potential I had, at that time,' he claims.

Before throwing his hat into the ring, Deenihan visited a lifelong friend to ask his advice. Should he go to San Francisco or make a bid for Leinster House?

If anyone knew what to do, then John B Keane would.

The celebrated playwright and novelist had been steeped in the Fine Gael tradition and he had held various organisational roles in the party over the years. More importantly, he had watched Irish politics for a lifetime.

'John B had been asked to run for Fine Gael himself. He had kind of a short fuse and he didn't have a high tolerance level as such but I am convinced he would have won a seat. It was lucky for him that he did not contest a seat as he would not have had as much time to write and he would not have left such a literary legacy.'

The conversation between Deenihan and Keane was very frank and to the point.

'He was absolutely honest with me. I'll always remember his words. He told me that politics was a very, very rough game and that your own people would be worse than the opposition,' recalls Deenihan.

'He had been involved in campaigns with the previous TD Gerald Lynch. He saw how that affected Gerald's time with his family and dragged him away from his business. So he mentioned that as an example.

'Then he said: "If you run for that nomination, not alone will I propose you but I will canvass with you for the rest of my life." '

With that, Deenihan decided to go for the party nomination against a number of people who knew a lot more about politics. On the night of the convention, Deenihan stood up in front of the room and gave his pitch. He explained how he had devoted so much energy to football for the previous 12 years from the time he played minor for Kerry in 1970 up to the night his leg snapped in Killarney.

'I told them that I was prepared to give the same energy and commitment to politics, which I have simply done. I just transferred that energy and motivation from football and training for it. It didn't change, it is just a different focus, a different commitment,' he says.

After being asked to run on the Thursday, Deenihan was selected as the candidate on the Saturday night. He ran a good campaign and narrowly lost out on a Dáil seat by just 140 votes.

'After that, people thought that I was just there to take the chance, that I wasn't really committed. The more people said that to me, the more it drove me to become a politician and win the next election, which I did.'

By initially dipping his toes into political waters, the sporting side of Deenihan's life changed forever.

'I just couldn't concentrate totally on my fitness. My whole schedule had changed and it wasn't conducive to training and eating and resting properly, so politics in that sense just changed my life.'

After narrowly missing out on the Dáil seat in 1982, Deenihan was appointed as a nominee of the Taoiseach, Garret Fitzgerald, to the Seanad in 1983.

Four years later, Deenihan garnered 10,087 votes and won a Dáil seat in Kerry North. Fine Gael lost 20 seats in that election so Deenihan bucked the national trend with his poll-topping performance.

He has applied the same philosophy to his politics that he employed during his football days.

'If you put time, energy and commitment into anything in life that is one of the elements that ensures success. I apply that to politics and I proved that in 1987 as I worked 14 hours a day.

'I found that, apart from name recognition, one of the great strengths being an athlete gave me was the fact that I had endurance. I could get up earlier in the morning and stay up later at night than the people that I was competing against. I could drive to Dublin in the middle of the night and I wouldn't fall asleep in the car and that was because of all the fitness I had built up as an athlete. That was possibly one of the most positive transfers to politics. The whole issue of being patient, disciplined and taking defeats are all part of politics as well as sport.'

Deenihan says that the media have always been fair to him in his political career but he has got adverse publicity at times.

'Sport teaches you to get used to the media. Although you had a good game, someone could name the best players in that game and leave you out. The football experience certainly was a great preparatory experience for politics. For that reason, there was a very positive transfer from sport to politics. A lot of the ingredients and elements that are necessary for the successful sportsman also apply to politics.'

Deenihan has been Fine Gael's party spokesperson on a number of issues, including Tourism, Culture and Sport; Youth and Sports; and Defence and Arts, since 1987.

In December 1994, then Taoiseach John Bruton appointed him junior minister at the Department of Agriculture, Food and Forestry but he has never held a Cabinet position. Is this a big regret?

Deenihan points out that there was a lot of talent on the Fine Gael benches in 1994 and some of this talent was overlooked altogether because Bruton had a limited number of Cabinet seats and junior ministries to give out.

He says, 'When you look at some of those who were overlooked, I was delighted to serve as a junior minister. Fine Gael does not get into power too often. Unfortunately, there are a large number of very talented people who will never get the chance of serving as a minister of state or as a Cabinet minister.

'In Fianna Fáil it comes a lot easier; they are far more casual about being a minister or minister of state because almost everyone with any ability in Fianna Fáil will be a minister at some stage in their political career. Unfortunately that does not happen in Fine Gael because we haven't been in power enough.

'Up until now, if we had been in government, I may have had a ministry. It is like winning an All-Ireland in Gaelic football. Being a minister is the culmination of your political ambition and that is something that I would like to have done.'

Deenihan has served under no fewer than five different Fine Gael leaders – Garret Fitzgerald, Alan Dukes, John Bruton, Michael Noonan and Enda Kenny – since he entered politics. He claims to have been close to them all but Noonan, from Limerick, is a very close personal friend.

Ask Deenihan about his regrets in football and he will immediately talk about his broken leg and Seamus Darby's goal in 1982. Ask him about his biggest regret in politics and he will talk about Michael Noonan.

Little over a year after taking over as Fine Gael leader in February 2001, Noonan led his party into a general election drubbing. Deenihan believes that the party was doomed from early on as Noonan did not have a solid network around him. There was 'a malaise hanging over the party' and they suffered badly in a number of pre-election opinion polls.

'The media destroyed him. They did not recognise the ability that he has,' claims Deenihan.

'He was just treated unfairly by them. Referring to him as a "clown" and "baldy Noonan" was very unfair. Everybody has some failings but the media demonised him.'

As the economic bubble was still alive, Bertie Ahern was very popular and it is doubtful if Fine Gael could have won that election with any other leader.

'Noonan certainly didn't get the opportunity to express himself and demonstrate his capability. He is still one of the sharpest TDs in the Dáil. The one regret I have in politics is that I would like to have seen Noonan fulfil his capabilities and talents.' This could yet happen as Noonan made a political comeback in June 2010 when Enda Kenny appointed him front bench finance spokeman after Richard Bruton's failed Fine Gael leadership heave.

Deenihan has always stayed loyal to Noonan. Loyalty is important to Kerrymen. The night he was asked to enter politics, John B Keane promised him that he would always be loyal, and he kept his word.

Fine Gael went into meltdown under Noonan in the 2002 election and lost 23 seats. As the party's campaign imploded in disarray on a national level, Deenihan had real fears that he would lose his seat.

In the days before the 17 May polling day, he was out canvassing in Castleisland when he got a call from John B. He said, 'Jimmy, I want to canvass for you in this election.' Keane came out and started knocking on doors with Deenihan. He died two weeks after the election.

Deenihan says, 'I remember coming in after the election in 2002. I had held on by about 500 votes but Fine Gael seats fell all over the place. We were in total meltdown and I hung on. That was by far the toughest election but it was because of people like John B that I hung on.'

Back to Garret Fitzgerald and his failure to recognise the Cork teddy bear. Deenihan believes that the stories about Fitzgerald's lack of interest in the GAA are over-exaggerated.

'It is wrong to categorise people. Garret, like most people, would appreciate the importance of Gaelic games,' says Deenihan.

'The teddy bear story was kind of used against him but he was clued in to the importance of GAA. In 1987, when I was running for election and Garret was down in Kerry, we got a bunch of previous Kerry captains who all happened to be Fine Gael, to come in with me and he was very clued in to the whole football story.'

Deenihan's defence of Fitzgerald flies in the face of the decades of scorn Fine Gael have endured over the teddy bear. Maybe Fitzgerald has been unfairly mocked over failing to recognise Pádraig Horan or the teddy bear? Fine Gaelers may still wince at the apparent awkward relationship Fitzgerald had with the GAA but they can stick out their chests and boast about the fact that they have in the party ranks, 'one of the great corner backs of our time'.

5

John Donnellan
Right Half-Back

GALWAY – FINE GAEL

'If it was raining soup, Alan Dukes would have a fork in his hand.'

W ales gave us the Tudors, Austria gave us the Hapsburgs, Scotland gave us the Stuarts and Galway gave us the Donnellans from Dunmore.

While Ireland's Medieval High Kings such as the O'Neills and the O'Donnells were the closest thing this country had to dynasties, a number of GAA families have also earned that title.

The McCartans in Down, the Ó Sés in Kerry and, in more recent times, the Brogans in Dublin fall into this category but the best-known dynasty in GAA has to be the Donnellans of Dunmore.

Michael, or Mick, Donnellan who won All-Ireland medals with Galway and set up the Clann na Talmhan party in the 1930s is selected among the forwards in this 'Dáil-Star team' and his son John, or Johneen, is the automatic choice for the right half-back position.

John Donnellan was born in Dunmore, County Galway in 1937, two years before his father Mick set up a political party that promised to give a voice to struggling farmers, Clann na Talmhan.

John's playing career started with Dunmore as a juvenile, as the other club in the parish, Carrantryla, had no underage teams. He returned to Carrantryla in 1954 and won a number of honours with the small club. But the tiny rural club was forced to amalgamate with the larger Dunmore MacHales club due to emigration.

Following in the footsteps of his father, 'Johneen' quickly emerged as a promising young footballer with Dunmore MacHales.

In his 1993 book *Football Captains: The All-Ireland Winners*, RTÉ Gaelic games commentator Brian Carthy wrote: 'His contemporaries agree that John Donnellan never asked anything of his players on the field of play that he himself was not prepared to give many times over. He was a tenacious defender, very strong, fiercely committed and renowned for his long, well-directed clearances.'

At club level Donnellan won five Galway senior club football championship medals (in 1961, 1963, 1966, 1968 and 1969), two county league medals (in 1962 and 1966) and three Connacht club championship medals (in 1963, 1968 and 1969).

The Dunmore MacHales team, of which he was a part, was one of the best club teams in the country as it boasted names such as Donnellan and his brother Pat, or Pateen as he is known, and other Galway county stars such as Bosco McDermott, Seamus Leydon, and the Keenan brothers, John and Tommy.

Jack Mahon, the 1956 All-Ireland winner with Galway who would later author scores of GAA books, also played on the same team when the twilight of his own career overlapped with the start of Donnellan's career.

In Michael Leydon's 1983 book, *Dunmore MacHales: A history of football in Dunmore parish*, he describes John Donnellan by saying: 'Fire, grit, determination . . . all of these can be applied with equal ease to the finest wing-back to don the green and white. At county level, the bigger the name, the greater the challenge. Winner of every honour in the game, from county championships to All-Irelands, his will to win has never been surpassed in the GAA. A worthy son of Mick Donnellan and a true champion in the Olympian sense . . . '

Donnellan may have been the 'finest wing-back to don the green and white' of Dunmore, but it was his exploits as an inter-county player that made him a GAA icon.

His first major honour with Galway came in 1958 when he won an All-Ireland Junior title. Galway beat Leitrim and Mayo before beating Sligo in the Connacht final. After beating Kerry by three points in the All-Ireland semi-final, Galway went on to defeat Meath by 1–10 to 0–7 in the 'home' final in Tullamore. They would later beat Lancashire in the 'final proper' in Ballinasloe. Donnellan played at right half-back on that team, a position he would later make his own on the senior side. Sean Meade, who later joined Donnellan in the half-back line on Galway's greatest ever team, played at left corner-back on the 1958 junior team.

Later in the year Donnellan played his first game for the Galway senior team in a league game against Roscommon, and in 1959 he played in Croke Park for the first time in a league tie against Dublin.

In Jack Mahon's 1965 book about Galway football, *Twelve Glorious Years*, he wrote, 'John Donnellan had a most unhappy Croke Park debut on Kevin Heffernan, and Sean Meade was not much happier on Johnny Joyce. Recently I reminded John Donnellan of his debut and he wondered how he could be so badly stricken with stage-fright.'

Over the next few years Donnellan put his baptism of fire firmly behind him as he became one of the first names on the Galway senior team sheet. Along with his brother Pat, John was on the Galway team that reached the 1963 All-Ireland final against Dublin in front of a crowd of 87,706.

Despite Mahon claiming that Donnellan 'looked after dangerous Dublin centre half-forward Mickey Whelan in capital fashion', Dublin emerged victors on a final score line of Dublin 1–9 to Galway's 0–10. The Dublin team was captained by Des Foley, who would later join Donnellan as a TD in Dáil Éireann.

The heartbreak of losing the 1963 decider acted as a catalyst to motivating

Galway to get back to the following year's All-Ireland final. Ahead of the 1964 championship, the Galway team made the journey to England to participate in the now-defunct annual Whit Weekend games at London's Wembley stadium.

Started by Cork native, Fr Tom McNamara, in 1958, Irish GAA teams used to travel to London annually on the weekend of the religious feast, Whit Sunday, to play exhibition games for Irish emigrants. The games continued until the mid-1970s when dwindling attendances saw the curtain brought down on them.

Donnellan's Galway exacted a small piece of revenge on Dublin in Wembley when they beat them by 0–10 to 0–4 in front of a live BBC television audience.

When the 1964 championship commenced, Galway beat Sligo, Mayo, and Meath to book a place in the All-Ireland final against Kerry.

As John's brother Pateen Donnellan had not recovered from a knee injury, he was included in the substitutes for the final. Aside from that injury, the Galway team of soon-to-be household names basically 'picked itself' for the final. The team was: Johnny Geraghty, Enda Colleran, Noel Tierney, John Bosco McDermott, the captain John Donnellan, Sean Meade, Martin Newell, Mick Reynolds, Mick Garrett, Cyril Dunne, Mattie McDonagh, Seamus Leydon, Christy Tyrrell, Sean Cleary and John Keenan.

The Kerry team boasted names such as Mick O'Connell, Mick O'Dwyer and Jo Jo Barrett, a son of the legendary Joe Barrett. But Galway humbled the Kingdom with a 0–15 to 0–10 win.

In *The Irish Times* the following day, Paddy Downey reported, 'Kerry met a Galway side who played magnificent football from start to finish, whose skill in all departments had seldom been equalled and who should have won the All-Ireland by 15 points instead of five.'

Jack Mahon wrote how he met 'a rather tired looking' Mick Donnellan on his way into the Hogan Stand before the minor match.

'Mick would not miss a kick of the minor final. That was Mick. A great lover of football, he was one of Galway's most loyal supporters down the years,' wrote Mahon. 'I hoped for his sake as well as our own that his son John would receive the Sam Maguire before the evening was over.'

Like every other GAA man, the Clann na Talmhan TD lived in the hope that he would see one of his sons win an All-Ireland. But, as Galway were demolishing Kerry in the 1964 final, he died suddenly in the Hogan Stand during the match.

In Raymond Smith's 1971 book, *Football Immortals*, he explained how John Donnellan went up to receive the Sam Maguire Cup without knowing that his father had just died. Afterwards, John was swept across the field by 'a tide of excited, exuberant supporters to the dressing room'. He turned to one of his teammates on entering the dressing room and said, 'Let's bring the cup across to the old man.'

With that, Donnellan intuitively knew that something was wrong. Legendary Dunmore MacHales clubman and Galway player Brendan Nestor, who had played on the first Connacht team to win the Railway Cup with Mick Donnellan in 1934, came over to him and put his hand on his shoulder.

Nestor said, 'It's your father John – it's bad.' To which John replied, 'Is he dead?' and Nestor said, 'Yes, I'm afraid so.'

Then a visibly emotional Donnellan poignantly said, 'I would have really loved if he had been alive to see me receive the cup, for he had said to me beforehand, "you'll have to let me carry the base of the cup home to Dunmore".'

Instead, it was Mick Donnellan's coffin that was carried back to Dunmore. It was carried to the grave by some of Galway's All-Ireland-winning players. A week that should have been one of jubilation in Galway was tinged with immense grief as a double tragedy hit the Tribesmen. As Mick Donnellan passed away in the Hogan Stand, another one of the county's GAA icons, Mick Higgins, who had captained the Galway team that beat Dublin in the 1934 final, died while watching the game at home on television.

When the new season arrived, the Galway squad was eager to prove that their 1964 title was no flash-in-the-pan win and they progressed to the 'home' league final against Kerry. That match had an added appeal, as the winners were guaranteed a trip to the United States to play New York in what was then known as the 'league final proper'.

Galway beat Kerry to secure a trip to the States, where they played New York twice on successive Sundays in June and July to win on an aggregate score of Galway 4–12, New York 0–17. Pat Donnellan was Galway's star player at midfield during the trip in New York.

As the Galway team was in New York in early summer, the Connacht GAA council gave them a bye to the Connacht final where they beat Sligo. Despite showing 'post-American trip staleness' they were now firmly in the chase for a second All-Ireland title in a row.

A three-point win in the semi-final against a Down team, many of whom had won All-Ireland titles in 1960 and 1961, saw Galway back in the All-Ireland final against Kerry. Match reports from the time suggest that, after a shaky start, John Donnellan 'contained the mercurial Paddy Doherty [one of Down's stars] better than ever in the past'.

Mayo in the 1950s, with stars like Seán Flanagan, who would later become a Fianna Fáil TD, and Roscommon in the 1940s, with future Clann na Poblachta TD Jack McQuillan, had both managed to win back-to-back All-Ireland titles. So, ahead of the 1965 final, every member of the Galway squad was obsessed with emulating what Mayo and Roscommon had previously achieved.

The final was a tough physical game that was marred by indiscriminate fouling and jersey-pulling. It came to be labelled a 'survival of the fittest encounter' where 13 of the game's total 21 scores came from free kicks. One of the few players to play well in the bruising encounter was Pat Donnellan. The Galway management switched him from marking Bernie O'Callaghan onto Kerry's other midfielder, Mick O'Connell. He managed to stem the performance of Kerry's best player and helped Galway to a three-point win as the final score was Galway 0–12 to Kerry's 0–9.

John Donnellan was one of three players, two from Kerry and one from Galway, to be sent off in one of the incidents that tarnished the game. Mahon wrote about how Enda Colleran delivered an outstanding speech from the Hogan Stand after the game and called 'for three cheers for Kerry in the traditional manner' to which he was 'greeted with many boos.'

An article in the following week's *Tuam Herald* under the byline JPB, proudly claimed, 'To beat Kerry once is worth two All-Irelands, to beat them two years running is Galway's greatest achievement.'

While the sixties may have become a period of social revolution across the globe, Jack Mahon's *Twelve Glorious Years*, published a few months after Galway's two-in-a-row, remarked how Donnellan's team had 'made it fashionable' to play Gaelic football.

The book's epilogue gives an unbelievably politically incorrect take on how the Galway team should be held up as an example against the long-haired 'sissy' generation of the sixties. Mahon wrote, 'As idols of the youth, they bear themselves well and are a credit to the county's maroon and white. What a pleasant contrast they are to the much idolised, long-haired gentlemen who seem to take queer pride in being effeminate.

'In my youth the worst insult one could offer to any lad was to call him a sissy. As long as the present Galway team are accepted as models, the 'sissy' craze will not emerge. For that relief, much thanks.'

In 1966 Galway were going for a three-in-a-row of All-Ireland titles. The great team managed to get to Croke Park on the third Sunday in September by beating Roscommon and Mayo in Connacht and Cork in the semi-final.

Raymond Smith's book, *Football Immortals*, described how the week before the All-Ireland was one of heartbreak for John Donnellan. During the 1964 final his father had died as he captained the winning team, then he was sent off in the 1965 final and now for the 1966 decider he was dropped from the team.

Smith wrote, 'John Donnellan was dropped for the final. Granted he had been nursing an injury but by the time the final line-up came to be selected it was felt that he was fit enough – he had been training hard to take his place in the side. The camp was rife with rumours of a 'split' . . . '

He added, 'Suffice it to say that when the prospect of a united approach to the winning of the three-in-a-row hung in the balance, John Donnellan put the honour of Galway first, sank his own feelings for the good of the team, stood in a tension-filled room and said that he would be with them fully . . . It was John's finest display for Galway.'

With Enda Colleran as captain, Galway went on to beat Meath in the final by 1–10 to 0–7 and Donnellan came on as a substitute for Sean Meade and won his third All-Ireland medal.

That same year, Dunmore MacHales completed the double of county league and championship victories, and a great run of club successes culminated with back-to-back county championship and Connacht club titles in 1968 and 1969.

By the end of his inter-county career, John Donnellan had amassed three Senior All-Ireland medals, six Connacht Senior medals, one Junior All-Ireland medal and a Railway Cup medal. As well as holding the distinction of being a part of Galway's three-in-a-row winning team in the 1960s, Donnellan also holds the distinction of being one of the few GAA players to win an All-Ireland medal while he was a sitting TD.

He was elected to the Dáil on 3 December 1964 in the by-election held to fill the seat left vacant after his father Mick's sudden death in Croke Park on All-Ireland final day – so he won the 1965 and 1966 titles as a TD.

In the weeks after Clann na Talmhan TD Mick Donnellan's death, attention turned to candidates to succeed him and as John had just captained Galway to an All-Ireland title, he was the obvious choice.

Dr Tony Varley, the NUI Galway academic who has studied the Clann na Talmhan party, explained why John Donnellan was not asked to stand for the party his father had founded.

Founded in 1939 Clann na Talmhan took the national political scene by storm when they won 10 Dáil seats in the 1943 general election. But the party's fortunes had dwindled away leaving the Dáil with just two Clann na Talmhan

TDs by 1961 – Joseph Blowick and Mick Donnellan.

Varley's study into the small party's history explained how John Donnellan was counselled into standing for Fine Gael. In view of Clann na Talmhan's financial and organisational weakness and the certainty of a Fianna Fáil by-election victory if Fine Gael and Clann na Talmhan were to field separate candidates, Donnellan was advised to accept an offer to stand for Fine Gael.

'A proposal that John Donnellan should go before the public as a Clann na Talmhan candidate could muster no more than five per cent support at the movement's last official gathering,' wrote Varley. So the Clann na Talmhan movement in north Galway was absorbed into Fine Gael, and the party that Mick Donnellan had set up was dissolved in 1965, after Blowick, the party's sole TD, decided not to contest that year's general election.

John Donnellan won the 1964 Galway East by-election with 20,920 votes compared to Fianna Fáil candidate Tom Hussey's 19,612 votes and Sinn Féin candidate Pádraig O'Ceallaigh's 1,497. The Donnellan GAA dynasty had just become a Donnellan political dynasty to match.

In Michael Leydon's history of the Dunmore MacHales club, he said, 'The Donnellan name, along with the fact that John had captained the All-Ireland team, all contributed to this astonishing win.' After the election win in December, Donnellan was led by a torchlight procession from Milltown to a huge reception in his native Dunmore.

Within weeks of his election, Donnellan became the subject of some controversy after he became the victim of a stinging verbal attack from Fianna Fáil Senator Mark Killilea Snr. in January 1965. The annals of *The Connacht Tribune* newspaper show how Killilea claimed that Donnellan won his Dáil seat on the back of his success as a GAA player. Speaking at the annual meeting of the Tuam Fianna Fáil Cumann, Killilea blasted, 'Fianna Fáil could have burst the GAA by putting up a footballer in the recent East Galway by-election . . . The Galway jersey was displayed in that election and there are none so blind as those who do not want to see.'

He claimed that Fianna Fáil candidate Tom Hussey had garnered 20,000 votes in the by-election and said, 'When the general election comes along, Fianna Fáil will again gain a majority.'

In comments clearly directed at Donnellan he added that 'elections are not won by kid-glove methods. Elections are won by hard work and availing of every opportunity.'

The Connacht Tribune reported how the outgoing secretary of the Tuam Fianna Fáil organisation P. Talty stated, 'A GAA official denied that the GAA was used in this election, but this we cannot agree with. It was most definitely used as an election gimmick by the Fine Gael hierarchy.'

The controversial comments sparked one of the paper's readers to pen a letter to the editor the following week, rebuffing the Fianna Fáil criticisms and listing a number of reasons for Donnellan's election. Among these were the claims that he 'was selected as a Fine Gael candidate because of his wide personal and general appeal' and that the GAA was non-political and no GAA official used their position to help Donnellan's election bid.

The letter added, 'Had the mysterious football candidate been put forward by Fianna Fáil he would not have burst the GAA but merely underlined the fact that the GAA shelters followers of both major political parties, as the Dáil already does in the persons of such exponents of the Gaelic code as Fianna Fáil's Jack Lynch, Fine Gael's Henry Kenny and Labour's Brendan Corish.'

Despite the early criticism from political foes, Donnellan proved himself to be an able TD who maintained that unique Donnellan brand of politics that his late father had created. His electoral record stands testament to his reputation of being a dogged constituency worker as he was returned to the Dáil in every one of the eight general elections he contested between 1965 and 1987.

The way he survived a constituency review that seemed to sound his death knell in the Dáil in 1980 was a remarkable achievement. He showed innate political shrewdness when he chose to transfer his political base from Galway East to the new five-seater Galway West constituency as he managed to keep his seat in the five-seater.

Retired RTÉ commentator Micheál Ó Muircheartaigh, known as 'The voice of the GAA', tells the story of the day Donnellan was appointed a minister of state or 'junior minister' at the Department of Transport and Posts and Telegraphs by Taoiseach Garret Fitzgerald.

Ó Muircheartaigh said, 'John Donnellan was appointed as a minister on 14 December 1982. Shortly after his appointment to high office, he walked out of the door of Leinster House where his new State car was waiting. There he was, having been appointed as a junior minister, and he would have been welcome in any of the big Dublin hotels or in any big venue that night. But he instructed his driver to hit for Ballygar [in Galway], so he called to his friend Mattie McDonagh. Mattie got the first spin in John Donnellan's new State car in 1982.'

Even though Donnellan had been a TD for 18 years at that stage, the friendship he forged with his three-in-a-row winning Galway teammate, McDonagh, was never forgotten.

When Alan Dukes took over from Fitzgerald as leader of Fine Gael in 1987, Donnellan was aggrieved to have been left out of Dukes' front bench. *The Irish Times* reported in March 1988 that 'personal relations between the two men have been bad since Dukes became party leader last year and ignored the former minister of state when he distributed portfolios.

'Donnellan's anger over his rejection was exhibited publicly at last October's Ard Fheis when, as chairman of the national executive, he refused to preside over one of the sessions when it would have involved introducing Dukes to the delegates.'

From the moment Alan Dukes became leader of Fine Gael after the February 1987 general election and omitted Donnellan from his front bench, the pair were on a collision course. And the smash was spectacular when it happened. Splashed across the front page of *The Connacht Tribune* on 25 March 1988 was a statement issued by Donnellan to journalist John Cunningham that will forever be remembered in Irish politics.

Donnellan was a harsh critic of the way Dukes had agreed the 'Tallaght Strategy' of conditionally supporting the government, provided it was doing what Fine Gael felt was correct for the country. In a statement dealing with the Fine

Gael party's policy on rod licences for trout and coarse anglers, he criticised the party for facilitating the passage of the angling licence legislation through the Dáil as one of a number of 'wrong options'.

In what appeared to be a statement on a relatively innocuous matter, Donnellan said, 'Fine Gael took the wrong option and they made a very poor decision when they accommodated the government to put through this legislation before Christmas, especially when one takes into consideration that free fishing had been advertised in the brochures that these people had been using for the coming season. They should forget it at least for this year and possibly for ever.

'We as a party have taken an awful lot of wrong options and this was another one of them. The political ground is very fertile for us and has been for the past 12 months, but we are making very little use of it.'

He ended the statement with the killer line: 'As a matter of fact, if it was raining soup, Alan Dukes would have a fork in his hand. He cannot pick up anything that is falling.'

The comments immediately sparked controversy as Cunningham's story was picked up by all the national newspapers the following day. *The Irish Times* reported how Donnellan's comments were dismissed as 'unimportant' and 'motivated by personal spleen' by a number of Fine Gael TDs. Dukes brushed off the attack and said Donnellan 'would be better employed directing his efforts to representing his constituency.'

Within days of Donnellan's outburst, the local Fine Gael organisation in his constituency, then Galway West, held a five-hour meeting before they issued a statement disassociating themselves from Donnellan's remarks. The controversy proved extremely divisive at local level as the Fine Gael's constituency secretary, Mark Concannon, resigned in protest at the way the organisation had distanced themselves from Donnellan's remarks.

Concannon said that he did not want 'to be part of a dictatorship in Galway West which only accepts policies as dictated from Dublin and which sees any other viewpoint as disloyal.'

A few weeks after Donnellan's incendiary comments, Dukes moved to assert his authority over the party by unexpectedly proposing that Donnellan should have the party whip removed. A Fine Gael spokesman told *The Irish Times* on 13 April that the 'raining soup' remark was not the sole reason for moves to expel Donnellan from Fine Gael. He cited Donnellan's unexplained absence from a Dáil vote on the future of Barrington's Hospital in Limerick in February and his refusal to chair the Ard Fheis session the previous October as reasons why the whip should be removed. He added, 'It was the straw that broke the camel's back, but the camel was already buckling considerably at the knees.'

The Fine Gael parliamentary party voted to expel Donnellan from the party at a meeting on 19 April 1988. Paddy Cooney proposed a compromise motion at the meeting, whereby Donnellan would be disciplined for his comments but not expelled. Cooney advocated the compromise instead of expulsion as Donnellan had expressed regret over his remarks.

The day after the meeting, *The Irish Times* reported, 'Donnellan gave a qualified apology to the parliamentary party for his remarks, saying that he recognised that they were not in good taste. He did not see his remarks to Dukes as offensive, and regretted it if they were.'

There is still a sense to this day among some Fine Gael figures that the 'raining soup' affair could have been handled better by Dukes as Donnellan's expulsion from the party in 1988 effectively ended his political career. Although the general consensus within the party at the time was that Donnellan would have had the party whip restored had he re-applied, he remained as an independent TD and did not contest the 1989 general election.

Donnellan still lives on the family farm at Cloonmore near Dunmore and his exit from the national political stage over 20 years ago certainly did not mark the death knell of the Donnellan dynasty.

Following in the footsteps of their grandfather Mick and their father John, John's sons Michael and John Donnellan proved themselves to be outstanding footballers and both played for Galway. It was a remarkable feat for the Donnellan family when Michael was one of the main stars on Galway's All-Ireland winning teams in 1998 and 2001. An amazing run from him, up the whole field in the first half of the match against Kildare that culminated in a point from Sean Óg de Paor, is regarded as one of the greatest scores ever in Croke Park and it was voted number 1 in RTÉ's *Top 20 GAA Moments* in 2003. He was named the All-Stars Footballer of the Year in 1998 and won a place on the 2000 All-Star team.

After leaving the Dunmore MacHales club, he went on to win an All-Ireland club championship medal with the Salthill-Knocknacarra club in 2005. The following year, Michael was appointed captain of the Galway senior football team. When he led the Tribesmen out onto the pitch at Pearse Stadium for a Connacht championship game with Sligo, he emulated his father and grandfather in becoming yet another Donnellan to captain Galway.

Austria may have had the Hapsburgs and Wales gave us the Tudors but Galway gave Irish politics and the GAA an amazing dynasty – the Donnellans from Dunmore.

Austin Stack
Centre Half-Back

KERRY — SINN FÉIN

'In an amazing twist of fate, the old rusty gun sitting on the Barretts'
table in 1968 was the same gun that Stack had concealed
on the night he was captured by pro-Treaty forces in April 1923.'

Kerry have won 36 All-Ireland football titles and the National Football League on 19 occasions. It riles people from other counties but a record like that gives Kerry supporters a licence to utter the perennial phrase: 'Kerry is the home of football.'

Detractors would say that William Moore Stack has a lot to answer for. On 31 May 1885, he and a number of others founded the first GAA club in Kerry at a public meeting in Tralee.

The following month the fledgling club sponsored a sports day, and the first athletic meeting under the auspices of the GAA took place in the town on 17 June.

This new event – involving hurling and football, as well as running, jumping and throwing events – caused quite a stir among the town's upwardly mobile sporting elite as it clashed with the annual jamboree organised by the County Kerry Athletic and Cricket Club under the auspices of the Irish Amateur Athletic Association (IAAA).

The GAA event managed to attract a crowd of 12,000 compared to the 1,000 who turned up for the IAAA event. The GAA had not only attracted the biggest crowd, the sports day in Tralee was also seen as a landmark event in the earliest chapter of Kerry's GAA story.

William Moore Stack's involvement in various other nationalist causes such as the Fenian movement influenced his son Austin who was also a separatist and supporter of physical force nationalism.

Born on 7 December 1879, Augustine Mary Moore Stack, or Austin Stack as he was better known, had a tough childhood. His father was jailed for a year for his involvement in the Land League when Stack was just two years old. Austin's mother died in 1889 when he was ten.

Between 1903 and 1905, six of Austin's sisters and his brother Jim all emigrated to the United States in search of work. Records show that they arrived in Ellis Island, New York, before ending up in Philadelphia. They emigrated one by one, with each one saving up money and posting it home so the next sibling could afford the passage to America.

Austin and his brother Nicholas remained in Tralee as they had both managed to secure employment as law clerks in separate solicitors' practices in the town.

Stack biographer Anthony Gaughan claims that 'Austin was quiet and reserved in nature' and during his teenage years he became a sporting enthusiast and member of the local GAA club that had been partly established by his father.

William Moore Stack died after a short illness in October 1899, four years after the GAA club in Kerry was founded.

Joe Ó Muircheartaigh and TJ Flynn in *Princes of Pigskin: A Century of Kerry Footballers* point out that by 1900 the arduous work of people like Moore Stack in establishing the GAA in Kerry had not paid off, as the organisation's popularity had waned somewhat. Clubs from other Munster counties were winning provincial titles between them while Kerry was in the doldrums. Erin's Hope of Waterford, Nils, Dohenys and Fermoy of Cork, the Commercials of Limerick and Arravale Rovers of Tipperary all won Munster titles in the mid-to-late 1890s.

'At this time Austin was appalled at the Cinderella status of the national pastimes, in particular Gaelic football and hurling, vis-à-vis rugby and cricket in his native town and resolved to do something about it,' according to Gaughan's biography.

In 1901 he founded the John Mitchell's GAA club in Tralee with Maurice McCarthy, and became the first secretary. The club enjoyed success on the playing fields almost immediately, winning the Kerry county football championship for eight consecutive seasons from 1902 to 1909. The success of the new John Mitchell's club had a knock-on effect across Kerry as the GAA was re-organised and revitalised all over the county.

As well as the role of secretary of the club, Stack was an accomplished footballer and he captained the club team from its inception. He was selected to play on the Kerry county side in 1902 and he quickly established himself as a half-back on the team.

That team was involved in a number of epic tussles with Kildare in the early years of the last century. GAA historians believe that this series of games did a lot to develop the GAA and popularise Gaelic football.

The games attracted record crowds and, due to the high standard of skills displayed and the good spirit in which the games were played, the GAA garnered much positive publicity from them.

The record gate receipts at games from then on meant that the organisation's Central Council had enough money to purchase their headquarters site, now Croke Park, at Jones's Road, Dublin.

The first chapter of the epic Kerry v Kildare battle unfolded in the Autumn of 1905. The two counties were actually playing the 1903 All-Ireland football final, two years late, when a number of spectators encroached onto the pitch.

Kerry were winning but the referee was unable to play the last few minutes of the game because of the spectators' encroachment. The referee awarded the game to Kerry but Kildare lodged an objection that was upheld by the GAA's Central Council. A replay was ordered and that fixture ended in a draw before Kildare went on to win the third fixture.

The following summer, 1906, Kerry met Dublin in what was the 1904 All-Ireland final. Stack captained Kerry to victory in that game.

He was joint honorary secretary of the Kerry County Board from 1904 to 1908 and he concentrated on the administration of the GAA after his early retirement from playing, due to injury.

He also became a member of the GAA's Munster and Central councils where he strived to improve the administrative side of the organisation. At the 1908 GAA congress, as a result of a motion proposed by Stack, it was decided that from then on all GAA accounts should be audited by chartered accountants.

In the early days of the GAA, players trained alone but, as a result of another Stack initiative, the Kerry football team collectively trained for a week before the 1913 All-Ireland football final against Louth. Collective training ahead of the final became the norm for teams after that.

In 1914 Stack was elected chairman of the county board, a position he held for two years. After a year-long lapse in 1916 he was re-elected chairman in March 1917.

After much prompting from Stack in 1921, the ancient Tailteann Games were revived and held in 1924, 1928 and 1932.

As well as following the path made by his father into the GAA, Austin Stack was also greatly influenced by his father's Fenian background and he became politically active in 1908 when he joined the Irish Republican Brotherhood.

Tralee-based auctioneer, Eddie Barrett, who is Austin's great-grand nephew (or Austin Stack's brother Nicholas's grandson), has studied Stack's life carefully. Barrett explains that in 1908 his great-grand uncle was living in digs in Rock

Street, Tralee. He was very involved in Conradh na Gaeilge and he used to give Irish lessons in his digs. He was also very politically alert and joined the IRB at that time. He combined his activities of being secretary of the Kerry GAA County Board with his role in the IRB and that made it easy for him to get around the country for IRB activity and meetings.

Marcus De Búrca in *The GAA: A History* wrote about the way in which figures like Stack infiltrated the GAA: 'particularly between 1907 and 1910 as Sinn Féin spread to widely separated parts of the country, prominent local members and supporters of that body, conscious of the value of the GAA in furthering their cause, pushed themselves to the front on several GAA county boards.'

Like so many other Irish republicans, such as Eoin O'Duffy in Monaghan, Stack used the GAA as a recruiting ground for the IRB. GAA clubs were also used as a cover for Volunteers to train, as they could practise military drills with hurleys.

Stack was the commandant of the Kerry Brigade of the Irish Volunteers in 1916, and he was involved in the planned landing of arms by Roger Casement at Banna Strand.

Stack biographer Anthony Gaughan pointed out that by the spring of 1916 it is doubtful whether there were 500 Irish Volunteers in all of Kerry and the general population in the county was 'generally unsympathetic' towards them.

Gaughan claims that if Austin Stack had succeeded with the arms importation it would have been a great surprise. The odds were against him from the start as *The Aud*, which was carrying the German arms, arrived sooner than expected by Stack and the Kerry Volunteers. This, along with other factors such as the Germans' failure to equip *The Aud* with radio, led to the British capture of the arms.

After Casement's arrest on Easter Saturday following the botched gunrunning plot, Stack was involved in an audacious attempt to have Casement released from RIC custody.

Eddie Barrett explains how Stack was well known in legal circles in Tralee from going in and out of court as a law clerk so he was able to go into the RIC station and enquire about Casement. It was initially thought that Stack might have been able to get Casement out of custody without a shot being fired. Stack had planned to use some of his contacts in the local RIC to get Casement released but the RIC Special Branch intervened, with Stack being arrested and imprisoned as a result.

He was sent to Spike Island prison before being court-martialled in Richmond Barracks and sentenced to 20 years in jail.

He was later released under the general amnesty by Lloyd George on 18 June 1917. Later that year Stack was jailed again in Mountjoy Prison, where he was involved in a hunger strike with founding member of the Volunteers and fellow Kerryman, Thomas Ashe. They went on hunger strike to demand prisoner-of-war status in jail. While Stack survived the protest, Ashe died on 25 September 1917 in the Mater hospital after being force-fed by prison authorities. When the jury at the inquest into Ashe's death criticised the 'barbaric' way the prison authorities had treated him, there was a public outcry and the ranks of the republican movement swelled with new recruits.

After his release in 1917, Stack became joint secretary of Sinn Féin with Darrell Figgis. He was also appointed deputy chief of staff of the IRA in March 1918.

However Stack was imprisoned again the following month in Crumlin Road Jail, Belfast. He was involved in orchestrating further prison protests and the prisoners won political status under his leadership. But the political status was gradually withdrawn so, in December 1918, Stack led 100 political prisoners in staging a revolt in the jail. They destroyed the prison by smashing it up, and a riot with the RIC ensued.

After what was dubbed the 'Belfast mutiny', Stack was elected, unopposed, as a Sinn Féin MP for West Kerry in the historic election of 14 December 1918. After that election, Sinn Féin's elected MPs boycotted the British parliament in Westminster and set up Dáil Éireann on 21 January 1919.

Stack was not at that historic first meeting of the Dáil in Dublin's Mansion

House as he had been transferred from Belfast to Strangeways Prison in Manchester for orchestrating the Belfast jail riot. He managed to thwart the prison authorities when he escaped from Strangeways with five others in October 1919. Michael Collins personally supervised that escape.

Even though he was elected to the first Dáil, it was November 1919 before Stack really entered politics. The president of the first Dáil, Éamon de Valera, before leaving to travel to America on June 1919, told Arthur Griffith, who became acting president in de Valera's absence, that Stack should be included in the Cabinet when he came out of jail.

About a week after Stack's arrival back in Dublin, Griffith offered him a place in the Cabinet as Minister for Home Affairs.

Anthony Gaughan wrote that the recent prison escapee accepted the offer and attended a meeting of the Cabinet in a lodging house in Fitzwilliam Street on 26 November 1919. His appointment as minister was formally agreed to by the Cabinet on 16 January 1920 and later ratified by Dáil Éireann on 29 June 1920.

After taking over the ministry from Arthur Griffith, who had held the post from the inception of the first Dáil in January 1919 until November in that year, Stack soon realised that little had been achieved.

A decree passed by the Dáil on 18 June 1919 authorising the establishment of a new arbitration courts system on a national scale, had gone nowhere. Stack set about a major reform that led to the establishment of the 'republican courts'. These were an integral part of the new administation's policy of undermining British rule in Ireland by attempting to replace the British legal system with a new courts system where local IRA figures, Catholic clergy or Sinn Féin figures who had authority, would act as arbitrators.

The courts existed until the Courts of Justice Act, 1924 was enacted, creating the Irish courts system that we still have today. Ken Loach's critically acclaimed 2006 film about the Irish War of Independence and subsequent Civil War, *The Wind that Shakes the Barley*, features a lengthy scene from a republican court session.

In 1921 Stack was returned as a TD for the new Kerry-Limerick West constituency in the second Dáil. He vehemently opposed the Anglo-Irish Treaty, and fought on the anti-Treaty side during the Civil War.

In early 1922 he travelled to the United States on a speaking tour and lived as a fugitive on his return to Ireland.

Throughout Stack's time on the run he always kept his gun, a .455 Webley revolver with him. When pro-Treaty forces arrived at the safe house near Sliabh na mBan in County Tipperary where Stack was hiding in April 1923, he could see that the game was up. Knowing that he was going to be caught, he quickly concealed his revolver in the attic.

Immediately afterwards he was captured by pro-Treaty forces and jailed. While he was in prison he went on hunger strike for 41 days before his release.

Although he was not as actively involved in the GAA in the early 1920s, the GAA never forgot him. In *The GAA: A People's History*, Mike Cronin, Mark Duncan and Paul Rouse explain that, even from behind prison bars, Stack had a significant impact on the organisation: 'In 1923 Kerry refused to play their All-Ireland final against Dublin in protest against the continued imprisonment of Austin Stack.'

After his release in July 1924 he remained a Sinn Féin TD for Kerry but he abstained from attending the Dáil. When Éamon de Valera founded the Fianna Fáil party in 1926, Stack was aghast.

Eddie Barrett says, 'Stack was hugely friendly with Michael Collins and de Valera but after Collins was shot the link was broken. When the Free State was established, republicans were ostracised and Stack found it difficult to come to terms with this.

'When it became known that de Valera was contemplating leaving Sinn Féin and founding a new party, Stack, could not get his head around this. He thought that the battle could be fought in an abstentionist manner and never joined Fianna Fáil.'

Stack was elected a TD in every election from the December 1918 elections up to 1927. He decided not to stand in the September 1927 general election, as his health had deteriorated as a result of his being on so many hunger strikes.

As a 14-year-old law clerk in Tralee, Stack had always dreamt of one day becoming a solicitor so after he bowed out of politics in 1927, he set about fulfilling his boyhood ambition.

Even though he had served as Minister for Home Affairs (a role akin to the modern day Minister for Justice) he was studying to become a barrister at the time of his death. He was due to sit his final exams when he passed away.

Stack married Una (nee Gordon) in August 1925 and the couple had no children. He died aged 49 on 27 April 1929 in the Mater hospital after years of ill-health.

He was buried in the patriots' circle in Glasnevin Cemetery and he remained in the honorary role of president of Kerry GAA right up to his death.

Nearly 40 years after his great-grand uncle's death, Eddie Barrett was sitting in his parents' home at 19 Princes Street, Tralee, doing his school homework a year before his Leaving Certificate exam, when he heard someone at the front door.

A strange man had come knocking on the door of the Georgian house near the Brandon Hotel. He said that he had travelled from his home in Tipperary, near Sliabh na mBan, to see Barrett's mother, who was a niece of Austin Stack and one of the few Stack relatives left in Tralee.

After the Barretts invited him into the house, he took something out of his pocket and placed it on the kitchen table. Wrapped in a very dry and aged oilcloth was an old rusty gun.

The Tipperary man, who was in his 60s, explained that when his father was on his deathbed a year or two earlier, he had told him that there was a gun in the attic of his house. The gun, a .455 Webley revolver, had been in the attic since the early 1920s and it had belonged to Austin Stack. Before the elderly man died, he asked his son to take the gun from the attic and make sure that it was returned to Stack's family in Tralee. The deceased man's son kept his word and tracked down the Barretts.

In an amazing twist of fate, the old rusty gun sitting on the Barretts' table in 1968 was the same gun that Stack had concealed in the attic of the house on the night he was captured by pro-Treaty forces in April 1923.

In 1968 a garda from Monaghan called Don Daly was stationed in Tralee and Eddie Barrett was friendly with him. Barrett asked Daly, who knew a lot about guns, to get Stack's revolver cleaned up and repaired.

Daly managed to restore the gun to perfect working order. A few months later he took the Barretts up to a beauty spot near Tralee, known as Scotia's Grave, where he allowed them to fire Stack's gun, almost 40 years after he had concealed it in the attic in Tipperary.

'The gun was a standard British Army issue weapon, so it obviously had been stolen from an officer by Stack. Garda Don Daly got it working perfectly and we went up to Scotia's Grave and fired it,' says Barrett.

Sometime in the mid-to-late 1970s Eddie Barrett's parents travelled to Dublin by train and handed the gun over to the National Museum. They gave it to the museum on condition that it would be returned to Kerry if there was ever a museum built in Kerry.

Barrett said that after the Kerry County Museum was opened in the Ashe Memorial Hall in Tralee a number of years ago, he still had the receipt for Stack's gun which his parents were given by the National Museum. He sent the receipt off in the hope that the revolver could be returned to the new Kerry museum but he claims that the National Museum had lost the gun.

The story of Eddie Barrett having Stack's gun returned is not Barrett's only link to the Civil War as his uncle, Joe Barrett, took the republican side during the Civil War and he was interned in the Curragh afterwards.

Joe Barrett was an accomplished Gaelic footballer and he captained Kerry to their 1929 All-Ireland final win over Kildare. Two years later he was involved in a symbolic gesture that helped to stitch up the open wound that the Civil War had left in Kerry. The GAA played the role of bridge builder between the two sides in the years after the Civil War and it stands testament to the strength of the organisation that it never split during the 1920s.

The GAA served as a neutral space where people from both sides could put their differences to one side. In 1931 Joe Barrett showed remarkable commitment to the GAA and football over politics. As his club, Rock Street, in Tralee had won the Kerry county championship in 1930, Barrett was made Kerry captain for the 1931 season.

Barrett accepted the honour but immediately offered the captaincy to his teammate Con Brosnan. The pair had been sworn enemies and had fought on opposing sides during the Civil War. The move caused much consternation among republicans but Barrett was willing to put politics aside for the good of football. His symbolic gesture paid off as Kerry won its tenth All-Ireland football title in 1931 with Brosnan as captain.

Barrett's GAA medals were later donated to the GAA museum at Croke Park by his son JJ, a well-known writer. When the GAA made the controversial decision to abolish Rule 42 and allow soccer and rugby to be played in Croke Park, JJ Barrett withdrew his father's medals from the museum in protest at 'God Save the Queen' being played ahead of the Ireland-England Six Nations Rugby International in 2006.

Joe Barrett's All-Ireland medal from 1931 was among the medals to be withdrawn.

On 1 May 1932, after renovations and the erection of a new stand, the main GAA field in Tralee was officially designated Austin Stack Park. To this day it remains one of Kerry's two main GAA grounds and the Rock Street GAA club was also renamed Austin Stack's GAA club. For that reason, Stack's name will always be synonymous with the GAA in the 'home of football'.

In 1935 the Office of Public Works commissioned Albert Power to execute a bust of Austin Stack, using Stack's death mask. The plaster model was completed by Power in 1941 but it was not possible to send it to Belgium to be cast in bronze due to World War II. Eventually, in 1950, a Swiss firm was contracted to make the bronze casting of Stack and the bust was placed in the National Gallery.

In 1952 the Office of Public Works was commissioning a series of political busts for Leinster House and another bronze bust of Stack was placed in the Dáil chamber where it remains to this day.

As much as his name is synonymous with the 'home of football', Stack's bust still towers over proceedings in the parliament he helped to create. For that reason his name will also forever be synonymous with the home of Irish politics.

7

John Wilson
Left Half-Back

CAVAN – FIANNA FÁIL
From the Polo Grounds to Perestroika

L ong before the late Dermot Morgan was adored by millions in Britain as Channel Four's 'Father Ted', he had his own cult following at home in Ireland with his *Scrap Saturday* radio programme.

Morgan's satirical RTÉ sketch show ran from 1989 to 1991 and its popularity stemmed from the way it lampooned figures such as Taoiseach Charles Haughey and his political advisor PJ Mara.

John Wilson, the Tánaiste at the time, was also a target. Morgan saw the funny side of the Tánaiste's regular use of Latin and Greek in the Dáil chamber and joked, 'John Wilson . . . I can almost see him in a toga spouting jokes in Latin in a Cavan accent.'

His satirical take on Wilson was not the most flattering but it was fairly accurate. Wilson will be forever remembered as an austere politician of remarkable intellect who effortlessly employed Latin and Greek phrases.

Wilson was also a Cavan GAA legend. He played for his county when they famously defeated Kerry in the only All-Ireland final played outside Ireland at the Polo Grounds in New York in 1947. Arising from his renown as a GAA star came a decorated political career that saw him hold seven different ministerial positions as well as serving as Tánaiste.

Of course, the caricatured image of Wilson is just a joke but he certainly had a tendency for 'spouting' Latin, Greek and an array of other languages. One of the finest examples of this came in May 1988 when the Fianna Fáil TD from Cavan found himself at the heart of *perestroika*.

In the mid-1980s Soviet leader Mikhail Gorbachev introduced a programme of economic, social and political restructuring, known as *perestroika*, which was a key reason for the fall of communism that followed it.

The story of *perestroika* and the subsequent fall of the Berlin Wall in 1989 is one of the greatest historical stories ever told and one GAA man enjoyed his own small but symbolic part in that story.

John Wilson was the Minister for Tourism and Transport from 1987 to 1989. Brendan Smith, the current Minister for Agriculture, served under him as his special advisor for many years.

One of Smith's most abiding memories from over two decades working under Wilson, occurred on 1 May 1988 when Wilson played his own little role in the fall of communism.

Gorbachev's *perestroika* ushered in a new era of seismic change in Soviet Russia and the decision to open a Western-style duty-free shop at Moscow's Sheremetyevo Airport was part of that momentous transition.

After an international tendering process, Aer Rianta, the forerunner to the Dublin Airport Authority (DAA) which had operated duty-free shops at Shannon and Dublin airports, won the contract to open a similar operation behind the Iron Curtain in Moscow.

Smith recalls, 'This really was *perestroika*, the Western world moving into Russia with a commercial venture. And there was a lot of cynicism with regard to whether this new duty-free shop would actually work.'

While the opening of a duty-free shop in most other parts of the world would barely garner any media attention, the symbolism of the opening of the Aer Rianta facility at Sheremetyevo Airport made it an international story.

As Minister for Tourism and Transport, John Wilson was sent over by Taoiseach Charlie Haughey to represent the Irish government at the event.

After the tape was cut to mark the official opening, Wilson and the other politicians were ushered into a room where a large number of journalists, photographers and TV crews had assembled for a press conference.

The tall figure of Wilson stood to make a speech entirely in Russian to the assembled crowd of Soviet business and political figures.

Smith recalls his surprise at Wilson's proficiency in the eastern bloc language and says, 'The rest of us from Ireland were at sea when John read his speech in Russian as we did not know what he was talking about. If you are familiar with a language, it is possible to read a script but it is what happened after the speech that really took us by surprise.

'The journalists were given an opportunity to ask questions. Without the use of any interpreter or prompting, John listened to all of their questions in Russian and responded to them in Russian.

'As an Irishman in that packed conference room in Sheremetyevo Airport, you would have to be extremely proud of that particular performance and it is something I will always remember.'

Languages were one of Wilson's greatest passions. As well as a lifelong *grá* for the Irish language, cultivated when he taught in Donegal, he spoke Spanish, Greek, Latin and Russian fluently, and also had a competent knowledge of Italian and German.

Born on 8 July 1923, John Patrick Wilson died one day after his eighty-fourth birthday on 9 July 2007. When expressions of sympathy were read out in the Dáil a few weeks after his death, his love of languages was fondly remembered. Then Taoiseach Bertie Ahern recalled how he would often find Wilson around Leinster House reading month-old newspapers in various languages.

'As a young member of this house I can remember asking why he read newspapers that were a few weeks or a month old. He said it was to keep up to date with the language rather than for the newsworthiness of the articles,' remembered Ahern.

As well as reading international newspapers, Wilson was also renowned for his use of foreign languages during Dáil debates where Latin or Greek phrases were used as weapons in the chamber.

Fine Gael and opposition leader, Enda Kenny, remembers Wilson's contributions to the Dáil as well-informed, eloquent and given in 'his particular staccato style'.

Speaking during the tributes following Wilson's death, Kenny recalled the way Wilson would whip the glasses off his face with more speed than any film star ever drew a six gun.

'Much of what is said in the House is Greek to many, but this was literally so in John Wilson's case. He was a distinguished linguist and livened up many dull days in the Dáil,' says Kenny.

Wilson's verbal jousts with Dick Burke, the extremely eloquent Fine Gael TD who preferred to be called 'Richard', are stuff of Dáil legend.

Kenny remembers, 'Whether they were talking about a two-teacher primary school in a remote part of a constituency or a major school development, the Wilson-Burke debates were a joy to behold.

'One might not know Agamemnon from Achilles or whether he was praising one or burying one but John Wilson had a way of doing so.'

A browse through Dáil debates between 1973 and 1992, when Wilson was a TD, show several examples of Wilson's grandiose oratory.

In early 1984, Taoiseach Garret Fitzgerald and his political adversary Fianna Fáil leader Charles Haughey were at loggerheads in the Dáil chamber.

As the joust between the two party leaders escalated, the usual exchange of jibes between backbench government and opposition TDs took place. Then Wilson piped up to shout out the Latin phrase: '*Roma locuta est, causa finita est?*' which is a quote from St Augustine meaning 'Rome has spoken, the case is closed'.

Wilson did not limit his use of the classics to Leinster House. *The Irish Times* journalist Michael Finlan wrote: 'That swept-back mane of silver hair above a noble brow, and his well-honed Graeco-Latin leanings have always endowed him with a dignified panache.' And Wilson showed that dignified panache when he addressed the European Committee for Catholic Education which visited Ireland in February 1979.

The committee was impressed when then Archbishop of Dublin, Dr Dermot Ryan, addressed them with a 25-minute speech in French. But he was followed by Wilson, who spoke first in English, then in French, before telling a few stories in Irish. This was followed by a series of Latin quotations before he finished off his speech in Spanish.

If his unconventional use of numerous languages was to give Wilson a particular status in the annals of Leinster House, it was his earlier career as a Gaelic footballer that gave him legendary status of a different kind.

John Wilson, or Johnny as he was known locally, was born in Mullahoran, County Cavan in 1923. In September 1937 he began secondary school at St Mel's College in Longford, an institution with which he would maintain a lifelong relationship. He followed the fortunes of St Mel's football teams throughout his life.

At St Mel's, Wilson shone academically and the 1940s was also a fruitful period in the school's football history as the college won eight Leinster Colleges Championships in that decade. Wilson forged his reputation as an exceptional footballer during this period and he was the full-back on the Leinster team in the inter-provincial colleges championship in 1942.

After St Mel's, Wilson went to Maynooth College where he developed into an outstanding debater and orator of note. His later use of Latin and Greek in Dáil debates was also born here as he obtained a first class honours degree in classics in 1945.

Third-level education in 1940s Ireland was much different to the modern-day system and it was unusual for a student to be released from their academic duties to play football. Wilson is reputed to have been the first ever student in Maynooth to be released, when he was granted permission to play for Cavan against Cork in the 1945 All-Ireland final.

Cork won that game. Playing in the Rebel County's full-forward line, future Taoiseach Jack Lynch won his only All-Ireland football medal that day while Wilson played on the losing Cavan side's half-back line.

'Now and then, John would remark about the huge coincidence that he played against Lynch in the 1945 All-Ireland football final. Little did he think that they would serve together in very senior political positions later in life,' says Brendan Smith.

As well as his achievements playing for St Mel's, Maynooth College and Cavan, it is no coincidence that Wilson's playing career was marked by a glorious period for his club, Mullahoran. He amassed county senior championship medals in 1942, 1944, 1945, and each year from 1947 to 1950.

On top of his successes with Mullahoran, he played inter-county football for Cavan from 1944 to 1948, winning All-Ireland medals in 1947 and 1948, as well as a National League medal in 1948.

The events of 14 September 1947 will forever be remembered in GAA folklore and Wilson was forever proud to have been involved. The Polo Grounds, which was the home of the New York Giants at the time, hosted the only All-Ireland final ever played outside Ireland. 35,000 people packed into the stadium on a blistering hot day. As the two teams stood on the pitch that had been baked hard from weeks of sunshine, two national anthems were played. The band started with 'Amhrán na bhFiann' before they played 'The Star Spangled

Banner'. Then the New York mayor, Bill O'Dwyer, threw in the ball. The fact that the pitch was smaller than a normal GAA pitch and had a baseball pitcher's mound posed problems for the teams.

Wilson's nephew, Kieran Harten, recalls how his uncle's recollections of the milestone event always involved him talking about the lengthy 29-hour flight the Cavan team took to New York via the Azores, Gander and Boston.

While Cavan had a gruelling flight route to the US, the Kerry team took a much longer and more painstaking boat journey to get there. The boat trip did not seem to affect the Kerry men, however, as they famously left the Cavan team eight points in arrears, just fifteen minutes into the game.

Wilson started the game in Cavan's half-back line and is said to have been given a torrid time by Kerry's Batt Garvey, before the Cavan management moved him to midfield where he had a much improved game.

Harten recalls how Garvey and Wilson became great friends in later years. They were both involved in setting up Ballyboden St Enda's GAA club in Dublin. In 1997 both men were honoured at a function organised by the club to mark the fiftieth anniversary of the Polo Grounds final. Then GAA president, Jack Boothman, made a presentation to them on the eve of the All-Ireland semi-final between Cavan and Kerry.

Of course Cavan recovered from their terrible start at the Polo Grounds, and won the 1947 final by 2–11 to 2–7. Wilson's teammate Peter Donohoe was Cavan's free-taker on the day and he was described in the *New York Times* as 'The Babe Ruth of Gaelic Football'.

Harten recalls how his uncle returned from New York and immediately headed to Kilkenny to take up a teaching post at St Kieran's College. Wilson is said to have been met in the corridor of the school by a shocked principal on the day of his return. The principal scolded the GAA star for not taking the week off to go back and enjoy the celebrations in Cavan.

Working as a classics teacher in St Kieran's College was Wilson's first teaching post after he completed his H. Dip. at University College Galway in 1947. After marrying Ita Ward the following year, the couple moved to Letterkenny, County Donegal where Wilson started to teach in St Eunan's College. It was here that Wilson's lifelong ties with Donegal began. He trained the school's football teams, did some refereeing and managed the Donegal minor team to the county's first ever Ulster title.

Charlie Haughey would later ask, while on an election canvass in Donegal, 'Is there anybody in Donegal whom John Wilson did not teach?'

Brendan Smith recalls how all later trips to Donegal would inevitably involve people who had played football under Wilson as a teacher, arriving to greet him. 'He always holidayed in Donegal and he enjoyed visiting Letterkenny as well so he could catch up on the college's football. No matter where he was in Donegal, some great characters would come and meet him to chat about football. I suppose he belonged to a golden era of Cavan football where John Joe Reilly, Tony Tighe, Mick Higgins, Big Tom Reilly and Simon Deignan were household names throughout the country.'

Wilson also got involved in the Association of Secondary Teachers in Ireland (ASTI) union during his time in Donegal. He served on the body's national executive council for a number of years and he was also elected president of the ASTI in 1959 and 1960.

After leaving St Eunan's College in 1960, Wilson took up a teaching post at Gonzaga College in Dublin where he taught a number of well-known people, including Peter Sutherland, who would later become EU Commissioner, and Michael McDowell, who later became leader of the Progressive Democrats and Minister for Justice.

Four years later he became a part-time lecturer in UCD and he was later appointed as lecturer in St Patrick's Teacher Training College in Drumcondra.

Despite his academic achievements, Wilson never forgot his roots in Cavan and kept in touch with the Border area. Brendan Smith recalls how the Northern question brought Wilson into politics in 1973.

'John was very passionate about the North and the need for political progress. He was passionate about the way the system in this country was not working – with our partition and the non-working political entity that the Six Counties had become. There had to be a better way for all the people on this island.

'He said that the difficulties that arose in the North after 1968, internment and all of that, gave him a greater belief in the need for politics to succeed and that was another reason why he sought election.'

Wilson had previously been involved in Fianna Fáil and he had been on the party's national executive. He had also contested a Seanad election and narrowly lost out in the late 1960s. He sought election to the Dáil in his native Cavan constituency in 1973 and he was immediately appointed a front bench member by party leader Jack Lynch.

It is often said of the GAA stars who go into politics that the high profile of being a local hero gives them an added impetus on the campaign trail. Wilson was no different. Although it was a heartfelt interest in the Northern question that spurred his entry into the political arena, being part of the great 1940s Cavan team certainly did not do him any harm on the hustings.

Smith recalls, 'John was extremely well respected by people and well known. A lot of times on a canvass, committed GAA people would quiz him about such a day in a county final or an Ulster final. There were always people reminiscing with him, particularly on the doorsteps at election time. And I would often say at times that you wouldn't get as many houses canvassed as you would like when the GAA chat started. He would keep delaying and enjoying the chat.'

Wilson was reportedly a 100-1 outsider with the bookmakers in 1973. But Fianna Fáil won two out of three seats in Cavan in that election. Wilson and his party colleague Paddy Smith won two seats for Fianna Fáil, and Fine Gael's Tom Fitzpatrick won the other seat. Cavan and Monaghan were two separate three-seat constituencies until 1977 when they were merged to form the five-seat Cavan-Monaghan constituency. Similarly, Erskine Childers and Jimmy Leonard were elected, giving Fianna Fáil two out of the three seats in Monaghan as well.

'Fianna Fail lost the election but they were the two results in the country that bucked the trend,' says Smith.

Some 28 years after the two men played against each other in the 1945 All-Ireland final, Jack Lynch spotted Wilson's potential and appointed him as his front bench education spokesperson on his first day in the Dáil. After Fianna Fáil was returned to power in 1977, Wilson was appointed as Minister for Education where he served until 1981.

Working directly with Wilson for so many years, Smith got to know him as well as any family member and Smith now has a good insight into Wilson's political philosophy.

'John was passionately committed from the point of view of a social conscience. He always believed that the potential of the individual should be achieved,' says Smith.

'He was a very committed educationalist because he always believed that education was the key to unlock the potential of the individual.'

Smith recalls how Wilson would often speak to him about how glad he was that more and more people were going on to third-level education and the opportunities this created for the individual and their family. Wilson remembered how few went on to third level education when he was growing up in Cavan and he was committed to increasing participation by developing the Regional Technical Colleges.

He relished the opportunity to hold the education portfolio at the Cabinet table from 1977 to 1981. After that ministry, he went on to serve as Minister for Posts and Telegraphs in the short-lived March to December government of 1982.

When Fianna Fáil was returned to power in 1987, he served as Minister for Communications from 10 to 31 March before he moved to the Tourism and Transport portfolio, where he remained until 1989. He briefly served as Minister for the Environment from 9 to 14 November 1991 and he was Minister for the

Marine from 1989 to 1992, and Minister for Defence and the Gaeltacht from 1992 to 1993.

While his political CV lists a range of ministries, Wilson was not without his flaws.

For example, his former pupil and later Minister for Justice, Michael McDowell, said in 1990: 'He never made as much of himself as he might have done; maybe it was due to the fact that he was concerned never to make a mistake.'

Before Charles Haughey retired as leader of Fianna Fáil in January 1992, there was some speculation surrounding Wilson as a possible successor. But he was first to dismiss the prospect of ever becoming Taoiseach. He said, in true Wilson-style, 'I'm not interested, *tout court!*' [meaning 'nothing else' or 'in short'].

As well as being Tánaiste under Haughey from 1990 until his retirement from politics in 1993, Wilson's name was connected with the office of President on two occasions in his political career – in 1983 and again in 1990. In 1983, before it became clear whether President Patrick Hillery was going to seek a second term in office, Wilson was mooted as a possible successor.

Smith plays down this as mere speculation. Wilson was the calibre of politician who would have been considered a suitable candidate but Smith is adamant that in 1983 Wilson's name was merely 'floated around' and he was more interested in staying involved in active politics at the time.

As it happened, Hillery stayed in office for a further seven years. Smith claims, 'I don't think that even if the opportunity arose in 1983 that John would have gone for it.'

Despite devoting much of his life to education and enjoying the role of Minister for Education, Wilson's proudest political achievement occurred during his tenure as Minister for Tourism and Transport, according to Smith.

Having an instrumental role in the restoration of the Ballyconnell to Ballinamore Canal was the accomplishment of which Wilson was most proud. The canal would later form part of the Shannon-Erne Waterway, which allows

Leabharlanna Poibli Chathair Bhaile Átha Cliath
Dublin City Public Libraries

travel by water from Lough Erne in Fermanagh all the way south to the Shannon estuary in Limerick. The huge infrastructural project opened up the disadvantaged areas of Cavan, Leitrim and Fermanagh to a new tourism market.

There was little money in the country and the public finances were in a perilous state when Wilson took office in the Tourism and Transport portfolio. The Troubles in the North were at their height in that year with an IRA bomb killing eleven people in Enniskillen on Remembrance Day, 8 November 1987.

'There was limited co-operation between North and South, and between Ireland and Britain at the time, yet here we had a flagship cross-border project supported by both governments and supported by the International Fund for Ireland at a time when the political situation on the island was very difficult,' recalls Smith. 'So it was a huge project to visualise and later achieve and implement.'

Wilson was appointed to the Transport and Tourism brief in March 1987 and he assisted the government in drafting a National Development Plan in the spring of 1989.

'The development plan had to be submitted to Europe to draw down Structural Funds. John had the Ballyconnell to Ballinamore Canal plan specifically included and identified in that plan. This marked a huge step forward and it was a huge project to initiate,' explains Smith.

Politics is a strange business which can throw up all manner of controversies. A dispute over the seemingly innocuous issue of anglers needing licences to go fishing became one such controversy when it ballooned into a major political issue in 1989.

Wilson found himself in the thick of it. The bitter dispute developed after the government attempted to impose licence fees on anglers before the 1989 general election and it escalated afterwards.

Upon appointing Wilson to the Marine portfolio, Taoiseach Charlie Haughey summoned the new minister to get the rod licence issue 'off the agenda as quickly as possible'. The dispute had dragged on for months on end and the people on both sides had dug in their heels and were refusing to compromise.

'They were in the trenches so it wasn't easy. But John devised the idea of the co-operative. Anglers could pay in to this particular co-operative and that funding was ring-fenced to go back into fisheries itself. The money could be used for re-stocking and developing fishing facilities so it was a fairly ingenious way of getting the issue settled because relationships between anglers and local communities had become very nasty.

'I recall that down around Athlone and back into Galway it had become very difficult. But he put a huge effort into it and came up with the co-operative idea totally himself and it worked.'

Also in that ministry, Wilson was involved in 1992 in the review of the EEC's Common Fisheries Policy. He dismissed suggestions that a small EEC member state like Ireland had little sway with the larger states at the negotiating table. In his eloquent style, he said, 'They say it's not the size of the dog in the fight that's important but the size of the fight in the dog.'

One day in early 1990, during his first year in the Department of the Marine, Wilson confided in Smith that he would like to run for the presidency. It was still very unclear who the Fianna Fáil candidate would be in that year's election to succeed President Patrick Hillery. Wilson told Smith that no matter who the Fianna Fáil candidate was, the party should have an internal contest beforehand.

Smith recalls, 'He did not talk to anyone else about it and he said to me, "I'll put my name forward when the time comes and whoever wins, wins. If I win I'll give it a good shot and if the party chooses another candidate they will have my absolute and full support." '

At 66, Wilson was the oldest member of the Cabinet and he made no secret that he wanted the party nomination. He actively canvassed Fianna Fáil TDs by letter and telephone and seemed to think that he had a good chance.

Speaking to RTÉ's Sean O'Rourke on the eve of the Fianna Fáil selection convention in September 1990, Wilson said, 'I am very pleased with the response up to date. I haven't counted the heads yet . . . but I think I am in there with a fighting chance.' But his reading of the battle with Brian Lenihan was ill-judged. Brian Lenihan would eventually win the internal Fianna Fáil race for the nomination by 51 votes to 19.

His reading of the presidential election was also ill-judged and he certainly did not see Mary Robinson coming when he said, 'With the history of Fianna Fáil, with their commitment to a campaign when they select somebody, I think that you could almost go so far as to say that it is a foregone conclusion. Fianna Fáil will win the election.' Robinson was elected Ireland's first female president the following month.

When O'Rourke put a question to Wilson suggesting that he or Lenihan would merely use Áras an Uachtaráin as a 'happy retirement home', Wilson retorted, 'Whoever makes that kind of accusation, I would take them on physically in a walking race around the Phoenix Park any time they want to!'

Looking back on Wilson's battle to win the Fianna Fáil nomination, Smith remembers, 'John thought he would have done better going on pledges of support he had received from individuals. But the minute it was over it was all about getting out and canvassing for Brian Lenihan.

'He was very friendly with Brian Lenihan and a great admirer of his so he canvassed in earnest for him. One of the highest votes Lenihan actually got was in Cavan-Monaghan.'

Exactly two weeks after Haughey sacked Lenihan, following the 'phonecalls to the Áras' controversy, he appointed Wilson to the role of Tánaiste.

As Wilson was the elder statesman in the party, with no ambitions to take over the party leadership, the appointment of his steady pair of hands to the second most powerful position in government had a calming influence on a party rife with grassroots discontent following Lenihan's sacking.

Smith does not recall Wilson being particularly close to Haughey and described the relationship between the two as 'businesslike'.

'It was a good working relationship but they were not close. In government you have your Cabinet meeting once or twice a week and then you go on about doing your business and minding your department. People might think there is more interaction than there actually is but everybody is doing their own job,' explains Smith.

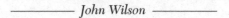

Wilson surprised colleagues and friends when, serving as Tánaiste and Minister for Defence and the Gaeltacht, he decided to bow out of politics in 1993.

Despite his retirement from Leinster House, he would later offer the country, North and South, some service in another role.

Almost 60 years after he played football for St Mel's College in Longford, Wilson enjoyed many weekday afternoons following the fortunes of his old school during his retirement, before he took on one of the most testing challenges in his life.

Just weeks after the Good Friday Agreement was signed in Belfast in April 1998, Taoiseach Bertie Ahern and Minister for Justice John O'Donoghue asked Wilson if he would head up the new Victims' Commission body.

Wilson's initial reaction was that he was too old to take on such a role but he succumbed to the encouragement of O'Donoghue who said that Wilson would command the respect of both communities and had a natural ability to listen to their concerns.

The commission started off by conducting a review of the services and arrangements in place in the South to meet the needs of those who had suffered as a result of the Troubles in the North. In 1999 the body produced a much-lauded report titled, *A Place and a Name*.

Along with his Northern counterpart Sir Kenneth Bloomfield, a former head of the civil service in the North, Wilson also had the particularly high-profile and sensitive role of tracing the whereabouts of the bodies of 'The Disappeared' – people killed by the IRA during the Troubles whose bodies were disposed of in undisclosed locations in the South.

Wilson, a first cousin of Fr Des Wilson in Belfast who was among the strongest supporters in the clergy of the Civil Rights movement in the North, had entered politics because of his interest in the Northern question. He was now given the unenviable role of Victims' Commissioner.

Smith says, 'He put his heart into it and he worked hard at it but he told me that it was an extremely difficult task emotionally. He was a very big, strong physical man but he said that at times it was very hard to deal with situations, because you could have an elderly or middle-aged person coming to you and outlining that they had lost a child or a sibling and there was no body, no final resting place, no place to put down a flower or say a prayer.

'He always said it was extremely difficult and you were dealing with people who had been through terrible trauma. He said to me that it was the hardest task he had ever undertaken in public life. It was extremely difficult. He met with individuals, groups, and families, and put a huge amount of work into it but found it extremely physically and emotionally demanding.'

Shortly before his death in July 2008, Cavan GAA County Board elected him as its honorary president. The Wilson name still features in Leinster House to this day as his nephew Diarmuid Wilson is currently a sitting Fianna Fáil senator.

John Wilson's life was decorated with achievements, from featuring in the Polo Grounds final to doing his own little bit to assist Mikhail Gorbachev's *perestroika* in the 1980s.

Back to his protégé Brendan Smith: 'The last match I saw him at was a county final shortly before he died. He was there with his Mullahoran flag like a youngster, full of enthusiasm even at that stage in his life.

'And I saw him at Ulster championship games in his later years and he had a Cavan flag with him then.'

Despite his epic political journey, Wilson never forgot the GAA.

Des Foley
Midfield

DUBLIN – FIANNA FÁIL
Clay-pigeon shooting, the Arms Crisis and the medal robbery

A rural Dubliner, a dual hurling and football star, and the winner of two Railway Cup medals in the one day – Des Foley was a rarity for more reasons than one.

Born in 1940, on a farm in Kinsealy, north County Dublin, Foley was the youngest in a family of nine children. His older sister Betty Ward, who lives in Cork, recalls Des as a child. 'It is hard to talk about Des without talking about Liam, or Lar as he was better known. They were the two youngest and the two of them did everything together.'

The two Foleys went to school in St Joseph's CBS in Fairview, where their lifelong passion for the GAA was born. They started playing hurling and football at the school, known as 'Joey's', and young Des quickly emerged as a promising player in both codes.

In 1956 Des and Lar were both on the All-Ireland winning Dublin minor football team. Two years later, Des won his second minor football title when he played at midfield and captained the team that beat Mayo. Lar featured at left corner-back on the Dublin senior team that narrowly beat Derry to win the Senior All-Ireland on the same day.

As Lar was two years older than his brother, he missed out on St Joseph's breakthrough achievement in 1959. Des captained the first ever Dublin college to win the Hogan Cup, the trophy presented to the All-Ireland senior colleges football champions.

The Foley brothers, dubbed the 'Kings of Kinsealy' by *The Evening Herald,* played club hurling and football with the St Vincent's club in Marino.

'Looking back now it is hard to separate them as they were never apart. In the early days Lar would have been a great protector of Des and in the end it was the other way around,' says Betty Ward.

'Our house was the same as any other house when we were growing up, as my mother used to be giving out to them about leaving their dirty gear stinking the house out.'

When they left school both Lar and Des started work on their father's farm before gradually building up their own cereal farms in the Kinsealy area. After farming together all week the pair would head off to play hurling or football for Dublin on a Sunday, but not before they engaged in their pre-match ritual.

Whether it was a league or championship match, hurling or football, the two brothers went to confession in Malahide on a Saturday evening and then they would go and get a haircut. The barber in Malahide used to say, 'What do you want another haircut for?' when the two brothers would arrive in. But Des and Lar were superstitious and feared that they would not win the following day if they did not adhere strictly to their routine.

They were always at home by 9.15 p.m. and in bed by around 10 p.m. On Sunday mornings Des and Lar would cycle to 8 a.m. Mass in Malahide and return home afterwards for breakfast. Sometimes after eating, Des would go back to bed for a few hours before getting up to wash himself in cold water and head to the match. The brothers followed the same routine ahead of every match they played and it certainly did serve them well.

Des won ten senior county football championship medals between 1959 and 1972 and four senior county hurling titles between 1960 and 1968, all with St Vincent's. But his playing career had its low points and losing the 1961 All-Ireland hurling final marked the biggest disappointment.

Lar played at left corner-back and Des at midfield on the Dublin team that suffered defeat by the narrowest of margins to a Tipperary team that included the legendary John Doyle. Dublin had not featured in an All-Ireland hurling final since their 1938 win over Waterford. They had not beaten Tipperary since the All-Ireland final in 1917.

For the first time ever, Dublin was no longer dependent on exiles from other counties as most of the players came from the Crumlin and St Vincent's clubs, with the exception of Paddy Croke from Tipperary.

Favourites Tipperary were winning the game 0–10 to 0–6 at the interval but Dublin's Billy Jackson scored an early second-half goal and they clawed their way into the lead shortly afterwards.

But Lar Foley and Tipperary's Tom Ryan, who had been introduced as a substitute, got involved in an incident that led to both players being sent off. Dublin were leading towards the end of the game but points from Donie Nealon and Jimmy Doyle brought Tipperary back into the lead. Jimmy Doyle scored nine of Tipperary's points in the game that ended in heartbreak for the Foley brothers as the final score was Dublin 1–12 to Tipperary's 0–16.

On St Patrick's Day 1962, Des Foley achieved a remarkable feat that had never been managed before nor matched since. He became the first player to win Railway Cup medals in both hurling and football on the same day. He lined out at midfield with Leinster in their two-point hurling victory over Munster for the first game in Croke Park on the day, and a short time later he played, in the same position, in Leinster's football win over Ulster.

Like any other game in his career, Des Foley followed his usual pre-match routine of getting confession, a haircut and going to Mass before the Railway Cup finals. He had a sore throat and a slight cold on the morning of the matches so his mother gave him fever-reducing quinine before he left Kinsealy for Croke Park.

As the Leinster team paraded around the field after their win over Munster, Foley was in the dressing room getting ready for his second game of the afternoon.

In an interview with RTÉ's GAA commentator Brian Carthy some years later, Foley said, 'There was very little time between the hurling and football so I had to race into the dressing room for a quick wash. I then changed my togs and put on a new Leinster jersey and while I was doing all this the footballers were parading around the field.

'I didn't come back onto the field until the second game was about to start. No one paid much heed to me winning the two medals. The hurlers were delighted to win their medal and the footballers likewise. What happened in between was a bit insignificant as far as they were concerned.'

Foley's Railway Cup feat was not the last record he set as he became the first player to captain Minor and Senior All-Ireland winning football teams when Dublin won Sam Maguire in 1963.

The first game of Dublin's campaign that year ended in a draw with Meath. With just minutes left in the game, Dublin were trailing by a point when Foley caught a ball in the centre of the field. He was tackled by two Meath players so he bounced the ball and side-stepped one of his opponents. When he got by the other player he illegally bounced the ball again before striking it over the bar some 50 yards away.

'I hopped the ball twice and got away with it! We won the replay by a point,' said Foley.

Des broke his wrist in the next game, a Leinster semi-final win over Kildare, and Lar took over the captaincy for the Leinster final against Laois as Des was still out injured. Dublin beat Laois by two points in that game and Des was fit to participate in his county's All-Ireland semi-final win over Down.

Lar Foley played at full-back and Des at midfield for Dublin against Galway in the 1963 All-Ireland football final. Two years after their heartbreaking defeat to Tipperary in the hurling decider, nothing was going to stand between the Foleys and a Senior All-Ireland title.

Despite Galway boasting an array of household names in their starting line-up – Enda Colleran, Seamus Meade, Bosco McDermott, John and Pat Donnellan, Martin Newell, Matty McDonagh and Seamus Leydon – Dublin emerged victors on a final scoreline of Dublin 1–9 to Galway's 0–10.

Betty Ward recalls how proud she was to see her brother lift the Sam Maguire. She says, 'He loved the Irish language and he gave his entire speech on the steps of the Hogan Stand *as Gaeilge.*'

After calling in to the Refuge in Donnycarney and Kyle's in Coolock, the cup was back in the Foley's farmhouse in Kinsealy by early evening.

Des had being going out with Malahide girl Rita Nugent since the couple were both 15 or 16 years old and they later married.

Rita Foley says, 'Des was not a party type. They used to say about Mick O'Connell being very quiet, well Des was very similar to him. He had won the All-Ireland and that was the end of the story. I can remember him having the Sam Maguire Cup sitting on the kitchen table on the evening of the match and everybody that passed by for weeks afterwards called in to see it.'

Foley went on to win Railway Cup hurling medals in 1964 and 1965, while continuing to win multiple hurling and football honours with the St Vincent's club.

As well as losing the 1961 All-Ireland hurling final, Des Foley's other great disappointment in his playing days came in 1973 when St Vincent's lost the All-Ireland club final replay to Nemo Rangers from Cork. Lucky to get a draw in the first game, Foley believed that St Vincent's were the better team in the replay. He used to recount winning a ball at midfield and passing it on to the club's 'big, long lanky fellow' in the corner-forward position who fumbled the ball and lost it. That player was a young Brian Mullins, who would later go on to become one of St Vincent's and Dublin's best ever players.

'We didn't get the goal we were looking for. He was only a "gasun" just after coming out of the minors. If it was five years later and I gave him that ball he would have put it in the back of the net, ball and goalkeeper,' said Foley.

His wife Rita recalls how Des and Lar maintained their passion for football throughout their lives. They were constantly involved in coaching and managing St Vincent's and Dublin hurling teams for many years.

One of Rita and Des Foley's sons, Des Junior, was an extremely promising young footballer and hurler in the early 1980s. Des Junior was involved in Dublin underage squads from the age of 14 and it was often said that he was going to be 'better than his father'. He was on the same team as future Republic of Ireland soccer star Niall Quinn when Dublin were beaten in the All-Ireland Minor hurling final in 1983.

Rita recalls, 'A week before the final, Des [Junior] went over on his ankle and tore ligaments. They injected him [with a painkiller] for the final and he has never been the same since. It destroyed his leg and he has had three operations on it since then.'

The Foleys other son, James, has a son called Peter who is currently playing on Dublin underage teams and proving to be a promising player. So the Foley name is still synonymous with Dublin GAA some 50 years since Des lifted Sam Maguire.

While playing for St Vincent's, Des became very friendly with Charles Haughey's brother Pádraig 'Jock' Haughey, who was a teammate. It was through this connection that he found himself increasingly interested in politics.

Both Des's sister and widow recall how Des and Lar were always doing odd jobs and helping out their neighbours in Kinsealy.

Rita says, 'From the time he was about 18, people were always asking Des to go and see Charlie Haughey about going into politics.'

Des used frequently send people to local Fianna Fáil councillor, Joe Dignam, to get help with their various concerns so Dignam eventually asked Foley's close friend Kevin Boland to approach Foley about standing for the 1965 general election.

Des's parents were Fianna Fáil supporters and the Foley family always debated politics at the dinner table when he was growing up. Betty says, 'Des's successes on the GAA field made him very well known so that helped him get into politics. It is easier if you are well known than if you are a raw recruit. It was a surprise to us that he decided to stand for the Dáil and I remember my mother wondering how he was going to have time to be a TD when he was so busy on the farm.

'But Des was married at the time so it was not my mother's province to be telling him what to do, if you know what I mean.'

Foley was elected to the fourth seat in the five-seat Dublin County constituency at the 1965 general election. Foley garnered 3,367 first-preference votes to get elected along with Fianna Fáil colleagues Patrick Burke and Kevin Boland. Labour's Seán Dunne and Fine Gael's Mark Clinton won the other two seats in the constituency.

Rita says, 'He enjoyed life as a TD but he worked day and night. I know people give out about politicians but people called here to the house 24/7. They would mostly call in or ring him at meal times when they knew they could get him in, so every family meal was interrupted.'

Rita recalls how the mid to late 1960s passed her by in 'a haze'; life was hectic for Des as a TD at the same time that the couple were rearing their young family of three daughters and two sons.

Four years after he was first elected, Foley increased his first-preference vote to 5,231 in the 1969 general election. He won one of the four seats in the Dublin County North constituency, along with Justin Keating (Labour), Mark Clinton (Fine Gael) and Patrick Burke (Fianna Fáil).

With this healthy increase in his vote in his second general election, Foley looked to have a promising future ahead of him in the Dáil – until 1970 when one of the biggest political scandals in the history of the State erupted.

There was widespread shock across the country when two Cabinet ministers – Charles Haughey and Neil Blaney – were sacked by Taoiseach Jack Lynch for allegedly attempting to illegally import arms for the IRA to use in the North.

Haughey and Blaney despised the cautious policies of Lynch on Northern Ireland and advocated a more vigorous approach as they felt nationalist civilians in places like Derry were left helpless. Lynch had set up a Cabinet sub-committee to organise emergency assistance and relief for Catholics in the North and had allocated £100,000 for the government's Northern Relief Fund. Haughey had been given sole charge of the fund and, along with Blaney, virtually given a free hand in looking after the government's policy on the North.

Money from the Northern Relief Fund was used to pay for a meeting in October 1969 in Bailieboro, County Cavan, of the Northern Citizen Defence Committees, which soon became fronts for the IRA. The meeting was told that £50,000 would be available to buy weapons to defend nationalist areas.

It was alleged that Blaney conspired to import arms, while Haughey provided the money for the purchase from the relief fund and tried to arrange customs clearance for the arms shipment.

The Garda Síochána's Special Branch was aware of the plot by April 1970 and they passed on the information to Lynch, who took no initial action. Fine Gael leader Liam Cosgrave was tipped off about the plan to smuggle arms into the North so he forced Lynch into action.

On 6 May 1970 Lynch sacked Haughey and Blaney from Cabinet after they refused to resign, and by 28 May the pair were on trial in what became known as 'The Arms Trial'. Haughey and Blaney were charged in court on the first day of the trial with conspiracy to illegally import arms for the IRA. The men denied any involvement in the affair and they were all found not guilty on 23 October.

The episode opened up bitter divisions in Fianna Fáil between supporters of Haughey and Blaney and supporters of the Taoiseach. Haughey was demoted to the backbenches, where he would plot his political comeback. Kevin Boland, Des Foley's lifelong friend, resigned from the Cabinet in solidarity with Haughey. He was expelled from Fianna Fáil later in 1970 and went on to found his own political party Aontacht Éireann which enjoyed little success at the polls.

Foley was vehemently opposed to Lynch's policy on the North and from the time of the Arms Trial he distanced himself from the party leadership and fell into the ranks of Fianna Fáil's dissident TDs. Then, after over a year on the verges of the party, came one of the most defining days in Foley's political career – Friday,

29 October 1971.

Speaking at a meeting of the Ashtown Fianna Fáil Cumann, Foley launched a bitter attack on Lynch. He told the meeting: 'If he [Lynch] had stood up and condemned British violence when it first turned against the Six-County minority, if he had roused the nation behind him and refused to back down to threats, if he had waged diplomatic war against Westminster throughout the world, if he had acted with manliness and courage, then many of the innocent dead in the North would possibly be alive.'

Foley added that history would condemn Lynch as an Irish leader who parleyed with 'the enemy'.

'I have decided to speak out because I feel that by any longer remaining silent I would be paying lip service to Mr Lynch's policy of washing his hands. I come from a Republican family and need no apology for speaking my views . . . It is a time for honesty and for an end to hypocrisy,' said Foley.

'The present Taoiseach has not only deliberately betrayed the nationalist minority in the Six Counties over the past two years, he has deviously misrepresented the silent majority in the 26 counties which sympathises with, and supports, the Northern minority in their final struggle for freedom.'

Continuing to denounce Lynch, Foley added that 'Mr Lynch has now made it clear that he intends to go on standing idly by'. Foley believed that Lynch was quick to condemn IRA violence while failing to condemn British Army actions in the North.

The outburst was a deliberate attempt to test Lynch to the limits as Foley added, 'The charade of standing idly by has gone on for too long. Mr Lynch adroitly plays on the fears of our people by implying that his policy of placating British terror is the only safeguard against the extension of violence to the 26 Counties.

'He stands branded as a hypocrite because it is now clear that his policy of washing his hands of responsibility has been a major contributing factor to the violence we now witness in the Six Counties.'

Foley's bitter public affront to the party leader was just one in a series of events that thrust Fianna Fáil into a major crisis.

Lynch issued a statement in the days after Foley's outburst where he said, 'If I felt as strongly as Deputy Foley appears to feel about the leadership of the party of which I was a member, I would resign from the party. Obviously Deputy Foley is seeking to have himself expelled.'

The reason for Lynch's cautious statement was that he needed to try to hold the party together for a crucial vote the following week. Fine Gael, sensing the crisis in Fianna Fáil, had tabled a motion of no confidence in the Minister for Agriculture, Jim Gibbons. The vote was regarded as vital to finally establishing the position of dissidents.

Foley, Wicklow TD and Minister for Labour, Paudge Brennan and Neil Blaney had not been attending Fianna Fáil parliamentary party meetings for over a year since the sacking of Blaney and Haughey from Cabinet. The votes of Haughey, Foley, Brennan, and Blaney were crucial, therefore, in the no confidence vote on Gibbons. They would either vote unconditionally with Lynch's government or face the consequences of going against Lynch.

On the Monday after Foley's outburst, Brennan also made a speech questioning Lynch's leadership. Speaking at a Fianna Fáil cumann meeting in Ballyshannon, County Donegal, he predicted a general election if Lynch could not obtain the complete loyalty of all the members of his party.

Brennan's remarks increased speculation within political circles that the country was about to be plunged into a general election. So the eyes of the nation were on the Fianna Fáil parliamentary party meeting on Wednesday, 10 November – twelve days after Foley's outburst and a week before the confidence motion in Gibbons.

But an overwhelming defeat of the dissidents at the meeting changed the whole character of the Dáil crisis. A decision was made to back Gibbons in the confidence vote, so Lynch's leadership was safe.

But Foley resigned from Fianna Fáil at the crunch meeting. When Foley's party colleagues came to consider how he would be disciplined after his outburst, Foley said that he had not intended to attack Lynch personally. Frank Aiken

A portrait of O'Duffy that appeared in the Garda periodical in the mid 1920s (*courtesy of the National Library of Ireland*).

O'Duffy and followers give the raised-arm salute, c. 1933 (*courtesy of the National Library of Ireland*).

Eoin O'Duffy with Minister for Justice Kevin O'Higgins at the Phoenix Park depot in the mid-1920s.

John O'Mahony minutes after the finish of the 1989 All-Ireland final (*Western People*).

John O'Mahony after managing Galway to a second All-Ireland title in 2001 (*The Irish Times*)

Count night in Castlebar after the 2007 General Election. Fine Gael TD Michael Ring, party leader Enda Kenny and newly elected TD John O'Mahony (*The Irish Times*)

Fine Gael's 'Dáil Stars' John O'Mahony TD, Jimmy Deenihan TD and Seán Kelly MEP with the party's Kerry South TD Tom Sheahan (*The Irish Times*)

Mayo captain Seán Flanagan (third from right)
with the Sam Maguire Cup.

Seán Flanagan: 'The original Roy
Keane', in pensive mood during
his playing days with Mayo.

Seán Flanagan at a Fianna Fáil Ard Fheis in 1979, with an image of party leader Jack
Lynch in the background.

Jimmy Deenihan in action for Kerry with teammate Jack O'Shea in the background.

Kerry captain Jimmy Deenihan lifts the Sam Maguire Cup after beating Offaly in the 1981 All-Ireland football final (*Ray McManus/ Sportsfile*).

Fine Gael Sligo-North Leitrim TD John Perry, party leader Enda Kenny, Jimmy Deenihan and unsuccessful Sligo-North Leitrim 2007 General Election candidate Michael Comiskey. (*The Irish Times*)

John Donnellan, Galway's jubilant 1964 captain, holds Sam Maguire aloft. The future Fine Gael TD is unaware that his father has just died in the Hogan Stand, a fact that is clearly reflected in the faces of GAA officials Fr Mahon (to his left) and Alf Ó Muirí (to Donnellan's right). (*Evening Press*)

John Donnellan goes to block down Derry legend Sean O'Connell's kick in the 1967 Railway Cup final.

John Donnellan on the day he was appointed junior minister in 1982.

Austin Stack; All-Ireland winning Kerry captain, a veteran of the 1916 Rising, the War of Independence and the Civil War who later served as Minister for Home Affairs, dressed in military uniform. (*Clare Express*)

Rory O'Hanlon, Charles Haughey and John Wilson canvassing during the 1981 general election campaign.

Taken in 1997, the surviving members of the 1947 All-Ireland football final played between Cavan and Kerry in the Polo Grounds, New York. From left: Mick Higgins (Cavan), John Wilson (Cavan), Teddy Sullivan (Kerry), Mick Finnucane (Kerry), Simon Deignan (Cavan), Tony Tighe (Cavan) and Gus Cremin (Kerry) (*Sportsfile*).

Dublin captain Des Foley and future Fianna Fáil TD leads his team in the pre-match parade behind the Artane Boys' Band ahead of his sides' 1963 All-Ireland football final win over Galway.

National Football League semi-final, Dublin v Kerry, Croke Park, Dublin, 1965, the Dublin team. Back row, from left, Sean Lee, Mick Kissane, Chris Kane, Lar Foley, Des Foley, Tony Donnelly, Jimmy Keaveney, Paschal Flynn, Brendan Quinn, front row, from left, Paddy Holden, Michael Whelan, Bill Casey, John Timmons, Gerry Davey, Brian McDonald and Noel Fox (*Connolly Collection / Sportsfile*).

Patsy Flannelly, Paddy Moclair, the captain of the ship, Henry Kenny and Purty Kelly sailing to America in 1937.

The Mayo 1936 All-Ireland team and officials pictured in New York in 1937. Back row: Paddy Mullaney, Bernie Durkin (chairman), George Ormsby, Patsy Flannelly, Henry Kenny, Patrick Collins, Tom Burke, Paddy Quinn, Purty Kelly, Gerald Courell, Tom Grier, Tommy McNicholas, Seamus O'Malley. Front row: Fr Eddie O'hara, Pat Brett, Jackie Carney, Jim 'Tot' McGowan, Paddy Moclair, Paddy ('Captain') Munnelly, Peter Laffey, Billie Mongey, Josie Munnelly, Tommy Regan, John Clarke.

The great 1936 Mayo football team: Back row – Paddy Moclair, Patsy Flannelly, Peter Laffey, Purty Kelly, Paddy Quinn, Paddy Brett, Tom Burke, Josie Munnelly, Jim 'Tot' McGowan. Front row – Georgie Ormsby, Henry Kenny, Paddy ('Captain') Munnelly, Seamus O'Malley (captain), Jackie Carney, Tommy ('Danno') Regan and Tommy Grier (*Western People*).

GAA president Sean Kelly with President McAleese prior to the Kerry v Mayo All-Ireland football final of 2004 (*Ray McManus/Sportsfile*).

Sean Kelly looks on as Kilkenny captain DJ Carey lifts the Liam McCarthy Cup after the 2003 All-Ireland Senior hurling final, Kilkenny v Cork (*Damien Eagers/Sportsfile*).

Sean Kelly celebrates with Páidí Ó Sé in Croke Park after Kerry's 1997 All-Ireland final victory over Mayo. (*Brendan Moran/ Sportsfile*)

The Galway football team 1922; Mick Donnellan
is fourth from the left in the middle row.

Mick Donnellan, Clann na
Talmhan founder and father
of the Donnellan GAA
dynasty in a pre-match pose.

Mick Donnellan pictured
in the Hogan Stand
minutes before his
death in 1964 during
the Galway v Kerry
All-Ireland final in which
his son John captained
the victorious Galway
side.

Kerry under-21 All-Ireland winners 1973. Martin Ferris is second from the left in the back row.

Martin Ferris leaving Bridewell in Cork for a court hearing in Dublin following his arrest for the 1984 'Marita Ann' IRA gunrunning mission (*Cork Examiner*).

Martin Ferris with Gerry Adams and Caitríona Ruane at a Sinn Féin Ard Fheis (*The Irish Times*).

Jack Lynch leads Glen Rovers in the Cork county senior hurling final 1949 (*Cork Examiner*).

Jack Lynch with the Liam McCarthy Cup (*Cork Examiner*).

Lynch with Margaret Thatcher while she was leader of the opposition. Behind them stand Airey Neave the Tory spokesman for Northern Ireland (left), later assassinated by the INLA, and Michael O'Kennedy, Irish Minister for Foreign Affairs (*Getty Images*).

The Kerry football team of 1940. Back row, left to right: Joe Keohane, Tadhgeen Drummond, Bill Dillon, Bill Myers, Jimmy O'Gorman, Bill Casey, Tadhg Healy, Charlie O'Sullivan, Seán Brosnan, Jerry Beckett, 'Doc' Reidy. Front row, left to right: Eddie Walsh, Dan Spring (captain, with mascot Harry McCarthy), Dan O'Keeffe, Murt Kelly, Tom 'Gega' O'Connor, Paddy Kennedy, Johnny Walsh.

With all the other living All-Ireland winning football candidates, Dan Spring is introduced to the crowd at the centenary All-Ireland in 1984 (*The Kerryman*).

Jack McQuillan sits on a bench on the plinth in front of Leinster House on his first day in the Dail as a Clann na Poblachta TD after his election in 1948.

Jack McQuillan (fourth from left with his shorts almost torn off) in action for Roscommon against Kerry in the All-Ireland final on 24 September 1944.

Jack McQuillan outside the Percy French Hotel in Strokestown, Co Roscommon in May 1968 with Donal Ó Connalláin, who was originally from Roscommon. The Dublin-based teacher was an Independent senator from 1961 to 1968 and heavily involved in the Roscommon Association in Dublin in the 1960s.

proposed that the party whip should be removed from him and other TDs suggested that a vote should be taken on Foley's future by open declaration.

At this stage Blaney called for a secret vote but the opposition against Blaney's suggestion was so strong that Foley took the initiative and resigned from the party himself. He said that he regretted having to leave the party but he had no choice as the meeting was conducted in such an 'undemocratic manner'.

In his statement issued after his resignation, Foley claimed that under the form of voting which was proposed at the meeting, deputies would not be at liberty to express their views freely. He outlined that he would continue to be a member of his local cumann and to sit in the Dáil, quashing rumours that he would be joining another political party.

It is often reported to this day that Foley joined Kevin Boland's Aontacht Éireann party but that was not the case. His widow Rita says, 'He was Fianna Fáil and that was it. He was never going to go and join another party.'

In his statement, Foley showed that he was very much a man of principle as he stood over his remarks about Lynch's stance on the North. He said: 'I did not withdraw my remarks because I could not withdraw what I firmly believe. I was not prepared to tell a lie to save my own skin or to satisfy the whims of individuals who prefer their £2,500 [TDs salary] to their principles.'

He remained outside the party fold until the end of the government's term of office, and in 1973 he stood as an Independent candidate in the Dublin County North constituency. He garnered 3,387 first-preference votes which was little over a third of a quota so he did not retain his seat. The four seats in the constituency were won by Ray Burke and Seán Walsh (Fianna Fáil), Justin Keating (Labour) and Mark Clinton (Fine Gael).

Recalling her late husband's seat loss, Rita Foley says, 'I don't know whether it was because of having lots of downers with the football, but he didn't let it get him down. To me it was the best thing that ever happened because he enjoyed life to the full after that.'

Foley continued his farming, going to GAA matches and managed to find time for his other great passion – shooting.

Charles Haughey had bought the Abbeyville mansion and extensive grounds, just across from the Foleys' home place in Kinsealy, in 1969. As Haughey and Foley were close friends, Foley used to go shooting on the lands at Abbeyville as well as on his own farm. While none of the Haughey children was particularly interested in farming, Eimear was the exception. She got on really well with Des and she spent a lot of time with him on the farm.

Foley reared pheasants in the woodlands at Abbeyville and he started annual clay pigeon and duck shooting competitions, which are still held there to this day.

In keeping with his nationalist stance in the political arena, Foley was the same in the area of clay pigeon shooting. He was chairman of the all-island Irish Clay Pigeon Shooting Association and Rita points out, 'Only for Des it would not have remained an all-island organisation, as the group in the North wanted to break away.' As well as being prolific GAA stars, Des and Lar shot for Ireland in numerous international clay pigeon competitions for many years.

5 February 1995 was the same as any other Sunday morning for 54-year-old Foley: he had planned to head to a football match later in the day. Rita woke before him and went downstairs to the kitchen to prepare some breakfast for the couple. While she was in the kitchen she heard a loud knocking sound on the ceiling above her. Foley had always kept a hurley beside his bed to protect himself if a burglar ever made his way into the bedroom in the middle of the night.

But the house was not being robbed. Des was having a massive heart attack and he was banging the hurley on the bedroom floor to alert Rita below. She ran upstairs and he was taken to hospital, where he died later that day. It was poignant that one of Foley's last acts before his death involved the GAA legend holding the hurley stick that had brought him so much joy in his earlier life.

About a year after his death, as the Foley family was coming to terms with Des's sudden death at a relatively young age, the family home in Kinsealy was robbed.

Rita Foley had had some of her husband's GAA medals made into various items of jewellery such as necklaces and bracelets.

'I had got a lovely rope edging put around his All-Ireland medal and had it put on a gold chain, which I always wore. The two Railway Cup medals that he won on the same day were on a bracelet and they were all stolen.

'It was in the year after Des died so it was terrible. There were other things taken but it was hard as the medals were of such sentimental value.'

The 1996 robbery got a lot of media attention and a public appeal for the return of the medals was made on the RTÉ TV programme *Crimeline*. But the medals have never been returned.

The medals may be gone but memories of the rural man from the capital will always live on in Dublin GAA folklore.

Henry Kenny
Midfield

MAYO – FINE GAEL

'Over 15,000 people did not vote for me. They didn't know who I was,
except that I was Henry Kenny's son.'

The old black and white photograph is grainy; it is not easy to distinguish the green from the red on the Mayo jerseys.

It is 1936. Charlie Chaplin has spoken for the first time in a film. African-American athlete Jesse Owens has just won four gold medals at the Berlin Olympics. The first Aer Lingus flight has taken to the skies. Franklin D Roosevelt is about to be re-elected for a second term as US President and Éamon de Valera is still drafting the Irish Constitution.

Back to the photo. Eight of the team stand in a line with their arms folded. In front of them are the other seven, all down on one knee.

Mayo midfielder Henry Kenny is on one knee in the front row. He is between Georgie Ormsby and Paddy Munnelly, his left hand resting on Munnelly's back.

There are 50,168 spectators in Croke Park when the photo is taken before the 1936 All-Ireland final. Most of the crowd are men. They wear long trench coats and fedora hats. Some of them have come by car, others by train and many more on 'high nelly' bicycles.

Before that day, Mayo had fallen at the last hurdle in the 1916, 1921 and 1932 All-Ireland football finals. But the county's fortunes took a U-turn in the 1934 National League, when they won the first in a record-breaking chain of six league titles.

1935 witnessed a landmark in the history of Mayo football, as one of the greatest midfield partnerships in Gaelic football was born. Patsy Flannelly and Henry Kenny formed the nucleus of the team that won the 1936 league title.

Mayo won the Connacht title a few months later and beat Kerry in the All-Ireland semi-final. Kenny would later tell the *Western People* newspaper, 'We reached our peak in 1936. We beat Kerry 1–5 to 0–6 in the best match of the year.'

With the semi-final win over Kerry under their belts, one game with Laois stood between Mayo and their first ever All-Ireland title.

Shortly after that grainy photo was taken, Mayo took to the field. The game was by no means a classic. It was actually one of the most one-sided finals in GAA annals.

Patsy Munnelly fisted the ball into the Laois net early in the game to score Mayo's first goal. This set them off on a scoring rout. When the final whistle was blown, the scoreboard read: Maigh Eo 4–11, Laoighis 0–5. Seamus O'Malley became the first Mayo man to lift the Sam Maguire Cup.

The day after the final, the *Irish Independent* reported: 'Bubbling with fire and energy, Mayo were into their work from the start and outpaced and outplayed Laois in all departments.

'They knew what was expected of them, set their hearts on victory, and the earnestness and will to win carried them to a triumph that leaves a new landmark in the records of the GAA and should have a healthy effect in further strengthening and popularising the game in the West.'

As one half of Mayo's midfield powerhouse, Henry Kenny garnered national recognition with his county's 1936 win. He revisited that national prominence with his election to the Dáil in 1954 and his subsequent 21-year political career.

One of the most popular TDs in Leinster House while he was there, Kenny would later attend what was effectively his own 'wake' in the Dáil bar before the curtains came down on his political career, a few months before his death.

⑨

Born in Main Street, Castlebar in 1913, Henry Kenny grew up in the town and went to school at the local St Gerald's College.

In the early 1900s Lord Lucan donated the Mall, which was originally a cricket ground, to the people of Castlebar. Kenny spent much of his youth playing football in the evenings after school on the Mall. Some evenings there were up to 200 children running around after one football. In later life Kenny used to recall that 'if you got a kick of the ball in the evening you were absolutely thrilled.'

He established himself as a midfielder on the school football team before finishing in St Gerald's and commencing his studies at the De La Salle teacher training college in Waterford in the early 1930s.

He played midfield on the De La Salle team with Seán Brosnan, who later played for Kerry and became a Fianna Fáil TD for Cork. De La Salle won their first Waterford county championship with Kenny and Brosnan on the team.

Kenny was six feet, one inch tall and he was around 14 stone in his playing prime. Tom McNicholas, the only survivor of the 1936 team, remembers Kenny being known as 'the man with the magic hands'.

Kenny's son Enda, the current Fine Gael leader, says, 'My father had a reputation for being a very clean footballer and he was never sent off. He also had an enormous pair of hands and a great spring to help him jump.

'He had a great skill of being able to catch the ball one-handed in the air and mid-flight he would land down at a different angle and be ready to move on.'

The Mayo team of the 1930s were tactically advanced as they were one of the first teams to work out a kick-out system.

'Tom Burke from Castlebar was the goalkeeper and he worked out a system whereby he would give a signal so that my father and the other midfielder, Patsy Flannelly, had a ten-yard advantage on the opposition's midfielders,' recalls Enda.

'This has happened since with the development of modern techniques. But Burke's idea was to signal in such a way that the midfielder would be moving and running by the time the ball was kicked, giving the Mayo midfielders more capacity to jump and win possession.'

When Kenny completed his studies at De La Salle college, he got a teaching post in Recess, Connemara. European Commissioner Maire Geoghegan-Quinn's father was the local bus driver in Connemara at the time and Kenny got to know him quite well. After finishing his week's work in Recess, Kenny used to cycle 60 miles home to Castlebar to play for Mayo.

The Mayo team did not meet up for midweek training in those days. Instead, the local county board sent telegrams to each member of the team ordering them to train on their own. One such telegram, sent from Claremorris on 7 July 1937, stated: 'It is important that each member of the team be fighting fit. It is not possible to bring the members of the team together, but the county board expects each member to do his part. Will you do your part?'

Kenny also taught in Polredmond, near Williamstown, County Galway and he played illegally a number of times for Dunmore before he secured a teaching post back in Castlebar. He won a number of Mayo county championship titles with the Castlebar Mitchel's club. The strength of the club was such that seven of the starting 15 players on Mayo's 1936 team were Mitchel's teammates.

Enda Kenny recalls, 'As members of the first team to win an All-Ireland for Mayo, those players were legends. My father had finished playing football by the time I was born but he used to talk to us about his football days. But then again, we were so small that we didn't ask the questions we should have been asking about the training methods and the carry on at the games.'

While Enda Kenny has some regrets that he did not ask his father more about football when he was alive, there are many stories from his contemporaries who obviously held him in high regard. The late Jimmy Murray, Roscommon's All-Ireland winning captain on two occasions, once said that Kenny was, 'the longest kicker of a ball I ever saw and the cleanest player I ever encountered.'

Known as 'Harry' Kenny to those who knew him best, he had some of his greatest battles as a Mayo player against legendary Kerry midfielder Paddy Kennedy. Some years after the pair finished playing, Kennedy said, 'The greatest footballers I met were Henry Kenny of Mayo and Tommy Murphy of Laois. If Kenny could swoop from behind you for a high ball you hadn't a chance. Both men were pure footballers and I loved playing on them.'

Enda Kenny recalls, 'My father had a great affiliation with the Kerry people because they would have played Kerry a lot in those times. In 1936 the Mayo team were invited down to play Kerry in the opening match after the official opening of Fitzgerald Stadium in Killarney.

'Seven or eight of the Mayo players were in one car when they left to return to Mayo that night. I don't know whether it was the road signs or the driver that was at fault, but they found themselves in Carlow the next morning.

'They were all starving and went into a café and ate breakfast only to discover that nobody had any money to pay for it. Paddy Moclair caused a diversion while the rest of them made a run for it.'

The Fine Gael leader adds, 'Another time they were driving home from a match and were dropping my father off in Connemara very late in the night when the car plunged into a stream. There must have been a few drinks taken because nobody was too worried and they all fell asleep in the car. When they woke there were forty or fifty people with shovels around the car. They thought that all the sleeping motionless players inside the car were dead.'

Enda recalls his father recounting how a man called Johnny Ruane, who worked in the bacon factory in Castlebar, used to cog his football boots.

'They didn't have multi-studs or anything like that in those days so you had to make the cogs using little circular layers of leather and nail them in to the soles of the boots,' explains Enda.

'The boots in those days used to have big shinguards on them and there was an extra strap outside them to protect the legs as the game was not as nice as it is now.'

A character in Castlebar, known as 'Boston Bennett', used to 'break-in' the local hero Henry Kenny's new football boots for him. Bennett would put dubbing that was also used for horse saddles on the boots. Then he would go out and kick a ball a few hundred times to soften the leather and break the boots in.

After Mayo won the All-Ireland in 1936, an Irish-American family called the McGoverns paid for the new champions to visit the United States. Although some members of the squad were unable to travel due to work commitments, Kenny was one of the lucky ones who embarked on the journey of a lifetime in early 1937.

The touring party left Cobh on the *SS Manhattan* and reached New York after a week at sea. The Mayo team trained on the deck of the ship during that week's voyage on the Atlantic. Henry Kenny's family still cherish an old sepia-toned photograph of Henry and his teammates Patsy Flannelly, Paddy Moclair and Purty Kelly, dressed in their Mayo kit, posing for a photo on the deck with the ship's captain.

The Mayo team spent four weeks in New York, Boston and Philadelphia. Another photo of the team, dressed in suits and standing outside a Manhattan casino, shows the tour was not all about football.

Enda Kenny adds, 'If you go into Mick Byrne's pub in Castlebar – he is a real GAA man. He is a cousin of the late Roscommon footballer Dermot Earley, who was actually born in that pub. Anyway, there is a picture on the wall in there of my father and three other Mayo players on the Empire State Building in 1937. That picture was taken when they were over on that trip and shows the links between Mayo and New York. The Mayo Association is still massive over there to this day.'

Henry played for Mayo in midfield from 1932 to 1948. They won seven

National League titles in that time, including six in a row. They won one All-Ireland and he won five Railway Cups for Connacht.

'You still go around the county and you meet older men who say, "Jesus, I remember I was at that match in 1947 or 1948", and they remember him playing.'

Henry Kenny hung up his boots after playing his last game for Mayo in 1948.

Two years later, Seán Flanagan captained Mayo to win their second All-Ireland title and, in May 1951, Flanagan was elected as a Fianna Fáil TD for the Mayo South constituency, four months before he captained Mayo to their third All-Ireland title.

Putting a GAA star up for election worked well for Fianna Fáil in Mayo South in 1951 so Fine Gael decided to give it a go in the same constituency in 1954.

Enda Kenny says, 'Seán Flanagan was still playing when he was elected in 1951 and that was probably it for Fine Gael. What they wanted was a name. So it was either going to be my father or the late Dr Philip Cawley from Swinford, who was a great friend of his.'

After the Fine Gael convention to select an election candidate, Cawley went home to find that his wife had two suitcases sitting in the hallway.

He asked her, 'What's this about?' and she replied, 'You can either have me or the job.'

Had Cawley's wife not packed the suitcases, he may well have entered political life and Henry Kenny may never have become a TD – but Cawley opted not to stand. Kenny stood in his place and the two of them remained great friends for the rest of their lives.

Prior to the 1954 election, Fine Gael had not held a seat in Mayo South since James Fitzgerald-Kenney held one of the five seats after the 1943 election.

Mayo South was a five-seat constituency again in 1944. Fianna Fáil won three of them, with Independent/Farmers Party TDs Dominic Cafferky and

Joseph Blowick (who were both Clann na Talmhan TDs in subsequent elections) taking the remaining two seats.

After 1948 the constituency was reduced to four seats. Fianna Fáil and Clann na Talmhan each won two of the four in the 1948 and 1951 elections. After enduring a decade of having no TD in the Dáil, the time had come for the Fine Gael organisation in Mayo South to fight back.

Enda Kenny says, 'So I suppose it was a case of Fine Gael having no seat for a number of years and saying to themselves, "Can we get somebody to stand here?" They encouraged my father to stand and he did.'

Henry Kenny won the fourth seat in the Mayo South constituency on 18 May 1954 with 4,983 first-preference votes.

Mayo's 1936 football hero became popular with TDs and senators from all parties in the Oireachtas. In an unlikely friendship, Conor Cruise O'Brien, who was elected to the Dáil as a Dublin North-East TD 14 years after Kenny, became very close to Kenny.

Enda Kenny recalls, 'The "Cruiser" used to like to talk to him because he [Cruiser] used to say, "It's a great thing for academics like me to talk to people like you." In many cases rural TDs like my father would be wiser to the world than a lot of the academics in the first place. I never came across anybody who served in here who had a bad word to say about my father.'

Henry Kenny was a backbench TD for most of his 21-year political career where he concentrated mainly on working for his constituents in Mayo. After the 1973 general election, when he was returned as a TD for the Mayo West constituency (established in 1969), he was appointed as a parliamentary secretary to the Minister for Finance by the new Taoiseach Liam Cosgrave.

During his tenure in this role, Henry Kenny took ill with cancer. After battling the illness for a number of months, he came to accept that he was not going to recover. He knew that he would have to wave goodbye to politics as the illness took hold.

The story of his last day in the Dáil reveals a lot about Irish politics, and even more about the way Irish society deals with death and bereavement.

Enda Kenny still has vivid memories of that day. He explains, 'I remember that morning when he left for the Dáil. I said to myself, "This is going to be his last trip." It was the end of June or early July in 1975. I remember it was a beautiful summer morning. He had failed physically at that stage. And that was going to be his last trip to the Dáil and he knew that. Everybody else up here knew that as well.'

While the Dáil chamber can be a loathsome cauldron where political adversaries engage in vicious debate, there are times when the TDs display altruism and empathy across party lines. Enda Kenny can remember when former Fine Gael Minister for Defence Oliver J Flanagan, whose son Charlie is currently a Fine Gael TD, had his last vote in the Dáil.

There is an electronic voting system in the Dáil nowadays, but in times gone past all votes were 'walk-through' votes whereby TDs walked up to the back of the chamber and turned one way to vote 'Tá' or Yes and the other way to vote 'Níl' or No.

'Oliver J stayed at the little gate where all the Fine Gael TDs were going out and shook hands with everybody,' recalls Enda. 'And after that the Fianna Fáil people, who had voted on the other side, all came out and shook hands with him as well because he wasn't going to be around afterwards. So I suppose it is camaraderie among thieves!' laughs Enda.

After Henry Kenny left the Dáil chamber for the last time on that day in 1975, he invited his friends from Fine Gael and other parties to have a drink with him in the Dáil bar. Kenny knew he was going to die soon so he effectively had his own 'wake', surrounded by the friends he had made in over two decades in politics.

Enda Kenny says, 'They drank all night in the Dáil bar and Seán Flanagan actually played 'The Coolin' (An Chúilfhionn) and a few more tunes on the violin until morning. And that was the end.

'He would not have called it his own wake. He would have called it recognition of moving on from here and saying goodbye to his role as an elected representative with his colleagues who were also elected representatives. He knew it was his last trip and they made a night of it.'

Even though Seán Flanagan was a Fianna Fáil TD and political adversary, Kenny was friendly with him in the Dáil. Enda Kenny recalls how the two Mayo All-Ireland winners 'got on very well'.

He adds, 'Flanagan used to joke that my father was the only one on the 1936 team who could read. Flanagan was a very bright man. He could be very gruff and very abrupt but he had a great brain. He was essentially, at the end of it all, a person really committed to his county. He had a great sense of pride in the county jersey as, indeed, my father had.'

Some time after Henry Kenny returned home to Mayo after that last day in the Dáil, the Taoiseach Liam Cosgrave, who was close to Kenny, came down to Mayo to visit him before he died.

Enda Kenny recounts how Cosgrave asked Kenny on his deathbed, 'This will be the last encounter we have. So is there anything you want done?'

Kenny made two final political requests of the Taoiseach. Firstly, he asked that money be allocated for the completion of the Robe-Mask Drainage Scheme. Kenny was in charge of the Board of Works in the Department of Finance and he had been lobbying for the scheme to be given the go-ahead. It had not been confirmed but after Kenny asked Cosgrave to do it, the Minister for Finance Richie Ryan ensured the money was provided for it in the budget.

'The process had been in train. They had done the cost-benefit analysis but it hadn't been confirmed so he asked Cosgrave to do that,' explains Enda Kenny.

Secondly, Kenny had been attempting to build a pier on the North Mayo coast for a long time. He had overseen a cost-benefit analysis on providing one at Ballyglass on Broadhaven Bay. So he asked Cosgrave to provide the funding for that as well. Cosgrave honoured the two requests after Henry Kenny's death.

On 4 September 1975 Islandeady played Ballinrobe in the Mayo intermediate football final. A match report in the *Western People* from that game described

how the team from the small parish of Islandeady, on the outskirts of Castlebar, used 'punch and crunch' tactics.

Enda Kenny played on the half-back line for Islandeady. His brother Kieran was also on the team and another brother, Henry, was on the panel. Islandeady beat Ballinrobe by two points in a proud day for the Kenny siblings. They were able to tell their father of the win that took place just eleven days before he passed away.

Enda Kenny recalls his father's final days. 'Well, you see, you don't believe that your father is going to die. You don't talk about what is going to happen after he dies. You don't bring those things up. Like any other family in the country, you know these things are going to happen yet you don't believe them. And then when it happens, you say, "Why didn't I say that or ask that?" It's the same for everybody.

'When anybody dies you are left with memories and personal recollections about what kind of person they were as a husband or as a father. Then you meet all the people who say, "Sure I knew him well. I saw him playing football" and all the rest of it, and you still meet people, who are obviously older people now, who would have remembered Henry Kenny playing for Mayo in the late 1940s.'

The Kenny family still have all of Henry's football medals mounted on a shield. They include his All-Ireland medal, Connacht championship and Railway Cup medals and a number of smaller ones from various exhibition games.

'My older brother played minor football for Mayo. My younger brother Kieran played for the senior team and played in the 1979 Connacht final where he marked the great Dermot Earley,' recalls Enda.

On 19 July 1979 *The Galway Advertiser* match report from that final stated: 'Kieran Kenny bids fair to emulate his late father in the art of fielding . . .'

Enda says that his father never put any pressure on his children to emulate him on the football pitch or in political life.

He claims, 'It was never a case of our father applying pressure on us to play football or get involved in politics. When you are growing up in a political household you see things going on and it sort of assimilates into you.'

When Henry Kenny died on 25 September 1975, the Cosgrave government or National Coalition, as it was known, was left with a majority of just one Dáil seat. This narrow majority forced Cosgrave to quickly hold a by-election in the hope that Fine Gael could win back Kenny's vacant seat.

But early talk of the by-election was not without controversy as a story on the front page of the *Mayo News* on 4 October shows.

Under the headline, 'RTÉ comment described as disrespectful' the Westport-based newspaper reported how members of Castlebar Urban Council condemned RTÉ and other sections of the media as 'callous' and 'disrespectful because of their haste in making projections, long before Mr Kenny's remains had been taken from Swinford Hospital where he died.'

Councillor Dick Morrin, who was actually a Fianna Fáil councillor, rang RTÉ to make a complaint. He said, 'As he was still lying on his deathbed in hospital, those people in RTÉ calmly and brutally discussed the future of the area and who was going to take his place.'

Shortly after his death, the local party organisation's attention turned to Henry Kenny's children as they were optimistic that a candidate with the Kenny name would be hard to beat in the by-election.

The *Western People* reported on 4 October that within days of the funeral 'the party made a formal request to the family to consider allowing one of the four boys seek the party nomination.'

In the same newspaper a week later, columnist John Healy stressed the need to have a Kenny contest the by-election as Liam Cosgrave had 'marked the Kenny family as the first family of Mayo in the Fine Gael hierarchy.'

Enda Kenny can remember mixing bags of sugar with water to make gum to stick up posters at election time for his father during his teenage years. Although he had never considered running for office before his father's death he had helped his father out with constituency clinics as his health deteriorated.

When the local Fine Gael organisation in Mayo formally asked the Kenny family to put forward a candidate, Enda still had no particular ambition to run. Just qualified as national school teacher, the 24-year-old was working in a small rural school in Knockrooskey near Westport and enjoying life.

But his two younger siblings were still at school, while of the two older sons, one was still at college and the other was working for a bank outside County Mayo. As the middle son, with the least commitments, Enda put his name forward and he was the party's automatic choice at the selection convention.

The by-election occurred within six weeks of Henry Kenny's death, on 12 November 1975.

After being selected to contest his father's vacant Dáil seat Enda Kenny embarked on a memorable campaign. He remembers, 'I was still grieving as he was only dead a few weeks. It was one of the last of the old style by-elections as the entire Labour party were down canvassing for Fine Gael. You had Brendan Corish, Justin Keating, Conor Cruise O'Brien, Michael O'Leary and Frank Cluskey. They were all down canvassing and it was a hilarious by-election when you look back on it – as by-elections are in any event.'

One of the iconic moments in the election came on the night Cosgrave visited Ballinrobe. The Taoiseach and the deceased TD's long-haired offspring walked from the racecourse on the outskirts of the town into Ballinrobe. As Cosgrave and Kenny walked in to the town, the road from the racecourse was lined on either side with people holding burning sods of turf high in the air at the end of hay forks.

'It was like a scene from an election back in the 1930s or 1940s. It is sort of pre-history now,' recalls Enda.

Just as the Fine Gael and Labour bigwigs were in Mayo for the campaign, Fianna Fáil leader Jack Lynch was down canvassing for the party candidate Michael Joe McGreal.

During the election *The Irish Times* claimed that it was an election 'without themes. No great national issue is being decided and none is likely to be significantly affected by the result. Instead, there has been a concentration on family loyalties, personal sympathy, tribal connections and gifts of patronage.'

But, midway through the campaign, the election was given an added national significance. Paper cuttings from the *Mayo News* on 8 November 1975 explain why. The paper reported, 'Fine Gael TD for North Tipperary, Tom Dunne, was seriously injured in a car crash and he is not going to be able to attend the Dáil for some time.

'Thus, in the event of Fianna Fáil winning the West Mayo contest, the Coalition majority would be wiped out and the possibility of an early general election almost a certainty.'

Fine Gael's predicament was simple; they had to win the by-election. The party's hopes rested on the shoulders of a 24-year-old novice.

When polling day came around on 12 November, the young teacher allayed Fine Gael's fears and topped the poll. His 15,584 first-preference votes got him elected on the first count with a 52% share of the vote.

The *Western People* said, 'His success put an end to a nagging fear that the government was going to go to the country to consolidate their position.'

Looking back, Kenny says, 'Over 15,000 people did not vote for *me*. They didn't know who I was except that I was Henry Kenny's son. They gave me the vote for the work he had done as a deputy over the years. It wasn't in respect of me as a novice, it was in respect of his legacy.

'He was elected in every election he contested. I learned lessons from him and one of them was to treat everybody the same. He really was a person with a great philosophy in life and his own philosophy was to help the lame dog across the stile. So if you are going to do something, let it be good.'

The RTÉ television programme *Reeling in the Years*, that takes a nostalgic look back through the broadcaster's archives, often shows footage of Enda Kenny arriving for his first day in the Dáil. In the footage, the new long-haired deputy walks up the plinth towards the doors of Leinster House where he is greeted by a crowd of supporters holding a large green and red banner with the slogan 'The West is Awake' blazoned across it. Cosgrave is there with the supporters to shake Kenny's hand and welcome him into politics.

On 22 November 1975 John Healy wrote in the *Western People*, 'Enda Kenny is on his own now and from here on in he'll be judged on his own performance. I have little doubt but that it will be a good one. He's his father's son.'

Kenny was very much on his own after the fuss created by his first day in the Dáil dissipated. He recalls, 'I was the same as anyone else who came in here in the middle of an electoral process. You get all the advice at the beginning that they are all going to help you, but the day you walk in the gate you are all on your own.

'So there was great excitement. That young fella you see on *Reeling in the Years* from time to time had become an elected representative and extended the lifetime of that government by about 18 months. But very soon you learn that the responsibility is on your own shoulders and it takes a long time to realise the way the mechanics of politics work and how this house works.

'That has changed over the years but, essentially, while they have programmes for people who are newly elected representatives to tell them about the facilities and how to get things done and whatever else, essentially you are on your own. You have to learn it from experience.'

Kenny remembers Jim Tully, who was a Labour TD and the Minister for Local Government at the time, telling him that the best way to learn the ropes in Leinster House is to go down into the Dáil chamber, sit down and listen.

'He told me not to say anything for a while, just sit there and listen and gain perceptions and reflections on what is going on.'

Kenny took Tully's advice and the Fine Gael leader has remained in the Dáil ever since his election in the weeks following his father's passing in 1975.

Enda Kenny's three children can boast that both of their grandfathers have won senior All-Ireland medals. Their maternal grandfather, Seán Kelly, won an All-Ireland with Kerry in 1953 while their paternal grandfather, Henry Kenny, was part of Mayo's breakthrough team in 1936.

Never sent off in his football career, Henry Kenny will always be remembered as a clean footballer, and by all accounts he conducted his politics in a similar fashion.

Following his death, respected journalist John Healy wrote in the *Western People*: 'Someone said Henry really wasn't a politician. It is nearly right – depending on how you define a politician.

'If you mean by the word a man or woman anxious to score off the other side, a man or woman who can tolerate no view but his or her own, a grasping person on the make, then Henry was a poor politician.

'Define it as a man who understands politics to be a game in which there are rules within which you must play, and in which there must be give and take in order to accomplish the greatest amount of good for people irrespective of your party leanings, and then you must agree that Kenny was a very fine politician indeed.'

Healy noted that political opponents shed tears at Henry Kenny's funeral. They mourned the loss of a political adversary who they held in high esteem.

Mayo's GAA community had lost one of the most ground-breaking footballers of his generation. They had lost 'the man with the magic hands'.

Seán Kelly

Right Half-Forward

KERRY – FINE GAEL

Rule 42, Europe and all that

It is 14 July 2009. Bastille Day. A date that has historic importance for France. On this date in 1798 the medieval Bastille garrison in Paris was stormed, symbolising the beginning of the French Revolution.

14 July 2009 is also a momentous day in the relationship between the GAA and politics. Former GAA president Seán Kelly has just been elected and today he will officially become an MEP.

When Ireland joined the EEC in 1973, six times All-Ireland winner and Taoiseach Jack Lynch appointed former Limerick hurling star and Limerick East TD, Michael or 'Mick' Herbert, to the first mandated European parliament.

Kelly is now following in Herbert's footsteps in becoming another staunch Munster GAA man to represent the province on the European political stage.

After flying from Kerry's Farranfore Airport to Frankfurt-Hahn in Germany, Kelly embarks on a three-hour car journey to the Rhineland city of Strasbourg.

The parliament sits for one week in every four in the French city when it is not in Brussels. Arriving at the European Parliament, Kelly is struck by the colossal size of the Louise Weiss building. Inside, he is taken aback when he sees the extent of the indoor amphitheatre, or 'hemicycle' as it is known, where Europe's 736 MEPs are to meet on the first day of a new five-year term.

'The only other similar experience I have had is the GAA Congress. But Congress is about half its size and is usually conducted in one language, with some Gaeilge,' says Kelly after his first week as an MEP.

He is happy that the other Irish MEPs have been so helpful to him. Without their co-operation, 'I would have got lost in a maze of corridors and rooms several times.'

The Kerryman is also pleased that most people speak English but he adds, 'The pronunciation of the Irish names is amusing as no doubt are our efforts to pronounce their names. Frequently, I am referred to as *Monsieur Seen Kellii*. 'Others think I am the great Irish cyclist from Carrick-on-Suir by the same name. They say to me – '*Sean Kelly, le cycliste, très bien!*'

In an interview with the *Sunday Tribune* after his first week in the new job, Kelly was asked if he found it a daunting experience. He replied, 'Ah now, Kerrymen aren't supposed to talk like that. If you can survive a GAA Congress you can survive anything.'

Kelly was elected as one of the three MEPs for Munster, or the Ireland-South constituency as it is now known, on 5 June 2009. Along with Fianna Fáil's Brian Crowley and Labour's Alan Kelly, Seán Kelly was returned as a Fine Gael MEP on the back of 92,579 first-preference votes.

After his first full week in public life, Kelly is already recognising the importance of the GAA as a platform for his new career in politics. At 57 he may be seen as a late entrant into the political arena, but the same cannot be said about his entry into the GAA family. It began over 50 years ago.

Born on New Year's Day 1952, Kelly's earliest memories of the GAA go back to kicking around with his brothers on the family farm in Kilcummin, near Killarney as a child.

Like rural villages all over Ireland in the 1950s, nobody had a television in Kilcummin when Kelly was growing up. He can recall the parish priest being the first person in the area to get a TV set. The priest used to put it into the parish hall on St Patrick's Day for people to watch the Railway Cup finals.

'It's amazing; even though Kerry is a football county, all I can remember is everyone talking about Christy Ring at that time. They all wanted to see the great Christy Ring. I have no recollection of the matches except people talking about Ring. He was a hero, even to people in Kerry, and that stuck in my mind. I think my interest in GAA developed from there.'

Kelly went on to start playing at under-14 level at a time 'when you were lucky to get two games a year'. He made it into the Kilcummin senior football team at 18 and he also played a lot of football as a student at St Brendan's College in Killarney.

After finishing school, Kelly studied to become a teacher at St Patrick's teacher training college, Drumcondra before going to UCD where he completed his studies. Afterwards he got his first teaching post in the capital at Cromcastle Green Boys National School in Coolock.

He wryly laughs now when he looks back on his club playing days in Dublin. The man, who would later rise to the highest administrative rank in the GAA, was one of the organisation's rogues in his earlier days.

Disregarding the rule that a player may only be affiliated with one club, he played with two clubs in Dublin at the one time – for one as 'Seán Kelly' and the other as 'Proinsias Ó Ceallaigh'.

He recalls a teammate at one of his Dublin clubs, asking him what the English translation of 'Proinsias' was and he replied 'Frank'.

'To this day some of them still call me Frank and I'd say they don't know I was president of the GAA yet!' says Kelly in his strong Kerry accent before laughing.

As soon as Kelly started teaching at Cromcastle Green he introduced football training to the school. 'It was a new school in a poor part of Dublin in Kilmore West in Coolock. They had never seen a football before so we started football in the school,' he recalls.

'I was joined by a very good friend of mine, Jimmy O'Grady, who is still there. We won a Dublin league and got them involved in Parnell's GAA club where some of them are still involved.'

In 1975 Kelly departed Dublin and moved home to Killarney where he took up a secondary school teaching post at his old alma mater, St Brendan's in Killarney. It was here that Kelly's rise through the administrative ranks of the GAA really gained pace.

He was chairman of Kerry's juvenile organisational board, or Bord na nÓg, from 1975 to 1978 and chairman of the senior board, Bord Sinsear, from 1978 to 1987.

After becoming vice-chairman of Kerry County Board in 1982, he was responsible for the development of hurling – in a county where there was little regard for any sport that was not Gaelic football.

With his characteristic tenacity, Kelly said it would be wrong to be responsible for developing hurling in Kerry without having hurling played in his own club, so he set up a club in Kilcummin and he started playing hurling himself at the age of 30.

Kelly won two Kerry intermediate championship hurling medals and played hurling until he was 40. He is convinced he would have played on much longer was it not for a serious groin injury. The groin injury was self-inflicted during a race with his son.

'I gave him odds that I would beat him in a race. I was just passing him when the groin went. A physio told me that it would never be right unless I got an operation on it. So I decided to call it a day,' recalls Kelly.

Through training teams in St Brendan's, playing hurling and his various administrative roles within the GAA, Kelly was very well-known across north Kerry by the early 1990s. And this had not gone unnoticed in the political world.

Explaining the appeal of GAA personalities to political parties, Kelly says, 'In many ways GAA transcends sport as it reaches out to all aspects of life. If you are seen to be a good player or a good administrator, people will always look at you from a political point of view. Political parties are always looking out with one eye, or half an eye, for people who might do a job for them in a particular area where they might be stuck.

'And even going away back 20 years they were talking about me standing for politics. I was asked more or less throughout the 20 years if I would become involved, by a number of parties, not always Fine Gael, but I really wasn't that interested.'

When John Bruton was leader of Fine Gael, he identified Kelly as a possible Dáil election candidate with a lot of political potential and sounded Kelly out about making a foray into politics. At the time, Fine Gael had an unwritten internal rule that general election candidates ought to be selected from the party's pool of existing county councillors. Against that background, Kelly was persuaded by Fine Gael to throw his hat into the ring for the Kerry County Council elections in 1991.

Looking back on the first time he dipped his toe into political waters, Kelly is thankful that he was not elected as he believes he would have 'done a George Lee on it' and fled the political stage immediately.

He recalls, 'I was chairman of the county board at the time, I was teaching and I had a young family. And a week or two into the election I said to myself, "I hope to God I am beaten in this." I didn't tell anybody that but that is how I felt internally.

'I remember the count was on in a place called the Áras Phádraig and I was hoping that I wouldn't be elected. I came down for a bowl of soup in Christy McSweeney's and somebody came in and said, "Seán, all you need is another 100 votes and that will elect you," so I nearly fell off the stool.

'But thankfully it didn't come true and quite frankly I was the most relieved person in the count centre that I wasn't elected. I think that I would have done a "George Lee" on it in terms of the county council. I wasn't ready for it.

'I don't think I was going to fit into the county council and I hadn't my work done in the county board. I was spreading myself a bit too wide.'

Kelly's early election failure had a silver lining: he believes he would never have become the president of the GAA had he been elected to the county council in 1991.

'Thank God I wasn't elected as I would not have become GAA president and I would not have been chairman of the Kerry County Board in 1997 when Kerry won the All-Ireland, which was as important as any political achievement.'

After 1991, Kelly was approached in each subsequent local and general election by Fine Gael, and other parties, who sought to add him to the party ticket – but he declined each invitation. When he became president of the GAA in 2003, the number of offers increased but he continued to turn them down and focused on the GAA.

He says, 'Once I stood in 1991 I got straight out of it. I felt very guilty, being a GAA county board chairman and being seen to be affiliated to a party.

'In fairness, the county took no issue as the year after I stood for the council I was challenged for the chair but my vote went away up. So it was satisfying that people did not hold my standing for Fine Gael against me.'

Kelly's eventual rise to his 2009 election as an MEP is certainly not something that was planned. Similarly, his rise through the GAA's administrative ranks to the role of president was not planned either.

Kelly claims that if he was the sort of person who would sit down and plan how to become GAA president, then he would have been the wrong person for the role. Instead, the opportunity just evolved after he served as chairman of Kerry County Board from 1987 to 1997 and subsequently rose to the rank of chairman of the Munster GAA Council from 1997 to 2000.

Kelly was the first Kerry person to be elected president of the GAA at the organisation's Congress in 2002. He had the highest margin of victory ever. He took up the reins as president the following year and served a three-year term of office that culminated in the passing of a highly controversial motion on Rule 42 which paved the way for the opening of Croke Park to rugby and soccer.

While Kelly would later become an elected politician in 2009, the way in which he presided over the relaxation of the most politically sensitive rule in the GAA rulebook during his tenure as president was truly historic.

Looking back he says, 'The highlights of my presidency were getting rid of Rule 42 and reaching out to the wider population. Looking back on Rule 42 now, it was even more important than I thought at the time with the significance of it.'

Rule 42 prohibits the use of GAA property for games other than GAA sports, so the GAA's vote on 16 April 2005, to relax that rule and allow soccer and rugby be played in the 82,500 capacity Croke Park stadium, was one of the most defining days in the history of Irish sport.

'The whole symbolism from the point of view of the maturity of Ireland, leaving the Civil War narrow-mindedness behind us and reaching out to different groups in Northern Ireland and transcending the divides there, I think that it encompassed all of that,' said Kelly in April 2010, five years after the GAA's landmark decision.

The seeds of the idea of opening up Croke Park were sown in Kelly's head long before that historic vote in 2005. He remembers sitting in the half-finished stadium over a decade ago when the Cusack and Hogan Stands had been completed and thinking how lucky he was to be involved in such a great organisation.

'Then I said to myself, this place will only be full three or four times in the year. It should be used for other sports.

'I always felt that we should be using Croke Park more. I just did not see the sense in having such an asset closed all the time. It was different to other venues. Take Fitzgerald Stadium in Killarney. It can be used 150 to 200 days a year. Croke Park was lucky if it was used ten or 20 days in the year.

'When they started to talk about building the "Bertie Bowl", I started to panic that Croke Park would be a white elephant. Instead of being an asset that would generate funds for the association, it would be the opposite. It would cost a bomb because there wouldn't be concerts or any matches there other than our own couple every year. So I became more and more certain that was not the way to go.'

Kelly's vision has been lauded in most quarters ever since with the Irish rugby team's Six Nations win over England in 2007 ranking among one of the highlights of the last decade in Irish sport.

There was stringent opposition within the GAA to allowing 'foreign games' into Croke Park, particularly from the Northern counties.

But Kelly says, 'I found Northern people very firm in their views, very outspoken but not personally bitter. Most of them would have respected the point of view of somebody else even though they were totally and utterly in disagreement with it.

'A lot of them argued strongly against it but they were able to see the other person's point of view. When the decision was made they accepted it and decided to get on with it.

'The Northerners' commitment to the game is stronger than the Southerners. The GAA was more of a badge of identity in the North during the Troubles than it was down here.

'We play football for the love of it and because we enjoy it but it meant more in the past to the Northerners. I always felt that because it meant so much to them that they respected everybody who was involved in the GAA and they never really became personal about it.'

Kelly is still invited to the North for various GAA functions and even though people do not agree with his stance on Rule 42 they often tell him he was 'a damn good president'.

But does he encounter bitterness over the issue from individuals elsewhere in the country?

'There are people who are totally rabid and who hate that Croke Park is opened,' he reveals. 'For instance, I can think of one person who was a great friend of mine until Croke Park was opened. I have been told by mutual friends that he absolutely hates my guts now. He would hardly say hello to me.'

In an unrelated incident, Kelly encountered personal hatred over the issue at a funeral in 2009. A well-known figure in Munster GAA circles had passed away so Kelly made a point of attending the funeral. The man's coffin had just been lowered into his grave and the prayers completed when Kelly started to make friendly chat with two men who were standing beside him. One of the men shook hands with Kelly and said to his friend, 'Do you know this man here?'

But the friend just looked Kelly in the eye and said, 'I wouldn't shake hands with you, you fucker, if it was the last thing I did. You are the bollocks that opened Croke Park.'

'Even during the European elections, I came across a bit of it. I was in Cork on the canvass and the cameras were coming behind me. Fortunately they had not caught up with me when I went around a corner and met a fella who had a few pints on board. He said, 'Go back to Kerry you British bastard!' so I kept going quickly.

'Overall I would have to say that there has been 95% positive reaction to it. For every one person who gives out, nine compliment me and say it was great for the GAA, thanks very much.'

Despite encountering the occasional insulting comment, Kelly has no regrets over the Rule 42 issue.

'I think that it is a privilege to have been given the opportunity and to be able to be part of the campaign to open it because it has done an awful lot for the GAA and a lot for this country,' he says.

Even though the redevelopment of the Lansdowne Road (Aviva) stadium has been completed, Kelly believes it would be 'crazy' not to leave Croke Park open so it could be used in the event of a soccer or rugby World Cup, a European Cup, or a game where the IRFU or FAI found themselves with 32,000 excess fans whom they couldn't accommodate in Lansdowne Road.

'If the IRFU or FAI find that they are losing a minimum of €2.5m on such a match, then there is no reason in the world why the GAA, rugby or soccer can't sit down together and say "Lads, €2.5m is a lot of money, let's do a deal here".

'Four years ago we did it out of patriotism as much as anything else, helping a friend in need, benefiting the economy. Now we are saying, "Here is our asset. It has worked out well. Maybe you might want to do it again in the future." So let's leave it open.'

The opening of Croke Park has coincided with a golden period in Irish rugby that culminated in Ireland winning the Six Nations Grand Slam in 2009. So is Kelly concerned that the success of Irish rugby will have a detrimental effect on the GAA?

He says, 'I remember when I was chairman of the county board in 1990. Kerry was doing badly because the great team was gone and we were struggling. I remember reading an article in the paper saying that the soccer was taking over from the GAA and all the kids were playing soccer because of World Cup '90.

'What happened ten years later? The GAA was stronger than ever. Once the GAA takes care of its own base at club level and at schools level, it will be okay. If someone comes to me and says that as a result of rugby or soccer getting so popular that we have no players, then I will be worried but I see no evidence of that.'

Looking at the challenges facing the GAA in the future, Kelly sees the problem of under-the-counter payments to managers and improving coaching standards, particularly in secondary schools, as paramount.

Back to politics. Ahead of the 2007 general election, Fine Gael leader Enda Kenny asked Kelly again if he would stand for the party and Kelly discussed it with him at length.

Having completed his presidency of the GAA the previous year, Kelly thought long and hard about the move. One day he was cutting the lawn at his Kilcummin home when he made his decision. He turned off the lawnmower and rang Enda Kenny immediately to say that he was not going to run for the Dáil.

Kelly says, 'I expected Enda to be disappointed or maybe annoyed. But he was most courteous and said that he respected my decision one hundred per cent. At the end of the phone call he said that he might get back to me at some point again in the future.'

In spring the following year, Kelly was attending the official opening of Lixnaw GAA club's new pitch when Fine Gael TD and five-time All-Ireland winning Kerry footballer Jimmy Deenihan turned to Kelly and said, 'Seán, you should stand for the European election next year and you will win a seat.'

Deenihan would become Kelly's director of elections the following year, but Kelly did not give Deenihan an answer at this point.

Enda Kenny, whose wife Fionnuala is related to Kelly, came back to him in early 2009 and asked him to run in the European elections the following June. Kelly's wife Juliette encouraged him to go for it.

Kelly had been based in Dublin working as the executive chairman of the Irish Institute of Sport at the time. He had been instrumental in setting up the institute but he was frustrated that it was not going to have the power he felt it should have. The fact that it was going under the wing of the Irish Sports Council and the lack of funding due to the poor state of the economy left Kelly 'pissed off with it'.

'I was also getting really cheesed off living in Dublin. Going home to an apartment on my own, living the life of a single person without being able to do what single people do, which is enjoy themselves.'

Kelly could not see himself stay in the role for another few years so he took Kenny's offer really seriously. He asked himself if he could make a contribution as a politician.

'I was very sceptical and quite frankly I didn't know that much about Europe. I have only learned since I went out to Europe about how little you actually know about spheres that you are not involved in.

'You can see that when you meet politicians like Gay Mitchell and Pat 'The Cope' Gallagher. Their depth of knowledge is only something you can acquire after being there for so many years. Anyway, I asked if I could make a contribution and spoke to a few MEPs first.'

Kelly spoke to Fianna Fáil MEP Brian Crowley and former Fine Gael MEP, and now TD, Simon Coveney about the job.

He recalls how Crowley, whom he knew from being with him on the judging panel for the Rose of Tralee, said to him, 'Seán I would be happy if you run but I would be happier still if you don't!'

After getting advice from Crowley and Coveney, Kelly decided to have 'a shot at it' without really knowing what his election prospects were.

'I really didn't know if I would be elected or not. I was wondering if there would be a transfer from sport to politics. As it turned out, in terms of the voting, there certainly was. I was delighted to be elected and now I am working like a beaver at it,' says Kelly.

He is enjoying his new life as an MEP but says that only certain people would be cut out for the lifestyle. He shares his time between Ireland, Brussels and Strasbourg, as well as spending much of his time travelling.

'We spend one week in four in Strasbourg which is a right pain in the arse altogether. It's hard to get to and it makes no sense as it costs a fortune as everybody has to transfer down there and get accommodation for the week,' says Kelly.

While the arduous trip to Strasbourg is one of the downsides to the job, Kelly finds airport delays and missing connections the worst part of his new life. After attending a conference in Budapest recently, Kelly was eager to get home to address a conference in Limerick one Friday evening. His flight from Budapest to Paris was delayed, leaving Kelly tight for time to catch his connecting flight to Dublin. Arriving late into the terminal building at Charles de Gaulle airport, Kelly started to run to catch his flight to Dublin.

'I ran all the way and I was just coming to the gate when I heard someone saying, "Stop!". And I looked around and there was a policeman holding a gun with it pointed at me,' recalls Kelly.

'I had not even seen the policemen as I had raced past them trying to get the flight. Some guy had left two bags unattended close to the gate where I was going. So they shut down the airport. My connecting flight to Dublin was delayed for an hour and a half and I missed the conference.'

Despite the hassle with airports, Kelly says he is enjoying the challenge of being an MEP and does not have any immediate ambition to win a Dáil seat.

'I'd rather master something than keep moving from one job to another. At this stage I am really enjoying the challenge so I will go two terms if I can.'

It will be 2014 before Kelly's first term in Europe is complete. That is a lot of Tuesday, Wednesday and Thursday nights away from home in Brussels and Strasbourg. It is also a lot of nights away from the cut and thrust of the GAA in his native Kerry.

So does Fine Gael's new MEP miss spending week nights at GAA meetings? The answer is 'No'.

Shortly after arriving in his new job, Kelly was sought out by the local GAA community in Belgium. He is now President of the Brussels' GAA club that plays in the European GAA leagues.

You can take the man out of the GAA, but you can never take the GAA out of the man.

11

Michael 'Mick' Donnellan
Centre Half-Forward

GALWAY – CLANN NA TALMHAN
A dynasty is born, Clann na Talmhan and an untimely death in the Hogan Stand

The deep wounds of the Civil War were very raw and the GAA's role in healing the bitterness it left behind cannot be underestimated.

A report of the Roscommon County GAA Board convention in the *Roscommon Messenger* in April 1922 referred to 'the necessity for a GAA revival as a useful and needful distraction from the strain of politics and as a means of bringing all Gaels together.'

By mid-1923 GAA activities began to resume as normal after the disruption of the Civil War and the organisation set about playing a backlog of fixtures that included the 1922 championship.

The Connacht Championship was played a year late; Sligo met Galway in the 1922 provincial decider at Parkmore, Tuam on 2 September 1923.

One of Galway's six forwards that day was Michael Donnellan, or Mick as he was better known. Born in Dunmore, near Tuam, County Galway in 1900, the 23-year-old was on the Galway team that suffered a one-point defeat at the hands of Sligo.

So the Tribesmen were out of the championship and Sligo beat Tipperary in the semi-final a week later to progress to their first ever All-Ireland final. But Sligo's excitement at reaching the final was short lived. In the first of a tumultuous decade of objections and counter-objections across the GAA, Galway objected to their defeat to Sligo in the Connacht final.

Galway's objection was upheld and a replay was ordered. Despite an appeal from Sligo against this decision, Sligo eventually agreed to a replay of the Connacht final at Croke Park on 30 September.

Galway won the replay by two points and played the 1922 All-Ireland final against Dublin on 7 October 1923 in Croke Park. The Dunmore MacHale's clubman, Mick Donnellan, played at full-forward for Galway in that game but his team were defeated in an extremely low-scoring final that finished on a score line of Dublin 0–6 to Galway's 0–4.

Galway were beaten in the 1923 and 1924 Connacht finals by Mayo so Donnellan had experienced a number of heartbreaking defeats before the Tribesmen won their first All-Ireland title in 1925.

While 1925 was a breakthrough year for Galway football, it will be forever remembered for another reason. The Connacht Championship that year was the most extraordinary played in the GAA's history and Donnellan's team were at the eye of the controversy.

In the same year that Benito Mussolini declared himself Il Duce in Italy and F Scott Fitzgerald published the classic novel *The Great Gatsby*, Kerry won the Munster title, Cavan won the Ulster title and Kildare emerged as Leinster champions. The Connacht Football Championship, however, descended into chaos.

A total of seven replays took place, many as a result of objections, with the most drama occurring between Roscommon and Sligo – the sides met six times before Sligo finally won. Donnellan's Galway side drew twice with Leitrim before Galway eventually prevailed.

As a result of all of the replays, the Connacht final between Mayo and Galway was not played until 18 October in Tuam. Meanwhile, owing to the extremely late finish to the Connacht Championship, the 1924 champions, Mayo, had been nominated by the Connacht Council to represent the province against Wexford in the 1925 All-Ireland semi-final. Mayo defeated Wexford by 2–4 to 1–4 in Croke Park on 30 August, while the other two semi-finalists were disqualified following objections.

At this stage, Mayo and Galway were the only two undefeated teams ahead of the Connacht final on Sunday, 18 October. With Donnellan playing at full-forward on the Galway side, they were trailing Mayo by a point towards the end of the game. Then Galway's right corner-back Mick 'Knacker' Walsh got a late goal to secure a Galway win. The final score was Galway 1–5 to Mayo's 1–3.

The 1925 championship was now in turmoil. Nominated by the provincial council, Mayo had gone on to beat Wexford in one All-Ireland semi-final while the other two semi-finalists had been disqualified so Mayo laid claim to the All-Ireland title.

But Galway had beaten them in the belated Connacht final in October. The morning after Galway's win, the newspaper headlines read: 'If Galway are champions of Connacht, then who are All-Ireland champions?'

At the next meeting of the GAA's Central Council, Galway were declared All-Ireland champions. A series of protracted meetings took place afterwards where appeals from Mayo were heard but Galway remained champions.

The Tribesmen may have won their first title in the most controversial circumstances but the presence of Donnellan in the forward line on the team signalled the birth of one of the GAA's greatest ever football dynasties.

They won another Connacht title in 1926 and after losing the 1927 and 1929 Connacht finals they were back to winning ways by 1933 when they beat Mayo in the final. Galway reached the All-Ireland final with Donnellan as captain but the Tribesmen lost out to Cavan.

The Dunmore MacHales' man proved himself to be such a prolific footballer that he featured in Connacht Railway Cup teams from 1926 onwards.

Primarily a wing-back, Donnellan was capable of playing in a variety of positions. When he lined out at right half-back for Connacht in the Railway Cup final in Croke Park on St Patrick's Day 1933, he is said to have scored a point with one of his trademark long kicks over 70-yards from the target. Connacht suffered a one-point defeat at the hands of Leinster.

Donnellan played on Connacht teams all the way up to 1934 when he captained the province to its first ever Railway Cup title.

There is a story told in Galway GAA circles about Donnellan being asked by two little mascots to have their pictures taken with him on the day of the 1934 final.

Donnellan asked the youngest of the two mascots what his name was and the boy replied, 'Sean.' The Connacht captain responded, 'Sean who?' 'Sean Purcell,' the child replied. That same child went on to become one of the greatest Gaelic footballers ever.

At the time, it was quite common for players to guest play for clubs in other counties and Donnellan is reputed to have won a Down club championship medal.

Such was his stature as a high-class performer that he played Sigerson Cup football with University College Galway (UCG), even though he was not a student at the college. Colleges were allowed to draft in a few guest players so Donnellan was regularly called upon to make the journey in from Dunmore to play for the university team.

Unfortunately for Donnellan, the Dunmore MacHales teams that he played for did not match the successes of the club at the turn of the century or later on in the 1960s, when his son John was playing. The club won seven Galway senior county championships between 1889 and 1912 but did not win another one until 1953. They were finalists in 1933 and they won a junior title in 1931.

Numerous footballers and hurlers have used their success on the GAA field as a springboard to get them into politics but the same cannot be said about Mick Donnellan. He was one of those young people who was always interested in politics and he joined Sinn Féin as a 16-year-old, after the 1916 Rising. The following year he was elected as a councillor on Glenamaddy District Council.

After Éamon de Valera founded Fianna Fáil in 1926, Donnellan was so impressed by the new party that he joined up and he served as a member of Galway County Council for the party from 1927 onwards.

In a 1988 interview with *The Connacht Tribune*, Mick Donnellan's son John said, 'He had tended towards Fianna Fáil but he seems to have fallen out with them.'

After falling out with Fianna Fáil, Donnellan was to leave an indelible mark on the Irish political landscape when, in 1939, he helped found a new party – Clann na Talmhan.

The party was born out of the Anglo-Irish Trade War, or 'Economic War', between the Irish Free State and the UK in the 1930s. After the Irish government refused to repay land annuities, which were loans given by Britain to Irish tenant farmers to enable them to purchase their lands, the two countries began to impose trade restrictions on each other. This economic war caused severe damage to the Irish economy and Irish farmers were among the worst hit. Prices received by farmers for their produce during this period collapsed while costs soared, and rural society suffered greatly because of this price-cost squeeze.

With the crisis in rural society came the birth of Clann na Talmhan, a political party which mainly drew its support from disaffected Fianna Fáil supporters like Donnellan.

In describing how Clann na Talmhan came about, Dr Tony Varley at NUI Galway said that there was 'a bitter realisation that farmers had done their patriotic duty by the Fianna Fáil-controlled state, manning the front-line trenches in the economic war only to find that their struggle had been all in vain.'

There was a growing sense that the Fianna Fáil TDs were not capable of representing farmers as they were disconnected from the harsh realities farmers were enduring.

Contempt for politicians and the establishment soared in 1938 after TDs voted to give themselves salary increases.

Mick Donnellan summed up the level of contempt when he said: 'You could take all the TDs, all the senators, all the ministers and members of the judiciary and all the other nice fellows and dump them off Clare Island into the broad Atlantic. Still, Ireland would succeed. But without the workers and producers the country would starve in twenty-four hours.'

There was a populist view that productive labour was the only real creative force in Irish society and Fianna Fáil did not realise it. So Donnellan set about creating a new movement that would tap into this view.

Donnellan believed that farmers had 'only themselves to blame' for the crisis they were in and he predicted 'a wholesale abandonment of agriculture was in prospect with farmers' sons flocking into the towns to get £3 a week for an eight-hour day.'

So an organisation styled as the county Galway branch of the National Farmers' Association held its first meeting in Dunmore on 22 January 1939.

Feeling betrayed by politicians and the political system, the activists involved in the new movement were initially intent on steering clear of direct involvement in politics. The intention was to become a trade union organisation.

Four months later, the Clann na Talmhan movement was formally launched at meeting in Athenry on 29 June 1939, to advance the cause of farmers.

Clann na Talmhan soon abandoned its initial strategy of organising along trade union lines and decided to turn to party politics by 15 August 1939. On that date, the organisation's executive in Galway decided to contest the Galway West by-election, brought about by the death of Fianna Fáil TD Sean Tubridy the previous month.

The by-election was held on 30 May 1940 and Donnellan believed that Clann na Talmhan had to contest it because the organisation's members would have divided along political lines had they not had a Clann na Talmhan candidate.

He said, ' . . . it was in order to kill that party spirit that we decided to contest the by-election'.

Donnellan believed that by ignoring the election, Clann na Talmhan would have 'flopped immediately' so he put his name forward for the by-election.

Having served as a Fianna Fáil councillor for some years and already been passed over for an Oireachtas election nomination, Donnellan was the party's obvious choice.

Varley, one of the few academics to extensively study the party, believes that Donnellan's entry into the 1940 by-election race caused a surge in the growth of the party as an anti-government movement.

'There was a sense in which the same heady mix of competition and the public expression of solidarity found in the Gaelic games at which Donnellan excelled, was recreated in that ritualisation of politics in powerful public spectacles that were marked features of Clann na Talmhan's early days,' wrote Varley.

Donnellan's brand of politics was totally different to anything seen in Galway for decades. Some contemporary commentators even remarked that the rallies he held echoed the Land League's demonstrations 60 years earlier.

He was a larger-than-life character. If local people in Dunmore, Milltown, Williamstown or Tuam heard that he was going to speak at a rally the crowds would soar.

Jim Hession, the late Fine Gael TD for Galway North from Donnellan's era, told *The Connacht Tribune* in 1988 that 'the basic driving force in Mick Donnellan was a hunger for power, a near megalomania'.

'If he was there [at a rally] you could expect three or four times the normal crowd. It wasn't that he was a good public speaker, but he had a remarkable charisma and power that attracted people to him as supporters.'

By standing in the by-election, Donnellan introduced his new party to the Irish electoral stage and he garnered nearly 6,000 votes. But his only other opponent in the by-election, Fianna Fáil's John J Keane defeated him with over 14,000 votes.

By 1942, the party had built on the by-election two years earlier, standing candidates in the local elections and building up a stronger branch network. Donnellan claimed in 1942 that over 80 per cent of the people of Galway had joined the party's 134 branches in the county.

The party became the second largest grouping on Galway County Council in the local elections and the foundations had been laid for the general election the following year.

Donnellan's reputation as a rabble-rousing speaker grew and he proved that he was not willing to shy away from controversy. Speaking at a party rally in a packed square in Tuam in 1943 Donnellan blasted: 'The politicians were deserters and turncoats. They turned away from rural Ireland and from the workers and turned to the money-grabbers, Jews and speculators.'

Donnellan was elected to the Dáil on the first count after he topped the poll in the four-seat Galway East constituency in 1943. His success was replicated in nine other constituencies as Clann na Talmhan won a total of ten Dáil seats in the party's most successful day at the polls.

The marginal party now found itself holding the balance of power as Fianna Fáil had failed to secure an overall majority in the June 23 election.

The Dáil's newest party had a mammoth decision to make. Should they go straight into opposition, in keeping with the platform on which they were elected, or should they do the unthinkable – get into bed with Fianna Fáil?

They did neither. World War II was still raging at the time and 'The Emergency' was in place in Ireland. So, 'swayed by the overriding interest of preserving stable government in wartime', Clann na Talmhan's national executive decided a Dáil strategy on 29 June. The party would support Fianna Fáil in forming a government but it would take no part in Cabinet, in return for a commitment from de Valera that he would 'resist anything that would injure agriculture'.

Donnellan met with de Valera on 1 July and this fuelled speculation that a secret pact had been agreed between his party and Fianna Fáil.

After they abstained from the vote that allowed Fianna Fáil form a minority government, Clann an Talmhan were bitterly attacked by the opposition parties.

Internally, tensions and divisions developed between the party's large- and small-scale farmers, and between TDs from the west of Ireland and those from the east. Personality differences also erupted between individuals.

Against this background, Donnellan's reign as leader of the party he had founded came to an end in mid-1944.

His contemporary Jim Hession admired the way Donnellan was able to tap into the mood that Fianna Fáil was no longer the party of the 'small man' and capitalise on it. But Hession also pointed out some of Donnellan's failings.

Hession said, 'He would be a lot more courteous to a Fianna Fáil man than he would to his own election workers . . . he was a tough man and treated his own people quite badly at times; he ordered them about and bullied them.'

On polling day one year, Hession witnessed him in a bar in Williamstown in North Galway. Donnellan went into the bar and ordered a few pints for some people there before he asked one of the men how he had voted earlier that day. When the man replied that he had not voted for Donnellan, he cancelled the order for the pints.

In praise of Donnellan, Hession added, 'But he knew the psychology of the people and had the charisma and appeal for them that only Fianna Fáil have seemed to capture apart from that.'

Varley wrote that by mid-1944 the large farmer element in Clann na Talmhan had 'come to see the dynamic, but volatile, Donnellan as too close to Fianna Fáil and the radical agrarian tradition, and too outspoken and undisciplined to hold the movement together.'

Joe Blowick, a large farmer and former Blueshirt from Mayo, was selected as Donnellan's successor. Donnellan remained as one of the most dominant figures in the party and even though Blowick was the leader, what Donnellan said 'went'.

The Connacht Tribune claimed, 'Joe Blowick might be staying in the Gresham Hotel as the leader, but Mick Donnellan would be living in less-exalted lodgings as the real leader.'

The Galway-based newspaper regularly referred to Donnellan's ability to manifest the type of charisma that Fianna Fáil politicians built upon.

It reported, 'He developed the Fianna Fáil style of charisma on the hustings. He saw that Sinn Féin had developed the idea of two-minutes silence at their meetings for the 'unknown soldier' and he did exactly the same thing himself though nobody ever knew what it was all about.'

Donnellan's athletic ability stood him in good stead as well, as he was known to regularly cycle from Dunmore to Ennis to political rallies before cycling home again.

The view that Donnellan was spurred on by megalomania is certainly substantiated by a poem, issued by Clann na Talmhan that was published in *The Connacht Tribune*:

> *Who says that Ireland's nearly done,*
> *And needs a healing plan?*
> *No fear! she's got a fightin' son –*
> *She's always bred strong men like Mick,*
> *Who answered to the call.*
> *So when you vote, be sure you pick*
> *Mick Donnellan for the Dáil.*
> *North Galway's on the march today:*
> *Productive schemes are growing.*
> *'Tis by your vote you can repay*
> *The man who set them going.*
> *Mick's always out to do his best,*
> *And to everyone pays heed,*
> *And if these words you wish to test,*
> *Ask those who are in need.*

In the 1944 general election Clann na Talmhan's Dáil seat tally was reduced to nine TDs and four years later the party was down to seven TDs.

After the 1948 general election, the party helped form the first Inter-Party government along with Fine Gael, the Labour party, Clann na Poblachta, the

National Labour Party and independent TD James Dillon.

During negotiations on forming the government, Clann na Talmhan looked for the agriculture and land portfolios at the cabinet table. Blowick got the Minister for Lands portfolio while Donnellan had to settle for the role of parliamentary secretary to the Minister for Finance with responsibility for the Office of Public Works. The Minister for Agriculture job was given to Dillon.

Despite being overlooked for a senior position at the Cabinet table, Donnellan used his position as a parliamentary secretary like no other TD and he flourished in the role.

Hession claimed that through 'open threats, cajoling and putting pressure on civil servants' he succeeded in getting money spent on schemes such as the Corrib–Clare drainage scheme. The scheme, talked about in political circles for many years, was a massive proposal that would see an area of 400 square miles of farmland drained.

Flooding was a constantly recurring problem in north Galway for centuries due to the relatively low-lying terrain and the high levels of rainfall in the West of Ireland.

In 1954, following years of Donnellan's haranguing civil servants and other politicians, the largest arterial drainage scheme of its kind ever undertaken in the country commenced. Known as the Corrib–Clare Drainage Scheme, it benefited farmers in Galway, Mayo and Roscommon as 400 miles of river and streams were widened and deepened to carry water off the 400 square miles of land.

In an interview with *The Connacht Tribune* some years after his father's death, Mick's son John Donnellan said, 'He proved that he could deliver by taking the Corrib–Clare drainage system from number 20 in the national priority plan to number four and then actually doing it.'

The £3,120,000 scheme took years to complete but it ensured Donnellan's Dáil seat was safe as it provided employment for 500 men for ten years. He was hugely popular with thousands of farmers as the field drainage scheme 'represented a dazzling political prize'.

The scheme was meant to start in 1951 but the Inter-Party government fell that year and Fianna Fáil were returned to power.

Back in office, Fianna Fáil TDs accused Donnellan of shamefully using his position as a parliamentary secretary to further the interests of his own constituency. But Donnellan had the last laugh. He returned to his role as parliamentary secretary for the Board of Works in the second Inter-Party government in 1954 so the project immediately commenced.

Donnellan was an astute political operator as well as he formed a remarkable voting transfer alliance with Fine Gael's Jim Hession between 1943 and 1954, before the pair fell out.

In a remarkable tribute to Donnellan's political nous, Hession said, 'Mick Donnellan was a Messiah-like figure. His major interest was heading the poll, but he achieved the best transfer performance I have ever seen, 96 per cent to me. It was incredible.'

Donnellan held his seat in the 1957 general election but Clann na Talmhan was firmly in decline as the party's Dáil seat tally fell from five in 1954 to just three seats.

By 1961 Donnellan polled 5,903 votes or 15 per cent of the vote but he had to wait until the third count for re-election. Fine Gael had virtually disappeared in Galway during the war years but the party's resurgence seriously damaged Clann na Talmhan's electoral performance from the late 1950s onwards.

Clann na Talmhan had just two TDs – Blowick and Donnellan – after the 1961 election and the party was hampered by financial and organisational weaknesses. Suggestions were made that the party should change its name and re-brand but they came to nothing and the party limped along with its two TDs.

Donnellan was one of the 76,498 people who packed into Croke Park on Sunday, 27 September 1964 to watch the All-Ireland football final between Galway and Kerry.

After being beaten in the previous year's final, the day should have been one of the proudest days in Donnellan's life as he watched his son John captain the Tribesmen to All-Ireland glory over a Kerry team that included Mick O'Connell and Mick O'Dwyer.

But it was not to be. Former Dunmore MacHales and Galway footballer Jack Mahon recounted in his 1965 book *Twelve Glorious Years* how he met 'a rather tired-looking Mick Donnellan' making his way to his seat to watch John, or 'Johneen', play, while another son Pat, or 'Pateen', was on the substitutes bench due to injury.

Despite being in failing health, the 64-year-old had insisted on travelling to the game and he died during the game as he sat in the Hogan Stand.

'Our All-Ireland victory had been won at a very heavy price,' wrote Mahon. 'Victory celebrations were few and our hearts went out to John Donnellan as we listened to him speak with so many of his father's mannerisms from the Hogan Stand. We knew that his father had died: he didn't. It was a tragic end to his greatest day.'

Photos of John Donnellan lifting the Sam Maguire Cup show him with a proud smile on his face. He was unaware of his father's death while the solemn expression on GAA President Alf Ó Muirí's face clearly shows how news of the death had filtered through.

In 1988 John Donnellan told *The Connacht Tribune* that his father did not talk much about Clann na Talmhan to him and that he had left little documentation behind after his death.

'I suppose it would be fair to say that it lost much of its identity when it went into coalition government. But he showed himself that he could bring in an enormous vote by working directly for the people,' said John.

'The people knew if you brought something to Mick Donnellan he would do his damnedest to get it done and if he didn't, he would kick up a hell of a stink about it.'

Donnellan had his own brand of politics. So much so that his Fine Gael constituency colleague, Jim Hession, even complimented his charisma.

Hession, who died in 1999, said, 'I suppose Clann na Talmhan lost their identity, but Fianna Fáil continue to keep their charisma, their ability to know the psychology of the people. For a while, Clann na Talmhan had that and no man understood that charisma better than Mick Donnellan.'

Martin Ferris
Left Half-Forward

KERRY — SINN FÉIN

'I was on the Kerry panel for the 1978 Munster final and the Friday before the game I was lifted by the gardaí and held for 48 hours . . .'

It's 15 June 2010 and Leinster House is a hive of activity. Fine Gael has put down a motion of no confidence in Taoiseach Brian Cowen after two scoping reports into the Irish banking crisis have criticised the government's fiscal policies when Cowen was Minister for Finance.

But the Fine Gael motion of no confidence is merely a sideshow to the real action. The Labour party has just become the most popular political party in the country for the first time ever in an *Ipsos MRBI/Irish Times* opinion poll. As a result, the Fine Gael leader Enda Kenny has become the victim of a leadership heave bid from his deputy leader Richard Bruton and a cabal of other key party figures.

As Kenny rises in the Dáil to outline the case against Cowen in the debate on the confidence motion, the knives are out for the Fine Gael leader.

As the high drama unfolds in the Dáil chamber, Sinn Féin TD Martin Ferris

167

has retired to his office. He is waiting until it is time for his party colleague Caoimhghín Ó Caoláin to stand up and argue the case for voting no confidence in the Taoiseach.

The television is on in Ferris's office and his eyes are fixed on the screen. Many other TDs have also returned to their Leinster House offices to work and to watch the proceedings in the Dáil chamber unfold on the TV screens.

But Ferris is not watching the live feed of the action from the chamber. His mind is elsewhere. Thousands of people have gathered in the sunshine outside the Guildhall in Derry. The final report of the Saville Inquiry into the deaths of 13 people in the city on Bloody Sunday in 1972 has just been published.

History is unfolding as the crowd in Derry burst into a spontaneous cheer. The relatives of the civil rights marchers who were killed are the first to see the Saville report and they hold their arms out of the windows in the Guildhall and give it the thumbs up.

RTÉ television has devoted a special live broadcast programme to the event and three words keep running across the ticker on the bottom of the screen: 'unjust and unjustifiable'.

Ferris keeps his eyes fixed on the screen and mutters the words 'unjust and unjustifiable'. He is delighted that the innocent Bloody Sunday victims have finally been vindicated.

This day means a lot to Ferris. A parliamentarian in Leinster House for eight years, his long history as a man of violence was directly connected to Bloody Sunday. Although he had joined the IRA two years before that, it was events like the atrocity in Derry in January 1972 that had goaded Ferris, and hundreds of other young men, into joining, or escalating their involvement in, the IRA.

Sitting in his Dáil office, Ferris says, 'This is some day for the British establishment. This report shows everybody what we have already known for a long time.'

The day the Saville Report is published is just a few days beyond the fortieth anniversary of Ferris joining the IRA in 1970 as an 18-year-old. Before that, he enjoyed a childhood not unlike that of any other young boy growing up in Kerry in the 1950s and 1960s. Born on 10 February 1952, Ferris had an enormous interest in the GAA and his earliest memories of the GAA are of Kerry playing Derry in the All-Ireland semi-final in 1958. The clash between Kerry's Mick O'Connell and Derry's Jim McKeever has become the stuff of legend and it helped to cultivate Ferris's lifelong interest in Gaelic football.

As well as following the fortunes of the Kerry team, Ferris used to accompany his father to local club championship games and he remembers being at all of the John Mitchell's GAA club's games in the late 1950s and early 1960s when they won five county championships in a row. Ferris's first trip to Croke Park is also very memorable as Kerry beat Roscommon in the All-Ireland final that day in 1962.

Martin Ferris's father, Patie, was apolitical while his mother Agnes was a staunch Fianna Fáil supporter. A Limerick woman, she always remembered her brother being tied to the back of a lorry and dragged through the streets of the city by the Free State forces during the Civil War. Éamon de Valera was her idol and she supported Fianna Fáil for most her life.

Agnes's interest in politics and her republicanism rubbed off on her son Martin who claims to have inherited his mother's interest in politics from an early age. A cousin of Ferris's father was a republican who was interned in the Curragh in the 1940s and there were a lot of republicans living in the area where Martin grew up. So it was a combination of these factors that spurred his interest in politics.

'A lot of very respectable and influential people in the area where I grew up were republicans; people like Mick Lynch and Liam Cotter in Spa, and Paddy Kelly in Ardfert. They were all strongly nationalist and republican minded people that influenced me,' claims Ferris.

'I got involved in the republican movement on the day my father was buried. That was on May 27 or 28, 1970. And I became really actively involved after Bloody Sunday in 1972. The optics of what was happening in the Six Counties encouraged me to join the IRA. You had television so it was in the room with you. We saw everything first hand that was happening. Bloody Sunday had a huge effect on people my age and it helped to make decisions on your future.'

While Ferris had made a life-changing decision to join the IRA in 1970, his interest in the GAA continued. He was on the verge of making the Kerry minor team when his father died that year. He had been called for a number of trials by the management but he missed the last trial because his father passed away.

That September, Kerry drew in the All-Ireland minor final and the selectors on the team, along with some of the mentors at Ferris's Churchill club, asked him to attend another trial. However he was too busy with work commitments at home to give his full commitment to the team and he declined the offer.

Two years later, as Ferris had come to terms with his father's death and the extra workload on the family farm that had been caused by his father's passing, he played at centre half-forward on the Churchill team that won the Kerry Novice county championship in 1972. It was Churchill's first major achievement since 1934 so Ferris was delighted to have played such a central role in the mammoth victory for his tiny club.

Around this time he earned himself a nickname that has stuck with him to this day – Martin 'The Pony' Ferris. He explains, 'There is a great character in the Churchill parish called Liam Cotter. We were playing a match one evening. I had very long hair at the time. I got the ball and one of the opposition jumped on my back. A free had been given, but I didn't realise it so I kept on running with the other player on my back.

'Liam Cotter joked at the time: "Would you look at the pony!" and that nickname has stuck with me to this day.'

As well as being involved in Churchill's historic win in 1972, Ferris finally broke into the Kerry county scene that year as he played on the under-21 team for the year.

Ferris scored the winning goal in the Munster final but the team was beaten by Galway in the All-Ireland semi-final a few weeks later.

From 1972 on, Ferris's activity in the IRA increased and by 1973 he found himself on the run from the gardaí.

Even though he was still eligible to play for the Kerry under-21 team in 1973, Ferris's IRA activity meant that he was not involved with the team for most of the year.

After Kerry won the Munster Under-21 title in 1973, former Kerry legend Joe Keohane, who was a selector on the team, contacted Ferris.

'I was on the run at that stage and I was not living in Kerry a lot of the time, but Keohane made contact with me to see if I would be available for the All-Ireland semi-final. The match was in Tralee and there was a possibility that I was going to be lifted by the gardaí so I didn't play,' recalls Ferris.

He had originally agreed to play the game so he was named to play as a corner-forward on the Kerry team. But fears that he was going to be arrested by the gardaí meant that Ferris discreetly watched the game from the crowd.

Standing there on the crowded terrace, Ferris found it amusing when some supporters shouted abuse at his replacement Michael O'Shea, who was wearing Ferris's number 13 jersey. Not realising that Ferris had been replaced by O'Shea, they shouted lines such as: 'Come on, Ferris, get into it! Wake up!'

Kerry did enough in that game to earn a place in the All-Ireland Under-21 final against Mayo in Ennis, County Clare.

As the game was in Clare, Ferris knew that the gardaí there would not pay as much attention to him so he was able to tog out in the Kerry colours, getting a lift to the game with his friend and teammate Batt O'Shea.

'I was on the run but it was probably only in Tralee that I would have been picked up. A lot of it would have been localised stuff that I was involved in, so there was no national hunt for me at the time,' he recalls.

Having missed the semi-final, Ferris started the game on the subs' bench. But as Mayo were winning by 0-9 to Kerry's 0-1, Ferris was put on a few minutes before half-time.

Future Fine Gael TD and Mayo manager John O'Mahony was playing in the left corner-back position and Ferris was sent in to play on him as Kerry's right corner-forward. Before he went onto the pitch, Joe Keohane said to Ferris, 'Let them know you are around' and he did just that.

'Within a minute there was a breaking ball and he (O'Mahony) caught it coming out of defence. I threw my arm across him and I hit him so hard that I broke the scaphoid bone in my wrist,' recalls Ferris about his first encounter with a man who would later sit a few seats away from him in the Dáil chamber some 34 years afterwards.

'I knew there was damage done but I didn't know that I had just broken a bone in my hand moments after I came on. There was murder in the second half as the game got very physical.'

Ferris was switched to play in the full-forward position, a few minutes into the second half, and helped Kerry pull off a major comeback and win the game by two points.

'I got a touch of a ball that ended up in the net. Mikey Sheehy took the credit for it and I couldn't argue with that as I could have been in the square when I hit it.'

Ferris still has his All-Ireland medal at home somewhere but he is not even sure where exactly it is. 'Medals do not really matter to me. But I suppose that All-Ireland title probably means a lot more to me now than it did then.'

The 1973 under-21 Kerry team was a who's who of young players who went on to become household names in later years. Among Ferris's teammates were Jimmy Deenihan, Ger Power, Páidí Ó Sé, John Egan and Mikey Sheehy, all of whom went on to win several senior All-Ireland titles.

So, looking back, does Ferris regret that the IRA got in the way of a fledging football career in the early 1970s?

He says, 'The level of commitment Mikey Sheehy, Tim Kennelly, Jimmy Deenihan and all of them had, was unbelievable. There was absolute commitment to football and they did not have any other distractions. My ultimate commitment was my involvement in the struggle.

'I don't know if I was ever good enough. I would like to know, and I will never find out if I was good enough. I made the choice and to this day I am convinced it was the right choice.

'At the end of the day, the management and my teammates would have to have asked if I had the necessary commitment. But my commitments were elsewhere. If I had the commitment necessary I would now know if I was good enough. But football was secondary, even though I loved competing and playing.'

In 1974 Joe Keohane contacted Ferris again and asked if he would play for the Kerry senior team in the national league but Ferris declined the offer as he was on the run and facing a prison sentence if the gardaí arrested him again.

On February 14, 1975 the gardaí arrested Ferris and two other IRA men in Youghal, County Cork and charged them with armed robbery of a co-op in Dungarvan, County Waterford and IRA membership. Ferris was acquitted of the robbery but sentenced to 12 months in Portlaoise Prison for membership of the IRA.

Two of Ferris's friends and teammates from the 1973 team, Páidí Ó Sé and John Egan, went on to become gardaí and were stationed in Portlaoise when Ferris was in jail there.

While in prison Ferris was involved in a failed escape attempt with a number of other IRA prisoners such as Kevin Mallon, Brian Keenan and JB O'Hagan in 1975. The prisoners managed to get explosives into the prison and they blew their way to the main door before the army started to fire at the would-be escapees. One IRA man, Tom Smith, was shot dead and four others including Keenan were wounded.

After he was released from prison in November 1975, Ferris was straight back into IRA activity and he was on the run from the gardaí again within weeks. Three months later on 14 February 1976 Ferris was arrested by gardaí. For the second year in a row, he was arrested on St Valentine's Day, and charged with membership of the IRA.

From March to May 1977, Ferris was among a group of 20 IRA prisoners who went on hunger strike in protest at the way they were being treated in jail. Ferris claims that the prisoners went on hunger strike because of the conditions in the prison that included 'brutality, strip searches, denial of visits from family or of paroles for serious illness and deaths in the family.'

Ferris stayed on hunger strike for 47 days and thought that he was going to die. After 32 days of the protest the hunger strikers were moved from Portlaoise Prison to the Curragh military hospital in Kildare as their health had deteriorated so much.

Ferris can vividly remember his mother, Agnes, coming up to visit him in the Curragh. 'I could see the shock on her face when she saw me. I will never forget her words. She said to me, "Whatever you decide, I will stand by you one hundred per cent." At that time I thought that it was all over – so she made things a little easier for me.'

Some of the prisoners who were on hunger strike with Ferris claim that after the first four or five days of the protest they found it easier. But Ferris certainly does not agree. He recalls, 'The sense of hunger never left me. I was craving for food right up to the forty-fifth day.

'We were moved to the Curragh military hospital into big dormitories and the military police were sitting across from us where they would have sandwiches brought in to them. They would be about 20 metres away from you. In fairness to them they had to eat and they were fairly discreet. Yet you would hallucinate that you could actually reach out and touch the sandwich even though it was 20 metres away.

'After we were moved to the Curragh, we just lay there waiting. You felt as if you were on a death sentence and you were just waiting and hoping for a reprieve,' recalls Ferris.

Kevin Mallon and Daithí Ó Conaill led the protest and they were dealing with intermediaries from the Catholic Church, trying to broker a deal with the government that would secure better conditions.

The Fine Gael Minister for Justice, Paddy Cooney, and the Labour Minister for Posts and Telegraphs, Conor Cruise O'Brien, were seen by republicans as two of the key figures who would not give in to the prisoners' demands. But there was a general election in the offing and Fianna Fáil hinted that they would deal with the problem if they were elected into government in the June 16 general election.

The protest ended in confusion before the elections. The protestors believed that their demands had been granted, yet the government claimed that this was not the case. After the election, O'Brien and Cooney both lost their seats and Fianna Fáil were returned to power with a majority. Ferris remembers that conditions gradually improved in the prison from then on.

Ferris was released from prison at the end of June 1977. He met his future wife Marie and the couple married in January 1978.

Around this time, Ferris returned to the football pitch. He played a number of challenge games with Kerry, including a game against Laois where a number of the prison officers from the jail in Portlaoise were lined out for the O'Moore county side.

He says, 'They were on one end of the field and I was on the other end. There was nothing said and we just played our game.'

Ferris got a call up to the Kerry panel on the back of his performances in the challenge games.

'I was on the panel for the 1978 Munster final and the Friday before the game I was lifted by the gardaí and held for 48 hours. I was released on the Sunday at about 1.10 p.m. and the match was on at 3.30 p.m. in Cork. I got there but there wasn't even a jersey left when I got there,' he remembers.

Mick O'Dwyer, the Kerry manager at the time, was building what is today widely regarded as the greatest Gaelic football team of all time; there was no place for a player like Ferris who was not able to give one hundred per cent commitment after that.

Ferris describes O'Dwyer as a 'very honourable person' and recognises that he, Ferris, did not have the necessary commitment to hold on to his place on the Kerry panel.

O'Dwyer claims, 'I have no doubt that Martin would have won many All-Ireland senior football medals if he had given football his one hundred per cent concentration. He had everything we would look for in a star player.'

But Ferris's playing days were ground to a halt with his involvement in the subversive activities of the IRA.

In September 1984 Ferris and four others were involved in a gunrunning plot to bring arms from America into Ireland for use by the IRA. Leaving the Kerry fishing village of Fenit on a trawler called the *Marita Ann*, they met up with another vessel in the middle of the Atlantic Ocean, the *Valhalla*, that had travelled from Boston. The arms and ammunition shipment was transferred from the Boston vessel to the *Marita Ann* before the Irish vessel set off on the return journey to Ireland.

After spending four days at sea, the Skellig Rocks off the coast of Kerry was the agreed point where the crew would make contact with the IRA units ashore. A number of IRA men were waiting on the shore for the shipment to arrive so they could take the arms and ammunition and conceal them in arms dumps.

But the *Marita Ann* never made it that far. The Irish Navy had been informed about the gunrunning plot. The navy vessels the *LE Aisling* and the *LE Emer* along with members of the gardaí were behind the Skellig Rocks waiting to pounce on Ferris and his cohorts. They used the Skellig Michael rock as camouflage so that the radar on Ferris's vessel could only pick up the rock and not the navy vessels concealed behind it.

As the *Marita Ann* got to within three quarters of a mile of the Skelligs and inside Irish waters they were intercepted by the navy and gardaí. Ferris was arrested and subsequently sentenced to 10 years in prison for the possession of explosives for unlawful purpose, and possession of firearms and ammunition with intent to endanger life.

Some days previously, as Ferris and his cohorts set off on the *Marita Ann* from Fenit pier on their way to meet the Boston vessel, IRA man Seán O'Callaghan was there to see them off. It later turned out that O'Callaghan, the head of the IRA's Southern Command, who was close to Ferris, was actually a Garda informer.

He had led a double life as an IRA volunteer and a Garda informer for many years and in 1999 he published an autobiographical account of his double life called *The Informer: The Real Story of One Man's War against Terrorism*. He was involved in foiling a bomb at a London theatre where Prince Charles and Princess Diana were meant to attend a Duran Duran concert in 1984.

After the *Marita Ann* had set off from Fenit in September of that year, the informer told his garda handler about the arms shipment and this led to Ferris's gunrunning mission being foiled off the Skellig Rocks a few days later.

O'Callaghan's work as an informer or 'the most important intelligence officer in the history of the Irish State' as he is dubbed by the gardaí in his book, directly led to Ferris's ten-year prison sentence.

Ferris recalls, 'It is obvious that he was, as he says himself, the informer. He was privy to the operation. When we got on the boat, he was on the pier with us. We left Fenit on the boat and we left him on the pier. He went off to do whatever he had to do, which was fairly obvious.

'That was on the Tuesday night and we were arrested on the Friday night. He was pretty close to me in that we were from the same area and he was from a prominent republican family. We were involved in republican activity together.

'While I didn't have any suspicions about him at all, my wife and my brother did. My brother and other people finally unmasked him.

Looking back nearly 20 years later, Ferris recalls, 'O'Callaghan is a person who has lived his life as a lie.

'I came out of prison in 1994 and by Easter Sunday 1995 it was common knowledge that Seán O'Callaghan was an informer. He hadn't admitted it himself publicly but he came to the Easter Sunday commemoration and he kept to himself in the background. He was very upset. I just went over to him and shook his hand and I walked down the town of Tralee with him afterwards. I went for a drink with him.

'By that time the allegations were proven internally within the movement that he was wrong. But O'Callaghan was still denying it.

'A few months afterwards, in the same week that Gerry Adams was granted a visa to visit America, O'Callaghan came out publicly and said that he was an informer. He went to America as well to try to undermine Adams and I would say that is why he came out publicly.'

When asked if O'Callaghan's double life had the effect of saving lives in the North, Ferris says, 'You could argue it both ways. At the end of the day, at that point in time, the IRA was at war. I was an IRA volunteer and I was with other volunteers on board the boat. We felt it was our duty to help in the campaign. It was an IRA operation and we were just doing what any other IRA volunteer would have done.

'The sole purpose was to arm the IRA volunteers so they could prosecute the war more efficiently and more effectively against the British presence.

'There was nothing going to stop the IRA. As Brian Keenan said, "The IRA was your next door neighbour. It was someone down the street. It was part of your community and it had the popular support which was necessary to prosecute the war in the Six Counties. That is how the IRA was able to get the British government to negotiate and take us from where we have come from to where we are now.'

The day Ferris was arrested on board the *Marita Ann* he was taken to Cork where he was held in Garda custody. His wife came down to Cork to see her husband and it was here that she told Ferris that she was pregnant with the couple's sixth child. Marie was left to rear Éamon (10), Eoin (5), Toireasa (4), Deirdre (3), Ciannan (1) and Máirtín (who was born in early May 1985) while her husband served his 10-year sentence for gunrunning.

Ferris claims, 'It was hard being away from my wife and family but I did have the comfort of knowing that the community in Ardfert, where we lived, and Churchill, where I am from, were absolutely brilliant and helpful to Marie and my mother.'

Back in Portlaoise Prison, Ferris was involved in another botched escape attempt with nine other republican prisoners in November 1985. The escape effort was led by Tommy McMahon, an IRA man from Monaghan who was serving a sentence for planting the 1979 bomb that killed Lord Mountbatten in

Mullaghmore, County Sligo.

After making their way through about 10 or 12 different sets of gates, Ferris and the other prisoners got as far as the final set of steel doors and used explosives to blow the door apart. The explosives blew the locks off the doors perfectly, except for one part of a lock that got jammed. The inmates were duly caught after that and Ferris served the rest of his sentence.

It was in prison, of all places, that Ferris rekindled his interest in playing Gaelic football with other prisoners.

'We played an awful lot of football in prison. We had some great matches and used to play interprovincial matches,' recalls Ferris. 'We used to play two or three times a year and it would end up in a Munster v Ulster final. There were some great footballers in there like Tommy McKearney from Tyrone. There was well over 100 gardaí in the prison and on the day of the final they would line the pitch and be looking out the windows at the game.

'It was only a 63 by 20 metres yard so the game would only be five or six a side. There were great games and they were very tough as they were played on concrete.'

Ferris explains that a 'senior respected republican' like JB O'Hagan, who was one of a group of IRA prisoners to escape from Mountjoy Prison by helicopter in 1973, or Dessie 'Snitchy' Ferguson would referee the games.

He adds, 'We used to play for a leather medal that was made in the prison workshop and we would die for it.'

Ferris was released from prison 11 days after the historic IRA ceasefire on August 31, 1994. On previous occasions Ferris had returned to IRA activity immediately after his release but this time was different and he embraced politics over violence.

Along with other Sinn Féin activists in the Kerry North constituency, Ferris set about building the party at grassroots level. He stood for the party in the 1997 general election and garnered 5,691 first-preference votes. This marked a massive increase on Sinn Féin's performance in the 1992 election when Billy Leen had got just 802 votes.

Ferris's 5,691 votes in 1997 put Sinn Féin ahead of Fianna Fáil after the first count. But it was not enough to get him elected because Sinn Féin did not get the transfers from other candidates. It did, however, provide Ferris with a good foundation for future elections.

In December 1997 Ferris was part of the first Sinn Féin delegation in over 70 years to meet the British government for talks in London. The delegation met British Prime Minister Tony Blair, his Secretary of State to Northern Ireland, Mo Mowlam, and her deputy, Paul Murphy, for face-to-face meetings in Number 10, Downing Street.

Describing that meeting, Ferris, says, 'Going in the door of Downing Street, I was nervous. I knew the hopes and expectations of everyone across the whole political divide were weighing on us. I was very honoured to be there representing Irish republicans.

'You were also conscious of the historical resemblance of what happened when Collins and his people were there before and what happened after that. It was symbolic in a sense that we knew we were sitting down across the table from the British government. They knew they had to find a settlement because if they didn't they were going to be locked into a continuous military campaign that they couldn't win.

'Those negotiations went on and they culminated in the Good Friday Agreement the following year and you had negotiations since then, right up until the transfer of policing and justice recently.

'When you look back on it, what has been achieved has been huge insofar as where we came from. It seemed awfully painful, slow and tedious when you were going through it, but when you look back it has been a huge move.'

Ferris won seats on Kerry County Council and Tralee Town Council in 1999 and he was confident of taking a Dáil seat in the 2002 general election. He topped the poll in 2002 with 9,496 first preferences, taking one of the three Dáil seats in Kerry North and edging out former Tánaiste and Labour TD Dick Spring in the process.

He claims, 'A lot has been said about me taking Dick Spring's seat. We took a seat and it didn't matter whether it was Fianna Fáil, Fine Gael or Labour – we just wanted to take a seat.'

There has been much made of the animosity between the Labour and Sinn Féin camps in Kerry North but Ferris rejects this and says there is 'nothing personal' between him and Spring. I have nothing against Dick Spring and wouldn't really know him. He is somebody from a big political family. I held his sister Maeve, who died recently, in high regard as I was on the council with her. I thought that she was an excellent councillor and a great battler.'

During the 2002 election campaign there was a lot of media coverage of the fact that Ferris was involved in an anti-drugs campaign in Tralee so he was heavily criticised for his involvement in vigilantism.

He claims, 'The motivation behind all those allegations in 2002 was to stop Sinn Féin taking the seat. I have never for one minute hid the fact that I led a campaign against drug dealers in a political way.

'I was to the forefront picketing their houses with Sinn Féin colleagues and others. I confronted them when they tried to bully and intimidate people. And we spent practically every waking moment for a number of years facing down these thugs.

'It was confrontational insofar as we were not going to back down from the drug dealers. I had the luxury of having a history that these drug dealers were afraid of anyway. Everybody knew who I was and where I had been. Everybody knew my history as it was something that had been in the papers on a daily basis locally. We had a very strong campaign against the drug dealers.'

Ferris has been caught up in a number of controversies and in February 2005 the Minister for Justice, Michael McDowell named him, Gerry Adams and Martin McGuinness as members of the IRA Army Council. It was later reported in July of that year that the three had left the Army Council.

Ferris says, 'McDowell had an insatiable appetite to have a front page in the paper and he named us. It was designed to damage Sinn Féin publicly.

'I had a history that is an open book. I have been in prison three times in Portlaoise. I have been arrested 50 or 60 or 70 times, I actually couldn't tell you how many times I have been arrested. I have been involved in IRA activity that I will take to the grave with me so it was very easy for McDowell to say that so he could damage Sinn Féin. He was Minister for Justice and if he had any proof he should have put it out there.'

When asked to look back on his IRA days and say if it was all worth it, Ferris replies: 'On a personal capacity it was never going to be worth it because there is part of your life when you were away from your family and your kids.

'Those of us who are still alive, who lived through it and have grown-up kids and grandchildren, try to do with our grandchildren what you weren't able to do with your own children.'

Was it worth it?

'It will never be worth it to the individual who gave up practically everything for it. The only thing that has made it worthwhile is the very fact that you now have an Ireland in a far better place. Political violence is no longer necessary and I don't think this whole thing is reversible or ever will be reversible. The reward is for our grandchildren. So I have no regrets.'

After Detective Garda Jerry McCabe was shot dead by an IRA gang in Adare, County Limerick during a botched post office robbery in June 1996, Ferris and other Sinn Féin figures were criticised for refusing to condemn McCabe's killers and for campaigning for their release under the terms of the 1998 Good Friday Agreement.

Looking back on the killing, Ferris says, 'We have all said it, even the lads that did it, have said that it was wrong and it should not have happened. The loss to Jerry McCabe's family is something that they can never get back.'

When two of McCabe's killers – Pearse McCauley and Kevin Walsh – were released from Castlerea Prison on August 9, 2009 after completing their full sentences, Ferris found himself embroiled in controversy and further criticism for collecting them at the prison on their release.

Ferris defends this on the basis that he had been Sinn Féin's spokesperson on prisoners for a number of years. He says there was a proposal that the men's families and supporters should be waiting at the prison gates to collect them but the Sinn Féin leadership rejected this idea.

'We thought it would be triumphalist so I agreed to collect them. We wanted to collect them in the middle of the night and take them away but they were not released until 7.30 a.m. and the press was there.

'We just took them out of the area and away from there to their families so that they were not carried shoulder high and met by a crowd of family and friends, like other republican prisoners were in the past. How would that have looked for the McCabe family?

'What we tried to do was genuinely not to inflict any further hurt on Mrs McCabe because we were quite conscious of what she and her family had lost and how difficult it had been for her and her family. We had the sole purpose of taking them away and trying to diffuse it and take away that sort of triumphant release.'

The year after Ferris was elected to the Dáil in 2002, the dual mandate whereby TDs could hold council seats as well as sit in the Dáil was abolished under local government reform legislation.

Ferris stepped down from Kerry County Council and his daughter Toireasa was co-opted onto the council in his place. So did Ferris encourage his daughter into politics?

He says that he did not persuade her to go into politics as she is 'her own person'. She was in ANC Youth from the age of about 12 and after her law degree she completed a Masters degree in Human Rights at Queen's University Belfast.

'Toireasa and I would clash a lot. We would have different views on a lot of things and she is stubborn. She is more like her mother. Did I encourage her into politics? No!

'When the dual-mandate rule came in, I was to step down from the county council as well. There was a strategy group and they had Toireasa as the third choice. The first choice said she couldn't do it because she had a big mortgage and a job, and the second choice after that couldn't do it either. Then they came up with Toireasa.'

After being co-opted onto Kerry County Council in 2003, she won a council seat in the 2004 local elections and retained it in 2009. She also polled a surprisingly high 64,671 first-preference votes in the 2009 European elections but failed to take one of the three seats in Ireland South/Munster.

In February 2006 Toireasa Ferris found herself embroiled in controversy after an interview with Pat Kenny on *The Late Late Show* on RTÉ. She refused to condemn the killing of Detective Garda Jerry McCabe and she also wore a very short skirt that hiked up when she crossed her legs during the interview. In the days that followed she was ridiculed by the tabloid media for wearing the skirt.

Martin Ferris was speaking at a Sinn Féin meeting in Coalisland, County Tyrone on the night of his daughter's appearance on *The Late Late Show* so he missed it.

He says, 'I remember I came back from Coalisland that night with Michelle Gildernew, and Michelle's husband said to me, "Your daughter was on and she was showing a lot of leg." And I didn't really take any notice of it until the next day when all hell broke loose. That shattered her.

'It happened in 2006 so she would have been about 26. When she sat down her skirt got caught up and she didn't take any notice of it. She was nervous and it did shatter her. She was very upset for a while but it toughened her up too.'

And 2006 was a memorable year in the Ferris household for another reason. Martin Ferris has always maintained his passion for the GAA and his family is heavily involved in the Ardfert club. He was a selector with the Ardfert team that won the All-Ireland Junior Club Championship in Croke Park in 2006. In an amazing feat, the club returned to Croke Park the following year to win the All-Ireland Intermediate Club Championship.

Ferris is extremely proud that he was a selector for the Ardfert team that had his sons Éamon play at centre half-forward, Máirtín at midfield and Ciannan on the panel.

He does not know for how long more he will stay in politics and if his daughter Toireasa will succeed him in his Dáil seat.

He says, 'To be quite honest about it, there are days when I think that I am

184

at this since 1970 and it would be nice, as my health is good, to spend a few years with my grandchildren before I go to the next world, whatever that is.

'Then there are other days I think that, Jesus, we have so much to do all the time with the struggle! And in most instances that takes precedence over everything.'

It is over 40 years since he chose the IRA and politics over football. Politics has always taken precedence. Old habits die hard.

Jack Lynch (Captain)
Right Corner-Forward

CORK – FIANNA FÁIL

'Jack Lynch was a gentleman. At one time he was the
most popular politician since O'Connell.'

After Adolf Hitler's German forces invaded Poland on Friday, 1 September 1939, Taoiseach Éamon de Valera called emergency Oireachtas sittings for the following day.

Dáil and Seanad Éireann sat overnight from 3 p.m. on the Saturday until 5 a.m. on the Sunday as the government declared an official state of emergency and enacted the Emergency Powers Act.

At 11.15 a.m. on Sunday, 3 September, British Prime Minister Neville Chamberlain announced on radio that Britain was at war with Germany.

As the news broke that our nearest neighbour was at war, de Valera called another Cabinet meeting at Government Buildings. Later that night he addressed the nation on radio and reaffirmed an earlier commitment, given in the Dáil, that Ireland would remain neutral.

But even the outbreak of the Second World War was not going to get in the way of the All-Ireland hurling final in Croke Park that afternoon, between the Cabinet meeting in the morning and his address to the nation that night.

The Cabinet meeting was wound up in time for de Valera and a number of his government colleagues to make their way from Merrion Street to Jones Road for the clash between Cork and Kilkenny. As the deadliest conflict in the history of mankind erupted abroad, the skies above Croke Park burst open with the torrential weather conditions in what became known as 'the thunder and lightning final'.

The final marked Cork's first hurling final since 1931 and the Leesiders were hoping to make a breakthrough with 22-year-old captain Jack Lynch playing at midfield.

In a 1982 radio interview with RTÉ journalist Mick Dunne, Lynch recalled, 'It was a raging storm and the rain came down like stair rods. At times it was impossible to see more than 20 yards from you.

'Conditions were almost unplayable. The ground conditions themselves were very difficult, and we felt a bit strange, as we had not been to Croke Park before, at least not as a senior county hurling team.'

Lynch's first All-Ireland final ended with Cork suffering a cruel one-point defeat to Kilkenny on a score line of Kilkenny 2–7 to Cork's 3–3.

While the 'thunder and lightning final' was one tainted by the heartbreaking defeat, it did mark the start of an extraordinary chapter for Lynch and the Leesiders. The war years, known as 'The Emergency', marked a golden era for Cork hurling. Over the next nine championship seasons Lynch would play seven All-Ireland hurling finals and win five, including a historic four-in-a-row. He also played in a football final, and won it, to put together a string of six successful appearances in All-Ireland finals, a record that has never been matched.

John Mary, or 'Jack', Lynch was born on 15 August 1917 within earshot of the bells of Shandon Cathedral in Cork city. The youngest son of Dan and Nora Lynch, he attended the local St Vincent's Convent primary school before he won a scholarship to the 'North Mon' (North Monastery CBS) school. It was at this famous Cork city school that he began to emerge as a superb sportsman. Lynch won three coveted Harty Cup medals during the North Mon's run of four-in-a-row victories from 1934 to 1937.

A *Cork Examiner* match report of the 1934 Harty Cup final highlighted Lynch as 'prominent all through, scoring long-distance points and, from his stirring play, set up the movements for the Mon goals.'

Even at this early stage in his playing career Lynch was showing himself to be a promising dual hurler and footballer as he was also on the North Mon team that won the 1935 and 1936 Munster Colleges football titles.

Following in the footsteps of his older brothers, Lynch started playing hurling with the local Glen Rovers GAA club at the age of 10. He also played for St Nicholas, the Glen Rovers' sister football club.

Lynch's club career was decorated with medals as he was on the St Nicholas teams that won minor football county championships in 1930, 1932 and 1933. In hurling he was on the Glen Rovers' minor teams that won the county championship four times between 1932 and 1937, and he captained them in 1933 and 1934.

This success was replicated at senior level as he went on to win ten senior county championship medals with Glen Rovers, including a remarkable eight-in-a-row feat from 1934 to 1941

At the age of 20, Lynch was captain of the Cork hurling team in 1938 and the following year he became the only player in history to captain both the inter-county football and hurling teams in the same year. That year he led Cork to their first Munster hurling title in eight years before they suffered defeat at the hands of Kilkenny in the 'thunder and lightning final'.

Following Chamberlain's announcement that Britain was at war with Germany on the morning of that final, the French announced they were at war during the match. But international events were not on Lynch's mind that evening as he came to terms with the defeat. Later in life Lynch was often heard saying that 'there were occasions in the 1930s when I thought I would never win an All-Ireland medal.' But all that was to change very shortly. In March 1941 Cork won the National League final when they beat Dublin, and the two teams met again in the All-Ireland hurling final that September.

If 1939 was the year of the thunder and lightning, then 1942 can be labelled the year of the 'foot and mouth'. A serious outbreak of foot-and-mouth disease severely hampered the championship as Department of Agriculture restrictions meant that some fixtures could not be played.

Cork's Munster semi-final tie against Tipperary was one of these fixtures and Lynch's team ended up advancing to the All-Ireland final having won just two games.

The fuel shortages during The Emergency meant that a relatively small crowd of just over 26,000 were in Croke Park to see Cork comprehensively beat Dublin on a score line of 5–11 to 0–6. Lined out at midfield, Lynch scored a few points in Cork's rout over Dublin, while a 20-year-old Christy Ring played in the half-forward line and scored three points.

Cork played Tipperary in the delayed Munster final the following month and lost the game, which meant they were All-Ireland champions even though they had lost the Munster final in the same year.

In 1942 Lynch resumed the role of Cork hurling captain that he had held in 1938–39. After beating a Limerick team that included the legendary Mick Mackey, and Tipperary along the way, Cork reached another All-Ireland final against a Dublin team that had trounced Kilkenny in the Leinster Championship. Although Dublin had improved on the previous year, Cork beat them and Lynch got to lift the Liam McCarthy Cup after Cork's 2–14 to 3–4 win over Dublin.

An *Irish Press* sports journalist writing under the pseudonym 'Green Flag' the following day wrote that: 'The challengers were outclassed at centre-field where Jack Lynch ruled the roost . . .'

Cork hammered Antrim in the 1943 decider, on a score line of 5–6 to 0–4, to complete their three-in-a-row.

Entering the 1944 championship Cork were favourites to capture a fourth successive title, something that had never been achieved in hurling history. It took a spectacular Christy Ring goal in the final minute of their clash with Limerick for the Rebels to win one of the greatest Munster finals ever played.

Lynch missed the All-Ireland semi-final with Galway but Cork managed to scrape past the Tribesmen with a one-point win to book their place in the All-Ireland final against Dublin.

Lynch and Con Cottrell, who had joined Lynch in midfield that year, both had outstanding games and Cork emerged victors on a score line of Cork 2–13 to Dublin's 1–2. Lynch was one of nine Cork stars to have played in each of the four-in-a-row All-Ireland victories.

The hurlers' unbeaten championship run came to an end the following year as they were beaten by Tipperary in the Munster Championship. But in 1945, the one year that Cork did not win the hurling title between 1941 and 1946, Lynch amazingly won a football title.

Given the professional approach now taken by GAA players to the modern game it is nearly incomprehensible that a player of Lynch's calibre, in the hunt for his fifth successive All-Ireland medal, would nearly miss the match. But that is what almost happened. Lynch recounted the bizarre story to *Irish Independent* journalist Raymond Smith for his 1971 GAA book *Football Immortals*.

Lynch was in digs in Terenure, on the south side of Dublin in 1945. As the digs were convenient to the bus route that ran by Croke Park, he told the Cork manager Jim Barry that instead of going to the team hotel before the match he would go straight to the Jones Road venue and meet the team there.

As he stood at the bus stop near Kenilworth Square on the number 16 bus route, bus after bus passed by him with the 'full-up' sign showing. Eventually one stopped but it only took on two or three people from the front of the queue.

Lynch could see hoards of fans making their way to the game. Time was passing and he was starting to fear that he would be late for the game. So he made his way to the top of the queue and anxiously told the bus conductor that he was playing in the All-Ireland final against Cavan.

The conductor quizzically looked at Lynch and gruffly said, 'I don't think that I have ever heard that one before.'

Lynch's story was so bizarre that the conductor thought that it may just be true and he allowed him to get on to the packed bus.

He eventually arrived in Drumcondra with only fifteen minutes to go to the start of the game, so he had to run around the back of the Cusack Stand to the dressing rooms. When Lynch knocked on the door of the Cork dressing room, most of the players were already fully togged out and ready to take to the field.

There was a deathly silence in the room. Jim Hurley, the Cork selector and Civil War veteran who was responsible for selecting Lynch on the team, had been pacing up and down as he wondered about Lynch's whereabouts. Lynch thought Hurley was going to take him to task for being late. But the selector put his hand on Lynch's shoulder and smiled. Having guessed that something untoward had delayed him he said, 'Jack Lynch, you were great to come.'

Lynch started the game in the right corner-forward position but he was later moved to midfield where he was instrumental in setting up a move that led to Cork's second goal from corner-forward Derry Beckett. Cork won the game by 2–5 to Cavan's 0–7.

During the game Lynch famously clashed with Big Tom O'Reilly and the Cavan star was knocked out after the two players collided in a tackle. Lynch was later accused by Cavan supporters of tripping him and kicking him in the head while he was on the ground. O'Reilly also went on to become a TD and when the pair would meet years after the 1945 All-Ireland final, Lynch would ask, 'Tom, did you ever straighten the record with the Cavan supporters?' To which O'Reilly would reply, 'I did, but they don't believe me.'

Lynch had achieved legendary status as a dual star with his football medal. The famous Cork GAA trainer, Jim 'Tough' Barry, recalled Lynch's response when he told him he was selecting him for the football side. Lynch remarked, 'I'm not a footballer at all.' To which, Barry replied, 'But you have the brains.'

It would be misleading to suggest that Barry was taking a big chance in selecting Lynch for the Cork team as Lynch had played for St Nick's club, North Mon and even played on Munster Colleges teams with Kerry football icons

Paddy Kennedy and Joe Keohane.

In 1946 Lynch was back in another All-Ireland final with the Cork hurlers, dispelling the view that the Rebel County's great team was finished. After beating Clare, Waterford, Limerick and Galway they renewed their age-old rivalry with Kilkenny in the All-Ireland final. Over 64,000 spectators packed into Croke Park for the first final between the two sides, since the 'thunder and lightning final' in 1939.

Captained by Christy Ring, who played at centre half-forward, Cork led at half-time by 1–3 to 0–5 after Ring scored what Lynch sporting biographer Liam Ó Tuama regarded as 'one of the grandest of the many great goals he scored in his career'.

With Ring firing on all cylinders and players of Lynch's quality supporting him from midfield, Cork ran out easy winners on a score line of 7–5 to 3–8. In a 1982 interview, Lynch pointed out that although Ring was a great hurler when he played for Cork in the 1940s, it was the following decade before he reached his peak.

Lynch said, 'He probably matured, although I don't know if you could ever say that Christy Ring matured, because he was a hurler from the day he was born practically, but he probably got more experience and was able to read the game better [and that made him] the dominant character in the 1950s.'

Lynch, the only player to play in seven consecutive All-Ireland finals, played for the Cork side that lost the 1947 hurling decider to Kilkenny by one point.

The midfielder, who had earned the reputation of being a hard but fair hurler and footballer, played the memorable Munster hurling finals against Tipperary in 1949 and 1950. At that stage Tipperary were in the ascendency. Cork's best days were behind them and Lynch finally hung up his boots in 1951.

In 1952 he was returning from a conference in Ottawa, Canada, via New York, when he met former Glen Rovers hurler Paddy Barry. Lynch's old friend invited him to Gaelic Park the following day to see a team, made up of Irish emigrants from Cork, play a similar team of Galway exiles.

Even though Lynch had not hurled in over a year, the Cork squad encouraged him to tog out and play. An unfit Lynch asked to be taken off at half-time but his new teammates cajoled him into continuing to play. In the last few minutes of the game he hit a ball and as he watched to see if it was going to go over the bar, he got a charge with a hurley in the ribs that left him lying on the ground in pain.

The following day Lynch set off for Ireland by boat as he had decided to try out the *Nieuw Amsterdam* vessel, which was the flagship boat of the Holland-America fleet at the time. The boat was small by Atlantic standards and it happened to be a very rough crossing. Lynch was in agony from the challenge the previous day and as he lay in his bunk, the pain was getting worse with every movement the ship made. Eventually, the ship's doctor visited him in his bunk and diagnosed him with broken ribs.

In an RTÉ radio interview some years later, Lynch recalled, 'That was the last hurling match I ever played, and I'm hardly likely to play one like it again!'

As well as his array of medals, Lynch was also named on the GAA's hurling Team of the Millennium in 1999, Team of the Century in 1984, the Cork Millennium Team, and Hurling Captain of the Forties.

In later life he would say, 'I think I learned from hurling and football a discipline and a self-control, how to cope with both victory and defeat.'

Lynch's highly-decorated GAA career was only one facet of an extraordinary life. After his Leaving Certificate, he opted for a career in the Civil Service and his first job was a brief spell in the Dublin District Milk Board in 1936 where his brother Finbarr worked.

After that he served as a clerk of the Cork Circuit Court from 1936 until 1943 and during this period he studied law at UCC at night. And after he was transferred within the civil service to Dublin, he completed his last two years of study at King's Inns before he was called to the Bar in 1945.

Professor Ronan Fanning of UCD has written how Lynch's early career in hurling opened the door to his first job in the Dublin District Milk Board. He was offered the temporary job in the newly established board by Seán Ó Braonain, later secretary of the Department of the Gaeltacht and a member of the Civil Service Hurling Club, who was as 'anxious to recruit new talent to the club as he was to the new Milk Board'.

In 1943, after Lynch had worked for seven years as a clerk in Cork Circuit Court, his prowess as a GAA player earned him a transfer to Dublin.

Fanning's entry on Lynch in the *Dictionary of Irish Biography* reveals: 'The last two years of his night course in law could only be taken at the King's Inns, and his sporting connections again proved their worth when Paddy Ó Ceallaigh, a principal officer in the Department of Finance and also the chairman of the Civil Service Football Club, arranged his transfer to the District Court clerks' branch in Dublin.

'Lynch duly joined the club, which in 1944 won the Dublin Senior Football Championship for the first time in their history.'

During this period he was promoted to become private secretary to the secretary of the Department of Justice, Stephen A Roche. Sport, work and studying at night took up most of Lynch's time in his early life and he was not viewed as being particularly interested in politics when he was in his twenties.

But Lynch biographer Dermot Keogh describes how the future Taoiseach caught 'his first glimpse of politics during the 1932 general election', which brought Éamon de Valera's new Fianna Fáil party to power for the first time. Lynch was fifteen when he took part in an old-style election rally in Shandon in Cork. His older brother Finbarr can remember Jack 'carrying a torch made of a burning sod of turf in the procession, accompanying de Valera through Blackpool into the city.'

His next significant brush with politics came in 1946 when he was asked by his local Fianna Fáil cumann to stand for the Dáil in a by-election but Lynch declined the offer. In that year he married Máirín O'Connor from Dublin.

Keogh's biography records how Lynch's sister Rena also says that her older brother had 'no overt interest in politics as a young man'. But his GAA prowess and notoriety made him the perfect target for political parties.

'The members of different parties had a path worn to the door trying to get him to stand in a by-election,' claimed his sister.

After former IRA chief of staff Sean MacBride founded Clann na Poblachta in 1946, his new party realised the political potential of GAA stars, and Roscommon's All-Ireland winning star forward Jack McQuillan was elected a TD for them in the 1948 general election. Attempts by MacBride's new party to have Lynch added to the party ticket in Cork proved fruitless as he opted to stand for Fianna Fáil in that election.

Helped by a band of election workers from the Glen Rovers club, Lynch garnered 5,594 first-preference votes in the Cork Borough constituency to take the second of five seats and become a TD for the first time. He was re-elected in the constituency in the eight general elections that followed from 1951 to 1977.

Lynch was not formally a Fianna Fáil member until the night he allowed his name go forward for the 1948 election. He joined the Brothers Delaney Cumann in Cork that night and remained a member until his active participation in the party ceased.

Upon his election de Valera appointed him researcher and secretary of the parliamentary party and after Fianna Fáil returned to power in 1951, de Valera made Lynch parliamentary secretary to the Minster for Lands. Lynch later described the role as one 'with roving responsibilities for the Gaeltacht and congested districts'.

Fianna Fáil lost the 1954 general election but Lynch retained his seat and during his time in opposition he focused on rebuilding his legal practice. It is often said that his wife Máirín would have been happier to see her husband turn his back on political life at this time and focus on law as she did not want to be 'a politician's wife'. But three years later Fianna Fáil got back into government and de Valera appointed Lynch to his Cabinet as Minister for Education. Lynch also held the Gaeltacht portfolio for a short period at the same time.

During his two-year tenure in the Education portfolio, Lynch introduced progressive legislation to remove the ban on married women teachers and initiated major building projects at St Patrick's teacher training college in Dublin. He also raised the school leaving age and introduced the Irish oral exams.

After de Valera became president of Ireland in 1959, the new Taoiseach Seán Lemass appointed Lynch to Lemass's old portfolio of Minister for Industry and Commerce. In this department Lynch played a major role in implementing TK Whitaker's first Programme for Economic Development which is universally regarded as the provider of the basis for the economic boom of the 1960s and early 1970s.

Lynch's performance in the Industry and Commerce portfolio, where he was involved in solving a number of industrial disputes, earned him a promotion in 1965 to replace the retired Seán MacEntee as Minister for Finance.

Evidence of Lynch's political weaknesses emerged when he held the Finance portfolio. The Minister for Education, Donagh O'Malley, made the monumental announcement that the government would provide free secondary school education for all. Lynch, whose department would have expected to have been instrumental in such a decision, had no prior knowledge of it. His authority was undermined when it emerged that O'Malley had agreed the decision with Lemass personally.

After Lemass's surprise 1966 announcement that he was going to retire as Taoiseach and leader of Fianna Fáil, the first contested leadership race in the history of the party came to pass. Lynch did not have any driving ambition to become party leader. He only agreed to put his name forward after he came under pressure from party colleagues who were concerned that bitter divisions would emerge between ambitious young TDs such as George Colley, Charles Haughey and Neil Blaney.

After Lynch entered the leadership race, Haughey and Blaney both withdrew their interest and Lynch comfortably beat Colley by 52 votes to 19.

At the time of Lynch's accession to the roles of Taoiseach and Fianna Fáil leader on 10 November 1966, many politicians and observers regarded him as a temporary, compromise figure in a party divided into rival groups that supported the other younger claimants for the leadership.

Lynch was often pilloried by political commentators, such as John Healy in *The Irish Times*, as a 'stop gap' leader. Stories of Lynch as Taoiseach driving home every day to have his dinner in the middle of the day with his wife Máirín, and Máirín even ringing up Government Buildings to leave a message for the Taoiseach to bring home lamb chops for the dinner were common. They helped his popular image but also fuelled the perception that he should not be taken too seriously as Taoiseach.

While he may have been regarded as a 'compromise Taoiseach' in some quarters, the people of his native Cork branded him 'the *real* Taoiseach', a name he kept for the rest of his political career, whether he was in office or not.

Despite reaching the dizzy political heights of becoming Taoiseach in 1966, Lynch never lost touch with the GAA.

Liam Ó Tuama wrote, 'During his illustrious playing career he had many memorable homecomings to Blackpool with victorious Cork, Glen Rovers and St Nicks teams but perhaps the greatest welcome of all was accorded him in 1966 when he came home as Taoiseach.'

Barrels of burning tar blazed outside the clubhouse on the night Taoiseach Jack Lynch returned to Cork. Two groups of schoolboys, wearing the Glen Rovers and St Nicks colours, greeted him singing Irish ballads before Lynch delivered his address.

The crowd was so big that it was hard for everyone to hear what the new Taoiseach was saying. One old GAA man at the back of the crowd asked a friend, 'What's he saying?' to which his old friend replied, 'Yerra, what's he saying, only that he's glad to be home and he'd play for the Glen in the morning if he could!'

Lynch was leader of Fianna Fáil for 13 years and Taoiseach for 10 of those years. While his leadership style at times gave rise to the stereotype that this warm, modest and self-deprecating man was 'too nice for politics' he led Ireland into the EEC and guided the State through a tumultuous period when violence erupted in the North.

As well as striving to be 'chairman rather than chief' of the government he initially attempted to reconcile Fianna Fáil's rival factions.

His predecessor Lemass had historically met the Northern Ireland Prime Minister Terence O'Neill in January 1965 so Lynch sought to continue this dialogue. TK Whitaker claims that one of his fondest memories of Lynch was the snowy day he went off to meet O'Neill at Stormont. On hearing the roars of 'No Pope here' from the Rev Ian Paisley as he got out of the car, Lynch turned to Whitaker and wryly said, 'Which of us does he think is the Pope?'

Des O'Malley's by-election win to retain the seat of his late uncle Donagh in May 1968 gave Lynch's leadership a boost. But his attempts to push through a referendum that would have scrapped the electoral system of proportional representation was seen by opposition parties and the electorate as an attempt to institutionalise Fianna Fáil in power and it was duly rejected. The referendum result cast doubts over Lynch's leadership and political judgment but all this was put to bed when he led Fianna Fáil to win the party's first overall majority (since 1957 under de Valera) in the 1969 general election.

While Lynch had proven his vote-winning credentials as a party leader in the June 18 election, the most defining challenge of his political career soon arrived with the Arms Crisis. The Troubles in the North began that summer with events such as the Battle of the Bogside between Catholic residents and RUC men in Derry.

After the violence erupted in Derry, there was a clear split at the Cabinet table as some ministers demanded that Irish troops be sent into Derry and Newry to protect the Catholic minority. Lynch argued against such a move and swayed the Cabinet to his way of thinking. That night he addressed the nation on RTÉ television in a famous speech where he said, 'The Irish government can no longer stand by and see innocent people injured and perhaps worse . . . ' This 'no longer stand by' comment was interpreted wrongly by unionists who believed it to mean 'we cannot stand idly by.'

In an effort to appease and satisfy the more radical elements within Fianna Fáil – people like Charles Haughey and Neil Blaney – Lynch set up a Cabinet sub-committee to organise emergency assistance and relief for the Catholics in the North and allocated £100,000 for the government's Northern Relief Fund. Haughey was given sole charge of the fund and, along with Blaney, almost a free hand in looking after the Dublin government's policy on the North.

Money from the relief fund was used to pay for a meeting in October 1969 of the Northern Citizen Defence Committees, which soon became fronts for the IRA. The meeting was told that £50,000 would be available to buy weapons to defend nationalist areas.

It was alleged that Blaney conspired to import arms, while Haughey provided the money for the purchase from the relief fund and tried to arrange customs clearance for the arms shipment.

The Garda Síochána's Special Branch became aware of the plot by April 1970 and they informed Lynch, who took no initial action. The leader of the opposition, Liam Cosgrave, was tipped off about the plan to smuggle arms into the North and he forced Lynch into action.

On 6 May Lynch made the most dramatic decision of his career when he sacked Haughey and Blaney after they refused to resign, and by 28 May the two men were on trial in what became known as 'The Arms Trial'.

Haughey and Blaney, together with two other men, Captain James Kelly, an Irish Army Intelligence Officer, and a Belfast republican, John Kelly, were charged in court on the first day of the trial with conspiracy to illegally import arms for the IRA. The men denied any involvement in the affair and they were all found not guilty on 23 October.

A bitter divide emerged in Fianna Fáil between supporters of Haughey and Blaney and supporters of the Taoiseach. Lynch's critics do not always point to the ministerial sackings when they appraise his tenure as Taoiseach, instead they point to the 15-minute telephone conversation Lynch had with British Prime Minister Ted Heath just hours after 13 civilians were killed in Derry in the 1972

Bloody Sunday atrocity.

Tapes of the conversation, played at the Saville Inquiry into the atrocity decades later, reveal that Heath displayed a condescending attitude to Lynch while the Taoiseach appeared to be more concerned about the effect Bloody Sunday would have on the stability of the South. The conversation began with Lynch saying in an apologetic tone: 'I am sorry to ring you at this hour but you will probably have heard the unfortunate news about Derry this afternoon.'

Despite his handling of the Northern question, Lynch displayed enough political nous to hold onto the leadership and achieved one of the high points of his career when he personally steered Ireland's entry into the European Economic Community in 1973. Ireland's first MEPs were directly appointed by the Taoiseach and former Limerick hurling star and Fianna Fáil TD Mick Herbert was among Lynch's ten nominees.

In February 1973 Lynch called a general election as he was confident he would be returned to power. Lynch topped the poll in his constituency, then called Cork City North-West, and Fianna Fáil increased its share of the vote from 45.7 to 46.2 per cent. But to the surprise of many, Fine Gael and Labour hammered out a coalition deal and the 'National Coalition' won the election.

Having staved off criticism for allowing Charles Haughey return to the Fianna Fáil front bench as health spokesman in 1975, Lynch remained leader of the party as they faced into the general election two years later. The National Coalition were expected to retain power as they had been buoyed up by the Minister for Local Government, James Tully's re-drawing of every constituency in Ireland. The 'Tullymander' was perceived to favour Fine Gael and Labour candidates.

Political commentators were unanimous in the view that the Fine Gael-Labour government looked set to defy Irish political history by securing a second consecutive term in office. And RTÉ political commentator Sean Duignan famously said that if Jack Lynch was to win the election it would be 'the greatest comeback since Lazarus'. Facing defeat, Fianna Fáil came up with a populist manifesto that included the abolition of car tax and rates on houses.

But the media had greatly underestimated how unpopular the coalition was and the Fianna Fáil slogan 'Bring Jack Back' became a reality as Lynch secured one of his great political triumphs with a 20-seat majority.

Lynch retained the Fianna Fáil leadership until 1979 when internal party discipline eventually got the better of him. A group called 'The Gang of Five' – Jackie Fahey, Sean Doherty, Tom McEllistrim, Albert Reynolds and Mark Killilea – were openly plotting against him in support of Haughey for the leadership.

Under pressure from this group, Lynch resigned as Fianna Fáil leader on 5 December 1979 and made no secret that he hoped that George Colley, and not Haughey, would succeed him.

He did not contest the 1981 general election and retired from politics. He became director of a number of companies and maintained his interest in the GAA for the rest of his life, which he spent with Máirín at their home in Rathgar, in south Dublin.

Towards the end of his life, when Lynch was in ill-health and had lost his eyesight as a result of a stroke in 1993, he decided to donate his GAA medal collection to the GAA Museum at Croke Park. During his career with Cork, and the Glen Rovers and St Nick's clubs, he won five All-Ireland medals in hurling and one in football, 10 Cork County Senior Hurling Championships (including eight in a row), three hurling National League medals, three Railway Cup medals, two Cork County Senior Football Championships and a Dublin Senior Football Championship with the Civil Service GAA club.

So in February 1996, three years before his death, Lynch gave all of those medals to the GAA, the occasion vividly described by Lynch biographer Dermot Keogh.

Con Murphy, a former GAA president and one of Lynch's former Cork teammates, Liam Mulvihill, the GAA's former director general, and Liam Ó

Tuama, a St Nicks and Glen Rovers club man who wrote a book about Lynch's sporting career, called to Lynch's Dublin home to collect the medals. Lynch was a shadow of the former towering sportsman that he had been in his early days.

In *Yes Taoiseach*, a book by Lynch's, and later Haughey's, government press secretary, Frank Dunlop, Dunlop describes how Lynch would always bring a bottle or two of his favourite Paddy whiskey with him on foreign trips. As the conversation flowed and more people joined the pair, Lynch would say, 'Let's see if we can get below Thurles' – a reference to the map of Ireland on the label. Dunlop wrote, 'Any night below Thurles was a good night.'

Echoing those days when he was in greater health, Máirín poured glasses of Paddy for his GAA visitors and a smaller amount for her husband that day in 1996. Keogh's biography describes how, even though he was blind, Lynch lifted the glass and turned to his former teammate Con Murphy and said, 'Who poured this out? Oh, Jesus, fill it up!'

Throughout his life Lynch possessed that inherent Irish male trait of not being one to show emotion. But he showed uncharacteristic emotion as he handed over his medal collection to his visitors. He said, 'Take good care of them. They were hard won.'

Lynch died aged 82 in October 1999, just months after the tunnel under the River Lee in his native Cork was named after him. In the days after his death, Liam Cosgrave, former Fine Gael Taoiseach and one of Lynch's main political adversaries said, 'Jack Lynch was a gentleman. At one time he was the most popular politician in the country since O'Connell.'

Like the medals, a compliment of that magnitude was certainly 'hard won'.

Dan Spring
Full-Forward

KERRY – LABOUR

The execution of Charlie Kerins, communists, contraception and Vincent Browne

A ll political careers end in failure. And most, if not all, football careers end in a similar fashion. A lot of players cling to, and live off, past glories. Few of them know the correct time to call it a day. But Dan Spring was different.

He said 'goodbye' to his inter-county football career on the steps of the Hogan Stand in Croke Park. The tall full-forward from Tralee captained Kerry to their fourteenth All-Ireland title in 1940. After beating Galway, Spring's acceptance of the Sam Maguire trophy was his final act in a Kerry jersey.

Spring decided 'to quit while he was ahead'. He retired after the game and never wore the green and gold of Kerry again.

The fifth eldest in a family of 14 children, Dan Spring was born on 1 July 1910 in Tralee. When his father Arthur, who was a butcher, became ill quite early in life, the frugal circumstances in the Spring household meant that Dan had to leave school at 14 years of age. While a number of his siblings emigrated, Dan was lucky enough to find work in Latchford's Mill in Tralee.

Getting this job had a major effect on his life. Firstly, it was through his work in the mill that he got involved in the trade union movement, which later edged him into politics. Secondly, finding work in Tralee meant he did not have to leave the town and his local O'Rahilly's GAA Club were not deprived of one of their biggest assets on the football pitch.

Spring was on the O'Rahilly's team that won the Kerry county championship in 1933 and his performances for the Tralee club earned him a place on the Kerry county team the following year.

Spring collected his first All-Ireland medal as a substitute. He was on the Kerry panel that won the 1937 All-Ireland title after a replay with Cavan, but he did not feature in either the drawn game or the replay.

The following year Spring, who was 6 feet, 3 inches tall and over 14 stone, emerged as one of the best full-forwards ever to wear the Kerry jersey.

In 1939 Meath won the Leinster title for the first time since 1895. This significant breakthrough was due in no small part to the Royal County's full-back, Tom 'The Boiler' McGuinness. After playing in the heart of the Meath defence for many years, it looked as if McGuinness was finally going to lead his county to an All-Ireland title as they faced into the 1939 final.

But Dan Spring dashed these hopes with one of the best All-Ireland final performances ever witnessed in Croke Park. Despite 'The Boiler' breaking two of Spring's ribs on the day, the Tralee man racked up a personal tally of 2–3 out of Kerry's total score line of 2–5. Kerry won the match, having scored two points more than Meath's 2–3.

A lot people in Tralee who had not made it to Dublin for the game gathered around radios to listen to the match. It was legendary RTÉ commentator, Micheál O'Hehir's second ever All-Ireland final behind the microphone.

Kerry fans were appalled throughout the first half to find out that Dan Spring was not playing. A man called 'Shine' appeared to be playing in his place. It was the second half before O'Hehir profusely apologised and referred to Spring by his correct name.

Back home in Kerry in the same year 1939, O'Rahilly's won the county championship. Under the captaincy rule in Kerry, whereby a representative of the club that won the previous year's county title captains the county the following year, Dan Spring was the captain of the 1940 Kerry team.

Dan's son Dick, the former Tánaiste and leader of the Labour Party, recalls, 'My father was made captain of the Kerry team in 1940 but I get the impression that being captain of a team did not mean a lot back then, other than the captain being the guy who walked up the steps in Croke Park if his county won.

'Nowadays the captain has a bit more authority but I suspect from what he said about those days, that my father had little say and the manager and county board had full control.'

Spring captained the Kerry team that beat Galway in the 1940 All-Ireland final.

'He retired from the Kerry team that day. He played club football until 1943 but he never told us why, at 30 years of age, he decided not to play any more inter-county football,' says Dick, who has made a number of attempts to research his late father's GAA career and found little information on his father's departure.

Despite quitting the game in 1943, Dan Spring remained a keen football and hurling fan. Dick says that his childhood memories are filled with going to watch Kerins-O'Rahilly's or Kerry matches on Sunday afternoons.

One of Dan's best friends was a Tipperary man who lived in North Kerry. For many years, he cut turf for the Spring family so his reward was a trip to the Munster hurling final each year with the Springs.

'For that reason we got to loads of Munster hurling finals as kids. Even though my father was always an avid GAA fan after he finished playing, I always got the impression that he did not have an awful lot of time for the administrators in the organisation,' recalls Dick.

'Whether he didn't get on with them in his playing days or not, but he often described a lot administrators as "fellas who never laced a boot". I think that can happen in a lot of organisations where you get guys involved in administration who never actually played.'

From his early days in Latchford's Mill, Dan Spring got involved in the Irish Transport and General Workers' Union (ITGWU). His association with this union got him involved in the Labour Party.

As the 1940 All-Ireland winning Kerry captain, his status as a local hero made Dan Spring a target of other political parties. He was even approached by Fianna Fáil and asked to stand for them in the local elections in 1942 but he declined the offer.

His ITGWU background meant that his preference was for the Labour Party, which was practically non-existent in Kerry at the time. He was elected to Kerry County Council in 1942.

Prior to this, John Joe Kelly was the sole Labour Party figure in North Kerry. Both Spring and Kelly stood in the Kerry North constituency in the 1943 general election. Spring achieved the unthinkable. On the back of transfers from Kelly, he managed to secure a Labour seat in a rural constituency where the party had made little or no previous impact. But the battle was far from easy. From the day Spring added his name to the party ticket for the 1942 council elections, he got a hostile reception. For a while, it appeared that Kerry North was no place for unfamiliar characters such as Labour election hopefuls.

Dick says, 'My father told stories about going out to places like Knocknagoshel canvassing on bicycles for the 1942 council election and the 1943 Dáil election. People were actually throwing stones at them as they thought they were communists.

'The Labour Party were regarded as communists even though communism is so far away from my father as he was a fairly straight conservative Catholic in social attitudes.'

A glance through the Dáil records from the time shows why the people of Kerry were roused to throw stones at the Labour party 'communists'. Fianna Fáil minister Sean MacEntee, one of the most prominent politicians in post-independence Ireland, warned people from the government benches about the 'Reds under the bed' and the 'Red scare'.

Some people in rural Kerry obviously believed these warnings about the threat posed by the Labour Party's 'communism'. As a result, Spring had to dodge the stones as he canvassed on his bicycle.

But the misconceptions about the Labour Party were emasculated by Spring's stature as a Kerry GAA star. Football overrides just about everything in Kerry.

Dick says, 'I would say that there was not a snowball's chance in hell of him winning a Labour seat in Kerry North if he did not have three All-Ireland medals and been captain of the Kerry team. There would have been no possibility at all.'

After his election to the Dáil, Dan Spring became friendly with the Clann na Talmhan, and later Independent deputy, TD Paddy Finucane, who represented the small farmers in north Kerry from 1943 to 1969. The pair used to travel to Dublin together and on the way home they used to stop in Loughill, on the coast road between Limerick and Listowel.

'They would stop for a whiskey or two in a pub in Loughill. At first they were treated very coldly in the bar. The publican would serve them drink and nobody would speak to them,' recalls Dick.

'One night as my father and Paddy Finucane sat in the bar, somebody came in and said, "Dan Spring, what are you doing here?" Everybody relaxed after that as they had previously thought that they were two detectives looking for information.'

Nowadays, if two TDs walked into a bar in an adjoining constituency to their own, they would certainly be recognised, as TDs enjoy much more media attention in the modern age. But in the 1940s, TDs were not nearly as well known. While Spring was elected on the back of his notoriety as a Kerry football captain, he later struggled to get re-elected in subsequent elections.

To this day, Kerry North is one of the most competitive political constituencies in the country for any politician. For a Labour TD to prove that his

1943 success was not just a flash in the pan, he needed to show that he was more than a former Kerry footballer.

The execution of Charlie Kerins was to have a seismic influence on Spring's political career. Kerins was born in 1918 and grew up on the same street in Tralee as Dan Spring. Although he was eight years younger than Spring, the pair played football together for the O'Rahilly's club, that was later named Kerins-O'Rahilly's in his honour.

Kerins was on the O'Rahilly's team that Spring captained to win the 1939 Kerry County championship. The following year he joined the IRA and became an active member of the organisation that was abhorred by Éamon de Valera's government.

On 9 September 1942, Garda Special Branch Detective Sergeant Denis 'Dinny' O'Brien was leaving his home in Ballyboden, south Dublin, when he was shot dead in front of his wife by IRA men brandishing machine guns.

A few weeks after the cold-blooded murder of the prominent Special Branch member and anti-Treaty Civil War veteran, Hugh McAteer was arrested and Charlie Kerins was subsequently named as the Chief of Staff of the IRA. Kerins went on the run and he remained at large until mid-June 1944, when he was arrested by gardaí in Rathmines, Dublin in a dawn raid. He was tried before the Special Criminal Court in Collins Barracks, Dublin for the shooting of Detective Dinny O'Brien.

Historian Tim Pat Coogan in his book *The IRA: A History* explained, 'At the end of the trial, the president of the Military Court delayed sentence until later in the day to allow Kerins, if he wished, to make an application whereby he might have avoided the capital sentence.

'When the court resumed, Kerins said: "You could have adjourned it for six years as far as I am concerned, as my attitude towards this Court will always be the same." He thus deprived himself of the right to give evidence, to face cross examination, or to call witnesses.'

After Kerins was sentenced to death there was much public revulsion and protests demanding a reprieve. This anger was reflected in a bitter row in the Dáil on 30 November 1944, the eve of his execution in Mountjoy Prison. During a heated debate, James Larkin Junior, the Labour TD for Dublin South, and Kerry North TD Paddy Finucane were suspended from the Dáil for protesting that Kerins did not get a fair trial and for condemning the media censorship of his trial.

After Larkin and Finucane were thrown out of the Dáil chamber, Spring rose to his feet and said, 'I stated last night and I still state, that this young person did not get a fair trial. This man is lying in Mountjoy awaiting execution in the morning. We have no one to blame only the Taoiseach [Éamon de Valera]. I can certainly say the Taoiseach or any of his ministers will not be too willing to address a meeting in Kerry in the near future.'

With that, de Valera stood up and moved a motion that Spring also be suspended from the Dáil. The vote was passed with 75 TDs backing de Valera, compared to the 18 TDs who sided with Spring. Even after the vote, Spring, who was fuming, said, 'I am leaving the House through a coalition vote between Fine Gael and Fianna Fáil. Fine Gael has 77 murders in Kerry (a reference to the Civil War) and Fianna Fáil has now nearly as many.'

From the time he came into government in 1932, de Valera took a very strong line against the IRA and there were many executions in the 1930s and 1940s.

Dick Spring says, 'A lot of families would have been Fianna Fáil supporters prior to the execution of Charlie Kerins. But they turned their backs on de Valera. They would not move to Fine Gael so they switched to the Labour Party.

'My father never had any time for what the IRA was doing. He was always very clear that there was the rule of law and you should accept the rule of law as democracy had done. But he was obviously opposed to the execution on a very personal, friendship level.'

Spring capitalised on the anti-de Valera sentiment in subsequent elections and actually managed to retain a Labour seat for eleven consecutive Dáil elections.

The year after Spring's initial election in 1943, there was a major split in the Labour Party. The 'ITGWU wing' of the party formed a rebel faction, claiming that communists had taken over the Labour Party in Dublin. Spring was one of six of the party's TDs who left the party and set up the National Labour Party. The new party had a short life as they came back into the Labour Party in 1948.

'After the party went into coalition in 1948 the divide between the ITGWU deputies and the others faded away but there was always that little bit of a niggle between the union and the party,' claims Dick Spring.

'I know that even in my own time there were often rows between ourselves and the union. I think they were all quite glad to get back in under the one banner in 1948.'

While Dan Spring spent most of his political career on the back benches, he did hold the position of parliamentary secretary to the Minister for Local Government from March 1956 to March 1957.

A vacancy arose for a parliamentary secretary in the second Inter-Party government in 1956. Instead of the leader of the Labour Party, William Norton, choosing who should fill the vacancy, the decision was made following a vote of the members of Labour's parliamentary party. The popularity of Dan Spring was such that he was elected.

The Minister for Local Government at the time was a Fine Gael TD from Donegal called Patrick, or 'Pa', O'Donnell. Spring and O'Donnell were good friends and the pair enjoyed a healthy working relationship.

'From my father's point of view, being involved in local government was all about building houses. He used to tell us that in the 1940s and 1950s there was an awful lot of slum clearances in Kerry,' says Dick Spring. 'Even in small towns like Castleisland, people were living in horrific housing conditions. So he got involved in building houses for people like that.'

Education was the other policy area that was close to Spring's heart, politically. Dick recalls, 'My mother was very involved. As a nurse she would have had a lot more formal education than my father so she was able to help him. They both saw education as a way of breaking down barriers as we came from the side of the town where very few people got access to education.' He remembers the late Labour TD David Thornley saying to him that Dick's mother was Dan's 'stage manager'.

Despite serving as a TD for some 38 years, Spring only served as a parliamentary secretary for one year and four days.

'I don't think he ever really had the ambition to be a Cabinet minister but he would have liked to have got back in as a junior minister,' says Dick of his father. 'But himself and Brendan Corish (the Labour leader who succeeded William Norton) fell out, quite stridently, after the 1973 coalition was put together.'

In the 1969 general election, the Labour Party adopted a strategy of running two candidates in constituencies where the party had a sitting TD. Party strategists believed if the party had the confidence to do this they could win two seats in some constituencies.

Two sitting TDs who were known to be independent minded and out of step with the leadership – Dan Spring in Kerry North and Michael Pat Murphy in Cork South West – rejected the strategy and had no running mate for the election. While Spring and Murphy retained their seats, the two-candidates strategy backfired on the Labour Party as they came back with four seats less than they had prior to the election.

It is understood that Murphy drove from Cork to Corish's house in Wexford after the 1969 election, in order to smooth the stormy waters between the two following Murphy's snub to the strategy. A few years later, in 1973, when Labour went into coalition with Fine Gael, Murphy was appointed by Corish as parliamentary secretary to the Minister for Agriculture.

Dick recalls, 'My father never forgave Corish for not appointing him too. He would have been in the Dáil for 30 years at the time and I think that he felt entitled, having held his seat for that length of time.

'But there were a lot of young Turks who had come into the Dáil in 1969.

I think he should have been made parliamentary secretary again in that 1973 coalition.'

Despite hitting a glass ceiling in terms of promotion, Spring led a colourful career in the Dáil and his approach to a vote on contraception has gone down in Leinster House folklore. Vincent Browne, in his early days as a journalist covering politics, rang a few backbench TDs in an effort to gauge political opinion ahead of the controversial vote.

Browne's youngest brother Malachy was Dick Spring's best man on his wedding day so Browne decided he would use this connection as a bargaining tool when talking to Dan Spring.

Dick recalls, 'Vincent rang my father, who would hardly ever be talking to journalists. When you are a rural backbench TD, the Vincent Brownes of this world would have no interest in talking to you anyway. But at this particular time, my father answered the phone and Vincent gave him a bit of soft soap about being Malachy's brother.'

Browne went on and on and eventually he asked Dan Spring what way he intended to vote in the following Wednesday's vote on the contraception issue.

Spring replied, 'Will you be in the Dáil next week Vincent? Well, you will see how I will vote then.'

Some months previously Spring had a very serious car crash on his way to Cork. The crash resulted in a massive High Court case that was actually scheduled to take place on the same day as the contraception vote. So Spring was in court and missed the controversial Dáil vote.

Dick recalls, 'At the time my father would not have voted for family planning. He just took his line from the Church but I am glad to say that afterwards he supported both family planning and the divorce referendum. So there was a big change there that was slightly influenced by his son and his wife.'

Politics was Dan Spring's life for almost 40 years. Dick recalls how everything in the Spring household started and ended with politics when he was growing up. The door was never locked and there was a constant flow of people calling in to the house to chat to his father, in an era before constituency offices.

'The house was like a railway station as our father worked out of it. You would have a fella coming in from a rural area like Kilflynn at 9 a.m. to do his shopping and other business in Tralee. He might be finished his business at 1 p.m. and his bus home might not be until 4 p.m.. So what would he do? He would call up and chat to Dan Spring,' laughs Dick.

'That was the kind of the house it was. Older people would call in and talk to Dan Spring about how the Labour Party was going or how the local organisation was going – so it was a kind of a network of information in from the rural parts of the constituency.'

Dick remembers, 'There were two cars on our street in those times and one of them was only ever taken out on Sundays to go for the family drive. However our mother was a nurse, so our car combined as the local ambulance, the local hearse, the local everything. So we were completely involved in the local community. Everything was very local.'

Growing up, Dan Spring's three sons Arthur, Donal and Dick played football for Kerins-O'Rahilly's and hurling for Crotta O'Neills, where their mother's family came from.

Dick recalls, 'I remember my older brother Arthur, my younger brother Donal and myself were playing for Kerins-O'Rahilly's against Lispole in the final of the West Kerry league. We thought we were only going out to collect the medals but they kicked the bejaysus out of us. It was a physical encounter and they beat us by a point. We came home that evening and we were having our supper and my father was sitting at the end of the table. He said that he couldn't believe how his three big fine sons were beaten by one parish out in West Kerry – because he used to go out and beat the pick of West Kerry when he was playing.

'The day wasn't long enough for us to play football and hurling,' recalls Dick, speaking of the years before he was sent to boarding school in Roscrea.

A decision was made to send the Spring children to secondary school and a choice had to be made between 'the Sem' (St Brendan's) in Killarney, a Gaelic football stronghold, or the Cistercian College in Roscrea, County Tipperary, a rugby school. His parents decided that their children should be sent to boarding school as they felt they would have no chance of doing well academically if they stayed in the hectic family home in Strand Street, Tralee. The Springs had no connection with Roscrea prior to that but the school was recommended by friends so Dick went there.

Dick did play both hurling and football for Kerry in the 1970s but a love of rugby blossomed in Roscrea and Dick went on to win three international rugby caps for Ireland. His brother Donal won seven caps.

Like their father campaigning for the Labour Party in 1943, the Spring children got many looks of bemusement from their neighbours in Tralee when they started to take a rugby ball home during their school holidays.

'My father was not really disappointed that we opted for rugby. His attitude was that as long as you are playing sport, it doesn't really matter,' recalls Dick. 'It could have been hockey for all he cared, as long as you were out doing the things that you should be doing as young men. So there was never really any regret or otherwise.'

Dan Spring did not push his sons into politics either. Dick says that he himself was always genuinely interested in politics and he was involved in election campaigns with his father from his early teens.

'I was putting up posters from early on and I'd say I was up on platforms from the age of about 15. I was doing after-Mass speeches at 15 years of age – no problem,' he insists. 'To be honest, he didn't encourage me one way or the other. That was very much the attitude, other than my mother who had a rule that if any of the six of us wanted to get into politics, the first requirement was that we would have a professional qualification to fall back on.

'That was the rule. Nobody was going to go into it as a full-time politician. And if you did go into it you would have something to fall back on, which was smart from my mother's point of view.

'It ultimately gave you a degree of independence because you didn't have

216

to say, "God I will lose my seat here if I vote in a certain way!" Instead, you could say that I am going back to the Law Library – or wherever you worked – if you lost your seat.'

⑤

By 1979, Dan Spring was 69 years old but he had absolutely no intention of bowing out of politics. The local council elections were coming up and Dick Spring was in the car with his parents on the way to the Labour Party selection convention for those elections when Dick and his mother convinced Dan to step aside.

Dick was elected to Kerry County Council in those elections (1979) and this paved the way for his election to the Dáil in 1981 where he took up the seat his father had vacated after holding it for 38 years.

'After he stepped down in 1981, he was still involved for the first few years. Constituents would contact him and he would automatically contact the county council or health board for them to sort out their concern.

'Then gradually he would take the messages from the constituents, write them down, pass them on to me and get me to do the work. Then it came to the stage that someone would call to him and he would say, "Why don't you go and see him yourself?" '

He had a short retirement as he died seven years later aged 78. But he did get to see his son become leader of the Labour Party in 1982.

'When I became leader of the Labour Party, he would have been both proud and tense. He knew it wasn't the easiest job in the world,' claims Dick. 'There used to be a rumour that Brendan Corish resigned about 17 times. He used to go back down to Wexford having resigned at a parliamentary party meeting. So the party would send a delegation down to tell him that nobody else wanted the job!

'The "Spring Tide" [referring to the 1992 General Election when the Labour Party led by Dick Spring increased their Dáil seats from 15 to 33, the highest number ever held by the party] was a few years after his death. He would have enjoyed that and been very proud of it but then he was proud of all his children and grandchildren in whatever they did.'

Three years after he retired from politics, Dan Spring was one of the Sam Maguire winning captains to be honoured by the GAA at the 1984 Centenary All-Ireland final.

Dick remembers, 'We were all very proud that day as we were all in Croke Park and he was one of the older captains at the time. But it is strange enough for a man who had been captain of an All-Ireland winning team and been a TD all his life, that he was actually a very shy man. I'd say he found walking out in front of all those people in Croke Park in 1984 a bit of an ordeal. He wouldn't have been a Teddy Kennedy type, going out waving his hands everywhere.'

Dan Spring will never be forgotten in his home town. There is even a road in the town called 'Dan Spring Road'.

Dick laughs, 'There's a good story about the road that is now named after my father. The road was being built in the early 1970s across an area, adjoining the town park, which was a swamp. So what they did, and it was the first time we had ever seen it, they put down lining like plasticine as the foundation rather than piling rocks into the swamp.

'My father said to his dying day, "That will never work. The road will sink." And many years later it is a handy little road between the roundabouts in Tralee. It is now an important road strategically in the town.'

The road never sank and it ended up being called after the man who said it would.

When Dick Spring was a student in Trinity College, the respected political scientist, Basil Chubb, was confronted by the young Spring. At every election the late Chubb used to predict that Dan Spring was going to lose his seat. The seat was never safe.

'People like Chubb could not understand that there was a Labour seat in Kerry North. But my father had no regrets about his political career. He was very proud that he had fought eleven elections and won them,' says Dick. 'He really struggled to get across the line in the 1973 and 1977 elections but he retained his seat because he got transfers from everywhere.

'He had a policy of not offending anyone and not taking a hard line. If you don't take a hard line, you will not offend.

'I think my politics might have been a little bit rougher and then you didn't get the preferences at the end of the day and you pay the price.'

Jack McQuillan
Left Corner-Forward

Jack McQuillan was a thorn in the side of numerous governments during a 21-year political career that spanned from 1948 to 1969.

One of the most radical TDs ever to grace Leinster House, McQuillan was paid the ultimate compliment by former Taoiseach Seán Lemass who said that McQuillan, and his confidant Dr Noel Browne, constituted 'the real opposition' in the Dáil. Opposition, revolt and protest are all words that are synonymous with McQuillan's political career. In fact, they were paramount throughout his life.

Born in 1920 in Roscommon, McQuillan's father was a sergeant in the RIC and his mother was a teacher. She came from a republican family in East Galway and had been taught by Éamon de Valera in Dublin. The family lived on a farm in Ballyforan, and like many other Irish mothers of the time, McQuillan's mother harboured notions that one of her sons would one day become a priest.

She sent Jack to be educated by the priests at St Clement's Redemptorist College in Limerick. After it quickly became obvious that her son did not have a vocation for the priesthood, he was sent to school in Summerhill College, Sligo.

The first indications of McQuillan's rebellious nature were evident in Sligo as he frequently found himself in trouble with the teachers in an era when corporal punishment was still permitted. When one of the priests in the school tried to hit McQuillan with a cane he grabbed it from the cleric and broke it. Soon afterwards he was expelled for organising a student strike in the school.

Speaking in a 2007 radio documentary, produced by Declan Coyne and titled *The Roscommon Rebel: The Story of Jack McQuillan*, Jack's widow Angela described how her husband's schooldays in Sligo came to an abrupt end.

'He was expelled, let's face it, because they couldn't control him and he incited rebellion against unfair treatment as he saw it,' said Angela.

After his expulsion from Summerhill College McQuillan ended up in the local Christian Brothers School (CBS) in Roscommon.

Jack's brother, Dr Bill McQuillan, believes that the uncompromising young Jack was happier at school in Roscommon and the fact that he began to excel as a footballer from then on helped him settle. Roscommon CBS won a Connacht schools championship with McQuillan playing in the forward line. They toppled the football kingpins of the schools in the province, St Jarlath's of Tuam, along the way.

After finishing school, McQuillan decided to move to England so he could join the RAF and fight Hitler in 1939. Driven by a sense of adventure, he was disappointed when his attempt to join the RAF was unsuccessful. He had a blue/green colour blindness deficiency that ruled out becoming a pilot. So he stayed in London and worked in pubs for a while before he returned to Ireland.

Upon his return, McQuillan joined the Irish army and rose to the rank of lieutenant. While stationed at the Curragh, he played football for the Defence

Forces teams in internal army tournaments and the Kildare club championship.

In 1943 Lieutenant McQuillan initially played with the St Patrick's club in Roscommon, as there was no senior club team in his home place, Ballyforan. By opting to play with the St Patrick's club, McQuillan played his early club football with Jimmy Murray, the Roscommon GAA legend who would later captain the county to All-Ireland Senior Championship success on two occasions, in 1943 and 1944.

Murray recalled how McQuillan could bend a four-inch nail with his hands as he was 'as strong as a racehorse, into body building in a big way and a keep fit addict.'

McQuillan won two Roscommon county championships with St Patrick's and his performances for the club earned him a call-up to the county senior squad where he played at full-forward in Roscommon's greatest ever team.

Roscommon won All-Ireland Minor titles in 1939 and 1941 and a Junior title in 1940 so the foundation was set for Senior success by 1943. After beating Leitrim, Roscommon overcame Galway to capture their first Senior Connacht title since 1915. Then a win over Louth booked them a date with Cavan in the 1943 All-Ireland Senior football final.

In a new departure for the GAA, following an initiative from county board chairman and future GAA president Dan O'Rourke, the Roscommon team engaged in collective training for two weeks before the final. They stayed together in O'Rourke's home as they prepared for the final with Cavan.

A record crowd of 63,023 packed into Croke Park to see Roscommon play their first senior final that ended in a draw: Cavan 1–6, Roscommon 1–6.

Two weeks later, the sides met for the replay and McQuillan scored one of Roscommon's two first-half goals to leave them two points ahead at the interval. A number of Cavan players were sent off in the second half and Roscommon won the All-Ireland title on a scoreline of 2–7 to Cavan's 2–2.

The following year, Roscommon beat Sligo and Mayo on their way to a second consecutive Connacht title. McQuillan was one of their star players in the All-Ireland semi-final win over Cavan where the final score was Roscommon

5–8 to Cavan's 1–3.

Beating Kerry in an All-Ireland final was the acid test of greatness for the reigning All-Ireland champions. For the second year in a row, the Roscommon team came together for a fortnight of intensive training before the final. This time they stayed at the Old Infirmary in Roscommon town, a building that is the present-day Roscommon County Library. A makeshift sign with the four letters K-T-B-L emblazoned across it was hung over the door of their temporary living quarters. KTBL was an acronym for Keep The Ball Low.

Roscommon followed the 'Keep The Ball Low' mantra in a final watched by 79,245 spectators in Croke Park, with thousands more outside who could not gain entry. McQuillan was marked by Joe Keohane, the Kerry player who is widely regarded as the greatest full-back of all time, in the game which Roscommon won by 1–9 to Kerry's 2–4.

Kerry exacted revenge, two years later, in the 1946 decider. After a replay and what is regarded as one of the best ever All-Ireland football finals, Kerry's 2–8 was enough to beat Roscommon's 0–10.

Jimmy Murray remembered McQuillan as a player of great vision who gave great full-backs such as Keohane from Kerry and Eddie Boyle of Louth a torrid time.

When the Roscommon Team of the Millennium was named in 2000, it came as no surprise to anyone that McQuillan was chosen as full-forward on the team that boasted football greats such as Dermot Earley, Donal Keenan, and Jimmy Murray among the six forwards.

McQuillan played inter-county football for Roscommon from 1943 to 1953 and it was his notoriety as a two-time All-Ireland winner that made him a target for the Clann na Poblachta party ahead of the 1948 election.

Founded by former IRA chief of staff Seán MacBride in July 1946, Clann na Poblachta was a radical republican party dedicated to achieving republican ideals by purely political means. The new party placed a heavy emphasis on the social issues that affected rural areas like Roscommon. These issues included the hardship of emigration, unemployment, rising prices and the lack of investment in the development of natural resources. After the new party won two by-elections in Dublin and Tipperary in 1947, Taoiseach Éamon de Valera, who was concerned that the new party was set to eat into Fianna Fáil's support base, called a snap election with a view to stifling the rise of Clann na Poblachta by catching them off guard.

McQuillan joined the new party as an organiser with a view to asking his football teammate Jimmy Murray to stand for election. But he ended up having his own name added to the party ticket for the 1948 election as Michael Igoe Kelly's running mate.

Ahead of the election, Kelly boasted that he was going to win a seat 'with my brains and McQuillan's boots'. He believed McQuillan's GAA celebrity status would attract votes that would transfer to him after McQuillan was eliminated from the count.

McQuillan garnered over 3,000 votes, 300 more than Kelly, so it was the All-Ireland winner who took one of the four Dáil seats in the Roscommon constituency ahead of Kelly.

Speaking on Coyne's documentary, Jack's brother Dr Bill McQuillan said, 'People were sick and tired of one-party government, which is what they had continuously since 1932. A lot of people welcomed the idea of a completely new party which clearly had leanings towards republican interest. But, at the same time, the ideas they were putting forward had strong socialist ideas behind them that appealed to a lot of people.'

After the election, 16 years of uninterrupted Fianna Fáil dominance in government was broken. De Valera's party was the biggest party after the election with 67 seats but he was six seats short of the majority needed to form a government in the, then, 147-seat Dáil. As a result, the first Inter-Party government was formed comprising Fine Gael, Labour, Clann na Talmhan, the National Labour Party, Independent TD James Dillon and Clann na Poblachta, which had won ten Dáil seats.

Fledgling young Clann na Poblachta TDs such as McQuillan and Dr Noel Browne had progressive ideas that helped form party policy. McQuillan was particularly worried about the way farming was the country's main industry yet cattle were being exported 'on the hoof' and slaughtered and processed elsewhere. The 'real industry' and process of adding value to the product was happening abroad. So McQuillan argued that meat should be processed at home to create jobs and stem emigration.

In 1950 McQuillan was elected to Roscommon County Council and he quickly earned the reputation of a politician who could 'get things done' locally. Parallels are often drawn between Dan Spring, the Labour TD from Kerry, and McQuillan. Both men entered politics on the back of their reputation and local hero status as All-Ireland winners but they were re-elected after they consolidated their vote on the back of arduous work for their constituents.

McQuillan winning a seat for the new Clann na Poblachta party in a conservative rural constituency like Roscommon in 1948 was akin to Spring's feat in winning a Labour seat in Kerry North five years earlier.

In the Dáil, McQuillan found a political soulmate in his indomitable party colleague Noel Browne. Speaking about the pair's political *modus operandi* in later life, Browne said, 'Our purpose was to harry the government by making radical proposals for all the unresolved issues in society. We put down questions on everything from public ownership of the whiskey distilling industry to gay rights.'

Both men had no respect for 'sacred cows' such as the Catholic Church and this was clearly shown with the controversial Mother and Child Scheme. Browne's brainchild, the 1951 scheme was a radical healthcare programme that proposed introducing free maternity care for all mothers and free healthcare for all children up to the age of 16.

The scheme caused a political storm after members of the conservative Catholic hierarchy, such as the Archbishop of Dublin John Charles McQuaid, argued that it was the exclusive right of all parents to provide healthcare for their children.

Browne, who had been made Minister for Health on his first day in the Dáil in 1948, refused to back down on the issue and he found himself at loggerheads with the Church leaders who believed the scheme 'opposed Catholic social teaching'.

He also received little support from his Cabinet colleagues, with whom he already had a fractious relationship. As he had failed to attend a lot of Cabinet meetings, he had become isolated from the other ministers and he had also fallen out with his own Clann na Poblachta leader Seán MacBride.

In April 1951, MacBride demanded Browne's resignation as a Clann na Poblachta minister and the outspoken minister duly submitted his resignation to the Taoiseach, John A Costello.

McQuillan was disgusted with the way Browne was treated and he resigned from Clann na Poblachta in solidarity with his friend. The Mother and Child Scheme was the breaking point for McQuillan who already had difficulties with MacBride.

Speaking in the radio documentary about her late husband, Angela McQuillan explained that Jack never got on with Seán MacBride: 'He absolutely detested him and everything he stood for. I remember Jack talking about committee meetings in Clann na Poblachta in the early days and the first thing they had to do when they went into a meeting was to take an oath of allegiance to the leader and that was something that Jack couldn't stomach.'

A general election was held in May 1951, a month after Browne's resignation, and McQuillan was elected as an independent TD.

In 1953 McQuillan piloted a private members' bill in the Dáil which ushered in new legislation that brought private and bog roads under the care of local authorities. The new legislation, contained in the 1953 Local Government Act, was extremely beneficial to all kinds of people especially small farmers in isolated rural areas like Roscommon.

There is a story told in Roscommon that during a subsequent election campaign a Fine Gael candidate was speaking outside a church to Massgoers. At the end of his speech, in a clear reference to McQuillan's hand in improving the by-roads in the area, the candidate concluded with the line: 'Don't forget about Jack McQuillan who took you out of the shit!'

The electorate in Roscommon did not forget about McQuillan as he was re-elected for a second term as an independent TD in the 1954 general election, and, again, in 1957. As an independent TD, McQuillan continued to be one of the most outspoken TDs in the Dáil and this was clearly shown when a controversy over a group of Hungarian refugees erupted.

Following a failed uprising against Communist rule in Hungary in 1956, a flood of refugees poured out of the country. Over 500 refugees were allowed into Ireland and placed in army huts at the Knockalisheen refugee camp in County Clare. The refugees became disillusioned with the lack of work and the cold army huts they were living in. To draw the government's attention to their plight, 371 of them went on hunger strike in April 1957 in the hope that they would be given visas enabling them to leave the country.

On 2 May 1957, when the Dáil debated the events at Knockalisheen, most of those who spoke, including Taoiseach Éamon de Valera, hinted at the ingratitude of the refugees. But McQuillan took a stand and suggested it was the Irish attitude to them that was the problem. He shouted at de Valera, 'Why were they brought here under false pretences? . . . It was a big show-off to show what we could do.'

A year later on 16 May 1958, McQuillan and Browne set up a new left-wing, secular party called the National Progressive Democrats. Although it was a tiny party with just two TDs, the new party punched well above its weight and played a vigorous role in the Dáil, where it tabled a number of contentious motions. They caused much controversy when they drew attention to the relationship between the Taoiseach and *The Irish Press* group of newspapers.

On 12 December 1958, Browne and McQuillan put down a motion about Éamon de Valera continuing to hold the post of controlling director of *The Irish Press* group while holding the office of Taoiseach. Their motion claimed that this 'could reasonably be regarded as interfering or being incompatible with the full and proper discharge by him of the duties of his office.'

They questioned de Valera's integrity as Taoiseach as he prepared to leave office to initiate his presidential campaign. The motion was debated into January

1959 before it was finally defeated by 71 votes to 49.

Browne and McQuillan relentlessly harried de Valera in the Dáil chamber and even though their motion was highly unlikely to succeed it did have the effect of landing a blow on the Taoiseach ahead of his bid for the presidency.

Between 1958 and 1961, seven of the nine motions discussed in Private Members' Time in the Dáil had been proposed by either Browne or McQuillan. They asked 1,400, or 17%, of all parliamentary questions between 1961 and 1962.

McQuillan enjoyed his electoral high point in 1961 when he topped the poll with over 5,289 votes at the general election as a National Progressive Democrats' candidate. He married Roscommon lady Angela Nolan in the same year.

In the 1960s, long before the advent of local radio, provincial newspapers were the key conduit used by rural TDs to convey their message to constituents. Roscommon had two provincial newspapers in McQuillan's era – *The Roscommon Herald*, based in Boyle, which mainly served the north of the county and *The Roscommon Champion*, based in Roscommon town which was the paper of choice in the south of the county.

One of McQuillan's best attributes was his bolshie stubbornness, where he was immovable if he took a stand on an issue. But this attribute also contributed to his downfall – as McQuillan's decision to sue *The Roscommon Herald* shows.

During the Cold War between the USA and the Soviet Union, the Soviet Premier Nikita Khrushchev came up with the idea of deploying missiles in Fidel Castro's Cuba, within range of the USA, in April 1962. By October, US reconnaissance photographs revealed Soviet missiles under construction in Cuba.

The crisis that ensued between Krushchev's Soviet Union and John F Kennedy's United States became known as the Cuban Missile Crisis. A year before Kennedy's visit to Ireland, at a time when thousands of Irish homes had a picture of Kennedy on the wall beside the Sacred Heart, there was widespread support for the US position in Dáil Éireann.

But McQuillan and Browne were different. The two TDs joined a demonstration outside the US embassy against the US policy on Cuba. The march was broken up by gardaí using Alsatian dogs and it garnered much national media coverage.

Hearing of McQuillan's involvement in the controversial demonstration, Roscommon Fianna Fáil councillor James Doherty, the father of the late former TD Seán Doherty, accused McQuillan and Browne of being communists.

The Roscommon Herald reported Doherty's comments and McQuillan was outraged at the accusation. Members of the Catholic clergy had already levelled the same allegation against McQuillan and Browne at the time of the controversy surrounding the Mother and Child Scheme.

Dr Bill McQuillan said, 'I think he thought it was bad enough having clergy calling him a communist, which they were doing, so he decided to sue *The Roscommon Herald* because they published it in full. I think it was a mistake that he did so.'

McQuillan won his libel action case against the local paper but he was only awarded a farthing, or quarter of a penny, in damages. So it was a pyrrhic victory for the TD as he had an extremely fractious relationship with *The Roscommon Herald* from then on, whereby one of the two local media organs gave McQuillan little or no coverage in its column inches.

In 1963 McQuillan and Browne joined the Labour Party but a by-election following the death of Fine Gael TD Jimmy Burke in July the following year had a worrying result for McQuillan – the Labour Party candidate Oliver Macklin only polled 5% of the vote. Burke's widow Joan took her late husband's seat with over 17,000 votes.

During the 1965 general election campaign, McQuillan, in his usual outspoken manner, publicly criticised Joan Burke's contribution to the Dáil in the two-year period since her election. As a new deputy, the nurse who had fallen into politics following her husband's death had spoken very little in the Dáil and McQuillan pointed this out to anyone who would listen.

Significantly, McQuillan managed to score the second highest first-preference vote of his political career on polling day, 7 April 1965. But the transfers failed to come his way and he lost his Dáil seat for the first time since 1948. Fine Gael votes had traditionally transferred to McQuillan but his criticism of Joan Burke backfired and the Fine Gael transfers never came his way. A realignment of the Roscommon constituency before the election, whereby a portion of McQuillan's support base in South Roscommon became part of the Galway East constituency, also hampered his performance.

McQuillan was elected for Labour in the 1965 Seanad elections that followed his general election defeat. He was frustrated in the Seanad as he felt that he had no power in what he believed was just a 'talking shop'. But his controversial approach to politics continued when he was approached by a group of disgruntled post office clerks who wanted to set up their own trade union in 1966.

He helped them set up the new breakaway union, the Post Office Officials' Association and he was duly selected as the new union's general secretary. As the new body was not affiliated to the Irish Congress of Trade Unions (ICTU), McQuillan came in for a lot of pressure from his Labour Party colleagues. There was a lot of agitation among the ICTU affiliated unions within the Labour Party and McQuillan lost the party whip in 1968 after he refused to resign his position as general secretary of the Post Office Officials' Association.

He did not seek re-election at the 1969 general election so he bowed out of national politics. In 1974 he retired from his Roscommon County Council seat and went off to enjoy early retirement in Spain with his wife Angela and their baby daughter Elaine. They lived in Spain for seven years before moving to Paris for a year. Then they returned home to Ireland and lived in Bray, County Wicklow.

Despite leaving the national political stage in 1969, McQuillan always maintained his interest in politics and he regularly had letters published in the Letters to the Editor page of *The Irish Times* during his retirement.

There were two recurrent themes to his letters. Firstly, he abhorred IRA violence in the North and he campaigned for the repeal of Articles 2 and 3 of the Irish Constitution, the articles that laid claim to the North. Secondly, he campaigned for the quashing of the GAA's Rule 21, which forbade RUC and British army personnel from playing GAA games.

After his death in 1998, as tributes were paid to McQuillan in the Seanad, Independent Senator David Norris recounted a story that showed how McQuillan was as rebellious and defiant in his retirement as he had been in his younger days.

In 1989, as the Troubles raged in the North, a campaign group called the Peace Train Organisation was set up in response to the repeated bombing of the Dublin to Belfast railway line. The organisation hired a train out for a day which brought hundreds of people from all over the country to the North in a symbolic gesture of protest against the bombing of the railway line. When the Peace Train was returning from Belfast to Dublin, it was stopped at Portadown. Everyone was told to leave the train as the IRA had planted a bomb on the line. All the activists, who included Senator David Norris, were asked to move onto buses that were parked beside the line.

Norris recalls, 'We were all like sheep, simply getting off the train. I saw Jack McQuillan sitting in the carriage and I thought that perhaps he was unwell.'

When Norris asked McQuillan if he was alright, the pensioner replied that he was perfectly healthy but he was not getting off the train and he fully intended to miss the bus.

'He said he had travelled on a Peace Train and he was returning to Dublin on it,' says Norris. 'The IRA would not put him off the train. I told him I thought he was right and asked if I could join him. From that the whole position unravelled. We refused to get off the train and 90 people stayed in Portadown station overnight.

'It was a remarkable tribute to his insight and courage. Without that, none of us would have stayed on the train. We scored a notable propaganda victory against the IRA on that occasion.'

As well as writing letters to newspaper editors about the reform of Articles 2 and 3, McQuillan constantly lobbied TDs and senators about it. He died in March 1998, just a month before the Good Friday Agreement, which finally amended Articles 2 and 3, was clinched in the North.

Speaking on *The Roscommon Rebel* radio documentary, Angela McQuillan said, 'Everything he proposed was before its time. It all came later. It was sad to see the things he was proposing 20 years beforehand coming in as if they were new policies that had just been conceived.'

On 8 March 1998 McQuillan, aged 77, died in Bray after a long illness. As the tributes poured in from politicians that day, then Labour Party leader Ruairí Quinn best summed up McQuillan's contribution to Irish politics.

Quinn said: 'During a very conservative period of Irish history Jack McQuillan tried to accelerate the pace of social change against all the odds. He will be remembered as a progressive politician who was ahead of his time.'

16

Substitutes and 'Also Rans'
Substitutes

Politicians who are named as substitutes have also played inter-county GAA or made significant contributions within the organisation's administrative ranks.

It is arguable that some of them should have been included in the Dáil Star team. But places were limited and the first 15 were chosen on the basis of the individual's achievements on the playing field, their influence on the GAA (such as Eoin O'Duffy's pivotal role in establishing the organisation in Ulster), their achievements in their political careers and those with compelling stories to tell (such as Martin Ferris).

Apart from the 15 Dáil Stars, some of the other politicians who were elected to Leinster House, via Croke Park, feature in this chapter.

John Doyle (Tipperary – Fianna Fáil)
Tipperary's John Doyle played club hurling for Holycross-Ballycahill from the 1940s up to the 1970s and inter-county hurling from 1949 to 1967. He won a

total of eight All-Ireland medals and eleven National League medals over three decades. His eight All-Ireland medals haul is a record he jointly shares with Christy Ring. From the late 1950s, Tipperary's full-back line of Doyle, Michael Maher and Kieran Carey gave the county one of hurling's most formidable back lines in history, famously known as 'Hell's Kitchen'. He was also named on the GAA's Hurling Team of the Century in 1984 and the Hurling Team of the Millennium in 1999.

A staunch Fianna Fáil supporter, Doyle was elected a county councillor in the 1960s. He stood unsuccessfully for the party in Tipperary North in the 1969 and 1973 general elections. He was one of Taoiseach Jack Lynch's nominees to the Seanad in 1969 and he served as a senator for one term up to March 1973. Doyle's close friend Sean McCarthy, a Fianna Fáil councillor in South Tipperary, said, 'John was always very friendly with Charlie Haughey. And after the Arms Trial when Haughey was going around the country on the "chicken and chips" circuit trying to rebuild himself, John's wife Ann used to drive Haughey around Munster to Fianna Fáil functions.'

He bowed out of Leinster House after he was defeated in the 1973 Seanad elections.

Dick Spring (Kerry – Labour)

Dick followed in his father Dan's footsteps as he also donned the Kerry jersey and became a Labour TD. Dick and his brothers played their club football with Tralee club Kerins-O'Rahilly's and hurling with the Crotta O'Neills club. Dick played briefly with Kerry in both hurling and football in the 1970s. Rugby became Dick's first sporting love as he attended boarding school at the Cistercian College in Roscrea, County Tipperary. He won three caps for Ireland and also lined out for London Irish in England. Elected to his father's Kerry North seat in 1981, he became leader of the Labour party the following year and held the post for 15 years. He was Tánaiste, Minister for the Environment, Minister for Energy and Minister for Foreign Affairs before his political career came to an end when he lost his seat to Sinn Féin's Martin Ferris in the 2002 general election.

Seamus Mallon (Armagh – Independent)

Seamus Mallon played his club football with the Mullaghbrack GAA club and after playing on the Armagh minor team, he broke into the Orchard County's senior team in 1954, a year after they were defeated by Kerry in the All-Ireland final. He played at centre half-back and midfield in 1955 and 1956 but his playing career was cut short in the late 1950s after he broke his shoulder in a club junior championship game.

On 1 September 2002, when Armagh beat Kerry to win their first ever All-Ireland final, lifelong Armagh fan Mallon was standing in the Hogan Stand beside President Mary McAleese, where he shook hands with the team captain Kieran McGeeney before McGeeney lifted the Sam Maguire Cup.

Mallon said, 'It was a moment when I looked back and thought about my father and all those people who didn't live to see an Armagh man lift Sam Maguire. Those people would have given their right arm to see that sight.'

Mallon served in the Seanad from March to December 1982, after he was nominated by Taoiseach Charles Haughey. The deputy leader of the SDLP party was the Westminster MP for Newry and Armagh from 1986 to 2005 and he will be forever remembered as one of the architects of the peace process in the North. After the 1998 Good Friday Agreement, Mallon became Deputy First Minister in the new Northern Ireland Assembly and he retired from the role in 2001.

Seamus Kirk (Louth – Fianna Fáil)

Ceann Comhairle Seamus Kirk played with St Bride's GAA club in Knockbridge near Dundalk, County Louth during a playing career that also saw him wear the

'Wee County' colours. He was on the Louth county minor team in 1962 and 1963 and played senior football for Louth from 1963. He was a member of the Louth team that won the Leinster Junior Football Championship in 1966 and the team that lost the 1970 Division One final. Kirk suffered a serious leg injury in a National League match between Louth and Down in Drogheda in October 1972.

'I remained in a plaster for nearly two years and I have had many subsequent orthopaedic operations since then, culminating in a fused ankle about eight years ago,' he said in 2010. He was first elected in November 1982 and he has been returned as a Fianna Fáil TD in each general election since. He was appointed Ceann Comhairle in October 2009.

Brian Cowen (Offaly – Fianna Fáil)

Was An Taoiseach Brian Cowen a good footballer? Eugene McGee, who managed Offaly to their dramatic win that denied Kerry the five-in-a-row in 1982, says, 'Put it like this, Brian Cowen played in a full-forward line at a time with Matt Connor and Brendan Lowry.' Connor and Lowry played in the full-forward line in that 1982 final and both players are widely regarded as among the greatest Offaly players ever. Cowen was not on the Offaly panel in 1982 but he did have a promising underage career where he played up to under-21 level with the Faithful County and played for seven years for the Clara club's senior football team.

Brian Cowen's uncle, Fr Andrew Cowen, was a goalkeeper with the first Offaly team to win a Leinster Championship in 1947. Brian had the reputation of being a dogged underage hurler and footballer with Clara and he would have featured more had he not been hindered by poor eyesight. At 24 years of age Cowen won the by-election in the Laois-Offaly constituency in 1984, following the death of his father Ber, and he has remained in the Dáil ever since. He has served as Minister for Labour, Minister for Energy, Minister for Transport, Energy and Communications, Minister for Health and Children, Minister for

Foreign Affairs, and Minister for Finance. He replaced Bertie Ahern as Taoiseach on 7 May 2008.

Michael 'Mick' Herbert (Limerick – Fianna Fáil)

Mick Herbert played hurling for the Ahane GAA club in Limerick where he won seven successive senior county championship medals between 1942 and 1949. He played in a number of Munster finals for Limerick and he was a member of the victorious National League team in 1948. Herbert's hurling career, where he played as a full-back, was cut short due to a serious head injury suffered in a club match in 1949.

Herbert was elected for Fianna Fáil to Limerick County Council in 1955. After unsuccessfully contesting the 1965 general election, he was elected a Fianna Fáil TD for Limerick East in 1969. Following Ireland's accession to the EEC in 1973, Taoiseach Jack Lynch appointed Herbert as one of the country's first MEPs. He served as a nominated MEP up to the first direct elections in 1979 when he narrowly lost out on the last Munster seat. He retained his Dáil seat from 1969 until his retirement from politics in 1981.

Herbert's brothers, Sean and Tony (who was a senator), were also prolific Limerick hurlers and his son Turlough was a member of the Limerick panel that reached the 1994 All-Ireland hurling final. Herbert passed away in 2006, aged 81, but the Herbert name still lives on in the corridors of power. One of Mick's daughters, Cathy, (a former RTÉ journalist) is now a special advisor to the Minister for Finance, Brian Lenihan.

Tony Herbert (Limerick/Dublin – Fianna Fáil)

Tony Herbert was a brother of former TD and MEP Mick Herbert. The Herberts' father and uncles played for Castleconnell and Limerick, while another uncle on the maternal side, Paddy Kenneally, played for Laune Rangers in Kerry and won two All-Ireland Senior football medals with Kerry. Tony won nine senior county championships in Limerick – five in hurling and four in football. He played for Limerick before he moved to Dublin for work reasons and joined the Faughs GAA club in Templeogue. He helped them win four Dublin senior hurling championships. He also played inter-county hurling with Dublin and won Leinster titles in 1948 and 1952. He marked his brother Sean on a number of occasions when he lined out for Leinster against Munster in the Railway Cup. Like his brother Mick, Tony was a Fianna Fáil senator from 1977 to 1982 before he bowed out of public life in 1983.

Paddy Lalor (Laois – Fianna Fáil)

Paddy Lalor is regarded as one of the finest hurlers ever to wear the Laois colours. The Abbeyleix club man, played both hurling and football for the O'Moore County and among the highlights of his playing days was being a member of the last Laois team that won the Leinster Senior Hurling Championship in 1949.

Lalor was elected a Fianna Fáil TD in 1961 and after the 1965 election he was appointed parliamentary secretary. Four years later he was appointed Minister for Posts and Telegraphs and in 1970 he was appointed Minister for Industry and Commerce. He did not contest the 1981 general election but he was elected as an MEP in 1979 and again in 1984 and 1989.

Maurice Hayes (Down – Independent)

Maurice Hayes played inter-county hurling for his native Down but his involvement in the administrative ranks of the organisation is where he really excelled. After becoming secretary of the Down County Board in the mid 1950s,

Hayes initiated a ten-year plan for the Mourne County's football team to become the first Northern team to win an All-Ireland. By 1960, Down made history by becoming the first team to take the Sam Maguire Cup north of the Border. The county won it again in 1961, 1968 and 1994 and Hayes's vision will forever be associated with Down's feat of being the only Northern county to win Sam Maguire before Derry's 1993 breakthrough. The highly respected author and political commentator was appointed to the Seanad as a nominee of Taoiseach Bertie Ahern in 1997 and he remained there for two terms until 2007.

Ted Nealon (Sligo – Fine Gael)

Ted Nealon played club football with three clubs in three different counties. He played initially with his native Tourlestrane club before his job as a journalist saw him leave Sligo and work in other areas. He won club and championship honours with Monaghan Harps and Dundalk Gaels before returning to play for Tourlestrane. He also played inter-county football for Sligo from 1953 to 1959. He recalls marking Galway's Frank Stockwell in the 1954 Connacht final and says, 'It was the same old story for Sligo. We came from 11 points down at half time and ended up getting beaten by a point after having a goal disallowed at the end.'

Nealon is probably the only TD to ever play rugby league. When he lived in Manchester for a short period he played rugby league for the Cadishead Rhinos club. The well-known editor of *Nealon's Guide to the Dáil* was a current affairs presenter on RTÉ before he was first elected as a Fine Gael TD for Sligo-Leitrim in 1981. He was a junior minister on three separate occasions in a political career that lasted up to his retirement in 1997.

Tom O'Reilly (Cavan – Independent)

'Big Tom' O'Reilly and his brother John Joe were Cavan GAA legends. Tom won a total of nine Cavan senior football championship medals with Cornafean. He won All-Ireland medals playing with Cavan in 1933 and 1945 and he was still on the county's panel when they won the Polo Grounds final in New York in 1947. O'Reilly was elected to Dáil Éireann as an Independent TD in 1944 when he took the fourth seat in the Cavan constituency with 5,000 votes. He stood for Fine Gael in the 1948 general election but failed to get elected and he did not stand for the Dáil again.

Dan O'Rourke (Roscommon – Fianna Fáil)

The late Jimmy Murray of Roscommon, who is among a select few captains to have lifted Sam Maguire on two occasions (1943 and 1944), held Dan O'Rourke in high regard. O'Rourke, who was chairman of the Roscommon County Board at the time, played a huge part in Roscommon's successes. He introduced 'collective training' to the Roscommon team and kept the team at his own house for two weeks to train for the 1943 final, and at the Old Infirmary in Roscommon town in 1944. In April 1946 he was elected President of the GAA.

A veteran of the War of Independence, O'Rourke also enjoyed a lengthy political career. He was first elected to the second Dáil as a Sinn Féin TD for the Mayo-South Roscommon constituency in 1921. He was re-elected to the third Dáil as pro-Treaty Sinn Féin TD in 1922. He was elected as a Fianna Fáil TD on five occasions between 1932 and 1948, and after unsuccessfully contesting three general elections in 1951, 1954 and 1957 he bowed out of public life.

Dr Hugh Gibbons (Roscommon – Fianna Fáil)

Dr Hugh Gibbons won his first All-Ireland when he featured on the Roscommon team that won the 1940 All-Ireland Junior title. Three years later he was on the Roscommon squad that won the Senior All-Ireland. In 1944 he played in Roscommon's full-forward line with Jack McQuillan when they won their second All-Ireland title in a row.

Gibbons, a medical doctor, was elected a TD for Roscommon on his first attempt for Fianna Fáil in 1965 and held his seat up to his retirement in 1977. The Gibbons family name remains synonymous with politics as his son Dr Brian Gibbons is currently a Welsh Assembly member and a former Minister for Social Justice in the assembly.

Harry Boland (Dublin – Sinn Féin)

Born in 1887, Harry Boland joined the Irish Republican Brotherhood (IRB) in 1904. At the time, he was also involved in the Gaelic League and he was one of the most influential figures in the GAA. He played hurling for Dublin and he featured for the capital's hurlers in the 1908 All-Ireland final. He refereed the 1911 hurling final and the 1914 football decider. In 1907 he became a member of the Dublin GAA County Board and when he rose to the rank of chairman he used his position to drive his IRB agenda. At the GAA's congress in 1913 he advocated the wearing of county colours and the establishment of 15-a-side games. He was also behind moves to expel any civil servants from the GAA who had sworn allegiance to the British Crown.

He was in London on GAA business in 1909 when he met Michael Collins for the first time. Collins was treasurer of London's Geraldines GAA club at the time and Boland suggested to Collins that he join the IRB. Boland brought him to Sam Maguire who initiated Collins into the organisation.

Harry, and his brothers Ned and Gerry, joined the Irish Volunteers at its inaugural meeting in 1913 and they all fought in the 1916 Easter Rising. Boland met Éamon de Valera in prison in England following the Rising and he was elected at the 1918 elections as a Sinn Féin MP for South Roscommon.

He was named by de Valera as the first Dáil's envoy to the United States in 1919 and he travelled to the US with de Valera as part of a campaign to raise awareness of the Irish cause abroad. He aligned with the anti-Treaty side after the Anglo-Irish Treaty and he was shot by Free State soldiers at the Skerries Grand Hotel in 1922. He died in hospital some days later and was buried in Glasnevin cemetery.

Tony Dempsey (Wexford – Fianna Fáil)

Tony Dempsey became chairman of Wexford County Board in 1976 at 35 years old. He trained the Wexford junior football team to a Leinster championship in 2000 and he was the manager of the Wexford senior hurling team in 2002 when he was elected a Fianna Fáil TD. He did not contest the 2007 general election but he was elected to Wexford County Council in the 2009 local elections.

Brendan Corish (Wexford – Labour)

Former Labour party leader Brendan Corish played for the St John's Volunteers GAA club in Wexford town in his youth and also played football for his county. Corish, who will forever be famed for a 1967 speech that blasted 'the 1970s will be socialist', was first elected to the Dáil as TD for Wexford in a by-election in 1945. He was Minister for Social Welfare from 1954 to 1957 and again from 1973 to 1977, when he was also Tánaiste. He was a TD for 37 years from 1945 until 1982, when he retired.

Batt O'Keeffe (Cork – Fianna Fáil)

Batt O'Keeffe won an under-14 football medal with the Cullen club and four minor football medals with Millstreet. In 1963 he won a Munster Colleges title with St Brendan's College in Killarney but lost out to St Mel's College in Longford in the All-Ireland Colleges final. Playing for Cork, he won Munster Under-21, Junior and Senior medals. He was also a Cork Intermediate Handball champion.

After being elected to Cork County Council in 1985, O'Keeffe was elected a Fianna Fáil TD for the Cork South-Central constituency two years later. He was a senator from 1989 to 1992 after losing his seat in the 1989 general election. The former lecturer in Cork IT was re-elected to the Dáil in 1992 and he has been returned in each subsequent election. He was appointed a junior minister at the Department of the Environment in 2007 and when Brian Cowen became Taoiseach in 2008 he appointed O'Keeffe as Minister for Education. Following Cowen's Cabinet re-shuffle in March 2010 O'Keeffe was appointed Minister for Enterprise, Trade and Innovation.

Liam Lawlor (Dublin – Fianna Fáil)

Liam Lawlor played minor and senior hurling for Dublin and for Leinster in the Railway Cup. He was renowned for his physical approach to the game and legend has it that he used to travel to Laois to play matches as the hurling in Dublin was 'too clean'. Lawlor was first elected to the Dáil in 1977 and although he lost his seat in the November 1982 election, he was re-elected in 1987 and held his seat until 2002.

A controversial character, he was one of the Dublin county councillors who appeared as a witness before the Flood Tribunal into planning and payments to politicians. He admitted receiving sums of money from lobbyist Frank Dunlop. He resigned from Fianna Fáil in June 2000 and did not contest the 2002 general election. Lawlor, who was imprisoned three times for failing to co-operate with the planning tribunal, was tragically killed in a car accident in Moscow in October 2005.

Michael Kennedy (Dublin – Fianna Fáil)

Michael Kennedy went to school in St Vincent's CBS in Glasnevin, Dublin and played for the nearby Na Fianna GAA club, in keeping with a long standing relationship between the school and the Mobhi Road club. One of Kennedy's proudest GAA memories was playing on the Na Fianna team that beat Marino club St Vincent's to win the Dublin senior football championship in 1969. He also played football and hurling at minor and under-21 level for Dublin from 1967 to 1969. After moving to north county Dublin, he subsequently played hurling with the Naomh Mearnóg club in Portmarnock where he won a junior hurling championship medal in 1991.

Bill Loughnane (Dublin/Clare – Fianna Fáil)

Bill Loughnane from Feakle, County Clare broke into the Clare hurling team in 1936. He was a medical student doing his final exams in UCD in 1938 when he got the bizarre news that he would not be playing for the Banner County that year. As a result of a secretarial error, Loughnane was not registered to play with Clare that year so he ended up playing for Dublin. At the time, Loughnane and his two brothers Paddy and Tom were all on the Clare panel. So Bill ended up playing for Dublin while his two brothers played for Clare.

Bill had won a number of intervarsity Fitzgibbon Cup medals with UCD at the time and he immediately established himself on the Dublin team that won the Leinster title and went on to book their place in the 1938 All-Ireland final. Meanwhile, his brothers Paddy and Tom were on a very strong Clare team that beat Cork and Tipperary on their way to the Munster final. They went into the

Munster final as favourites but Waterford took them by surprise and beat them. Waterford ended up playing Dublin in the All-Ireland final.

Had Clare beaten Waterford, two of the Loughnane brothers could have ended up playing against their brother Bill in the All-Ireland final. In the end, Bill played at left corner-forward on the Dublin team that beat Waterford in the final. After his sojourn with Dublin, he returned to the Clare colours and he was captain of the Banner men by 1942.

He was elected to the Dáil in 1969 and remained as a TD up to the November 1982 general election. His son Bill Loughnane Jnr unsuccessfully contested the 1982 election as an Independent and the 1989 general election as a Fianna Fáil candidate.

Sean Brosnan (Kerry – Fianna Fáil)

Dingle man Sean Brosnan won All-Ireland medals with Kerry in 1937, 1940 and 1941. An exceptionally good fielder of the ball, he was renowned for his high one-handed catches. He played at midfield with Johnny Walsh in the 1937 All-Ireland final and the following day *The Irish Press* reported how Brosnan 'brought down ball after ball with a reach that was magical.' He was due to captain Kerry to their 1939 All-Ireland triumph when he fell sick with flu the day before the game. As he lay on his sickbed at the Grand Hotel in Dun Laoghaire, he listened to the match on the radio before Tom 'Gega' O'Connor lifted Sam Maguire in his place.

Brosnan was a barrister and ended up living in Cork. He was elected to the Dáil as a Fianna Fáil TD for Cork North East in 1969 and lost his seat in the 1973 general election. He was then elected to the Seanad but he returned to the Dáil in 1974 after he won a by-election following the death of his party colleague Liam Ahern. He was re-elected to the Dáil in 1977 and he also served as an MEP, appointed by Taoiseach Jack Lynch after Ireland joined the EEC in 1973. He was due to contest the 1979 Euro elections but he withdrew from the campaign a few months before polling day due to ill-health and died on 18 April 1979.

Patrick 'Fad' Browne (Waterford – Fianna Fáil)

Waterford's Patrick 'Fad' Browne is often described as the 'greatest hurler never to win an All-Ireland'. He played for Erin's Own, a Waterford city-based club, and won eleven county titles with them, including nine-in-a-row from 1927 to 1935. He played midfield for Waterford for many years and also starred on Munster teams alongside Jack Lynch, Mick Mackey and Christy Ring, where he won a number of Railway Cup medals.

His son Tony says, 'When he was a child he was very picky or "faddy" about his food so his mother gave him the name 'Fad' and that stuck with him for life.' Fad Browne was elected as a Fianna Fáil TD for Waterford in a by-election in 1966 and remained in the Dáil until 1973 when he lost his seat. He was a senator from 1973 to 1977 when he retired from politics. Fad, who was the grandfather of the Waterford inter-county and Mount Sion club star Tony Jnr, died in 1991.

Michael Lowry (Tipperary – Fine Gael/Independent)

Although he is not renowned for his playing record, Lowry's prowess in the administrative ranks of the GAA served to launch the Tipperary North TD's political career. Starting out as secretary of the Holycross-Ballycahill GAA club, Lowry became the youngest ever Tipperary County Board chairman. During his three-year term he was responsible for the appointment of 'Babs' Keating. Keating led Tipperary to a Munster title in 1987 after a 16-year drought, and the county won the All-Ireland in 1989.

After he was appointed chairman of the Semple Stadium Management Committee in 1986, he helped the stadium come back from the brink of insolvency. His brainchild the Féile and 'Trip to Tipp' pop festivals helped repay debts of €1.5 million. The reputation Lowry garnered in GAA circles helped him get elected to the Dáil as a Fine Gael TD in 1987 and he has remained there ever since. He has served as an Independent TD since his controversial 1996 resignation from Fine Gael.

GV Wright (Dublin – Fianna Fáil)

Thomas Wright, known to everyone by his nickname GV, played football for the St Sylvester's GAA club in Malahide. He also donned the Dublin jersey for the capital's under-21, junior and intermediate teams in the late 1960s and early 1970s. Wright's sporting prowess did not stop with the GAA as he is a former international basketball player and coach.

He was one of Taoiseach Charles Haughey's nominees to the Seanad in 1982 and remained there for a year. He returned to politics in 1985 as a member of Dublin County Council and two years later he was elected a Fianna Fáil TD for Dublin North. He lost his seat in 1989 and returned to the Seanad, where he served as leader of the Seanad from 1992 to 1994 and Fianna Fáil's leader in the Seanad from 1994 to 1997. He was re-elected to the Dáil in the 1997 general election and held his seat until he retired from politics ahead of the 2007 general election.

Jack Wall (Kildare – Labour)

In 1966 the Lilywhites won the All-Ireland Junior hurling title after they defeated Warwickshire in Glebe Farm, Birmingham. Labour TD Jack Wall was on the winning side. Wall played hurling for Kildare from 1964 until 1974 and won All-Ireland Junior (1966), Intermediate (1969) and Senior B (1974) titles along the way. He also won a National League Division Two medal in 1969 and a range of county hurling and football championship medals with the Castledermot and Castlemitchell clubs.

Wall held a number of positions in the administrative ranks of Kildare GAA, including a ten-year stint as chairman of the Kildare County Board from 1989 to 1999. An electrician by trade, Wall entered politics when he was elected to Kildare County Council at the 1991 local elections and he was nominated to Seanad Éireann in 1993. He was elected a TD for Kildare South in 1997 and he has remained a TD since then.

Billy Timmins (Baltinglass – Fine Gael)

A rarity in Wicklow, current Fine Gael TD Billy Timmins has an All-Ireland winning medal. While Rathnew featured in the All-Ireland Senior club final in 2002, Baltinglass is the only Wicklow club to win the title – back in 1990. Although he did not feature as a Wicklow inter-county player, he deserves a mention as he was on the Baltinglass winning panel in 1990 and came on as a substitute in the final. Timmins was first elected as a Fine Gael TD for Wicklow in 1997 and was returned in 2002 and 2007.

Jim Tunney (Dublin – Fianna Fáil)

When Jack Lynch got a civil service job transfer from Cork to Dublin in 1943 he was immediately drafted into the Civil Service GAA club in the capital. He played football with a promising young Dublin player called Jim Tunney at the club and they won the Dublin senior football championship for the first time in their history in 1944. Tunney and Lynch would become close political allies in later years. Tunney broke into the Dublin team at this time and the high point of his playing career was playing at midfield with Kevin Heffernan on the 1948 team that won the All-Ireland Junior Football Championship.

Tunney was first elected a Fianna Fáil TD for the Dublin North West constituency in 1969. He was re-elected in every election from then until 1992, when he lost his seat. He was a parliamentary secretary for two periods in the 1970s and a junior minister for two further periods. He also served as Leas Ceann Comhairle and Lord Mayor of Dublin. Seen as a protégé of his former GAA teammate Jack Lynch, he was, nevertheless, retained by Lynch's successor Charlie Haughey and he became a close ally of Haughey. He was always known as a stylish dresser who wore a flower on his lapel, gaining him the affectionate title, 'the yellow rose of Finglas'. He died in 2002.

James 'Jimmy' Griffin (Meath – Fianna Fáil)
The Royal County's first ever All-Ireland success came in 1927 when they won the junior hurling title and Trim man Jimmy Griffin was on that team. Griffin was elected a Fianna Fáil TD for Meath in 1957 but died two years later.

Mark Clinton (Meath – Fine Gael)
Mark Clinton's playing career started off with the St Mary's club, an amalgamation of Moynalty and Kilbeg, before he played for Kells. He was a Kells player in 1939, when he came on as a sub for Meath in their All-Ireland final defeat to a Kerry team that included Dan Spring, Dan O'Keeffe and Joe Keohane. Clinton was elected a Fine Gael TD for County Dublin in 1961 and he was re-elected in every election up to 1981 when he retired. He was Minister for Agriculture from 1973 to 1977 where he negotiated Ireland's entry into Europe's Common Agricultural Policy (CAP). He was an MEP from 1979 to 1989, and he held the office of vice-president of the European Parliament for a period during this time. He died in 2001.

Jim Fitzsimons (Meath – Fianna Fáil)

Navan O'Mahony's clubman Jim Fitzsimons, won six Meath senior championship medals and played at centre half-forward on the Meath senior team in the early 1960s. Unfortunately Fitzsimons suffered a back injury that ended his inter-county career a few years before Meath won the All-Ireland in 1967.

In the late 1960s Fitzsimons was elected to Meath County Council for Fianna Fáil and elected a TD in 1977. He was returned in every election up to 1987 when he retired from national politics. He served as a junior minister from October to December 1982. He was elected an MEP in 1984 and he served as an MEP for 20 years until he retired at the 2004 elections.

Colm Hilliard (Meath – Fianna Fáil)

Colm Hilliard played for Navan O'Mahony's during a golden period for the club in the 1950s and 1960s. He played for Meath at minor level in the 1951 All-Ireland Minor final defeat to Roscommon.

Hilliard's father Michael had been a TD for 30 years and Colm was first elected as Fianna Fáil TD for Meath at the February 1982 general election, when he replaced retiring Labour TD James Tully. He was elected in every election up to 1997 when he retired. He died in 2002.

The Also-Rans

The GAA may have provided the perfect launch pad for many Oireachtas careers but success on the GAA field does not automatically transfer into Dáil votes as some of the 'also-rans' listed below found out.

Peter Donohoe (Cavan – Clann na Poblachta)

John Wilson was the best-known and most successful politician derived from the Cavan team that won the famous 1947 All-Ireland final in the Polo Grounds in New York. But Peter Donohoe, the full-forward on that team who scored eight points from frees in the game, did not enjoy as much success in politics. Donohoe, who was labelled 'The Babe Ruth of Gaelic Football' by *The New York Times*, stood for the Clann na Poblachta party in the 1948 general election in his native Cavan constituency but the 2,253 votes he garnered was not enough to elect him.

John O'Leary (Dublin – Fianna Fáil)

The former goalkeeper, who captained Dublin to an All-Ireland football title in 1995, was a five-time All-Star winner. He contested the 2007 general election as a Fianna Fáil candidate in Dublin North and polled 5,074 first preference votes but failed to get elected.

Graham Geraghty (Meath – Fine Gael)

Geraghty, who won All-Ireland titles with Meath in 1996 and again in 1999, when he was the team captain, was Fine Gael's surprise 'celebrity' candidate in the Meath West constituency in the 2007 general election. On 12 December 2006,

Geraghty appeared on RTÉ radio's *Morning Ireland* programme the morning after the Fine Gael convention that selected him as an election candidate. When asked why he was going into politics, he replied, 'Why not?' After that, he was asked: 'Why Fine Gael?' He replied, 'Why not?' He was eliminated in the first count after he polled little over 3% of the vote and failed to win any significant number of transfers.

Eamon Cregan (Limerick – Fianna Fáil)

Cregan was a dual hurling and football star with Limerick before going on to manage both Offaly and Limerick's senior hurling teams in the 1980s and 1990s. The Claughaun clubman gave up football to concentrate on his inter-county hurling career and won three hurling All-Stars in the 1970s. He won an All-Ireland hurling title with Limerick in 1973. He became the first outside manager to defeat his native county when he managed Offaly to their 1994 All-Ireland hurling title where they snatched victory from Limerick's jaws with two goals in the last five minutes of the game. In the 1981 general election, Cregan stood as a Fianna Fáil candidate for Limerick East but his 1,636 first preference votes (3.4% of the vote) was not enough to elect him.

Brian Whelahan (Offaly – Fine Gael)

Whelahan played for the Offaly hurlers from 1989 to 2006, winning All-Ireland titles in 1994 and 1998. He was the only player still playing in 1999, when he was named on the GAA's hurling Team of the Millennium. He has also won four hurling All-Star awards and he won four All-Ireland club hurling titles with Birr. In late 2008 he was announced as a Fine Gael candidate for the Birr electoral area for the 2009 local elections to Offaly County Council. He polled just 628 first-preference votes (8.7% of the vote) and failed to win a council seat. It has been speculated that he may contest retiring TD Olwyn Enright's seat.

Pádraig Horan (Offaly – Fine Gael)

Pádraig Horan captained Offaly to their first All-Ireland Senior hurling title in 1981. The St Rynagh's clubman won a second All-Ireland medal in 1985, when he won an All-Star award. He also managed Offaly, Laois and St Rynagh's. In 1995 he managed Birr to their first ever All-Ireland club hurling title.

Following the death of Fianna Fáil TD Ber Cowen in 1984, he contested the subsequent by-election for Fine Gael and polled over 18,000 votes but the deceased TD's son Brian Cowen garnered a massive 26,022 votes to top the poll and get elected to his late father's seat on the first count.

Seán Purcell (Galway – Fine Gael)

Seán Purcell and Frank Stockwell are widely regarded to have been among the greatest Gaelic footballers of all time. Galway's 'Terrible Twins', as they were affectionately known, won ten Galway club championships with Tuam Stars, including seven-in-a-row from 1954 to 1960. He won an All-Ireland title with Galway in 1956 and he was named on both the GAA's Team of the Century in 1984 and Team of the Millennium in 1999. But the 'Master', as he was nicknamed, failed to get elected for Fine Gael in Galway East in both the 1961 and 1965 general elections.

Luke Colleran (Sligo – Fine Gael)

Luke Colleran Snr was one of the famous seven brothers from the Tubbercurry GAA club to play for Sligo from the 1920s to 1940s. He won a Fine Gael seat on Sligo County Council in every local election from 1942 to 1974. He contested the 1957 general election but failed to win one of the five seats in the Sligo-Leitrim constituency.

Seamus Durack (Clare – Fine Gael)

Seamus Durack was the Clare hurling goalkeeper in the late 1970s and early 1980s when the famous curse of Biddy Early was still in train as the Banner County had not won an All-Ireland title since 1914. Durack had long retired when the curse was finally lifted with Clare's 1995 breakthrough but he did forge an impressive career between the posts that saw him win All-Star awards in 1977, 1978 and 1981 and league titles with Clare in 1977 and 1978. He unsuccessfully contested the November 1982 general election for Fine Gael in Clare.

Barney Rock (Dublin – Progressive Democrats)

Barney Rock is regarded as one of Dublin's greatest ever players and he was a Hill 16 fans' favourite throughout his inter-county playing career that stretched from 1980 to 1991. He won three All-Star awards, four Leinster titles and one All-Ireland title in 1983. The former Ballymun-Kickhams clubman also ran unsuccessfully for the Progressive Democrats in the 1991 local elections in the Finglas ward.

Mick O'Connell (Kerry – Independent)

One of the greatest footballers of all time, the man from Valentia Island won four All-Ireland titles and one All-Star award. He was also named on the GAA's Team of the Century in 1984 and Team of the Millennium in 1999. O'Connell was elected to Kerry County Council as an Independent councillor in the local elections in June 1979. Two years later he contested the 1981 general election as an Independent candidate in the Kerry South constituency after turning down approaches from Fine Gael and Fianna Fáil. But he failed to win a seat and garnered just a 4.6% share of the vote or 1,600 first-preference votes.

Joe Keohane (Kerry – Independent)

Joe Keohane played for Kerry from 1936 to 1949 and he is widely regarded as the greatest full-back of all time. He was named in that position in the GAA Team of the Century in 1984 and the Team of the Millennium in 1999. The John Mitchell's clubman won five All-Ireland medals and ten Munster titles and he was also involved as a selector on Kerry teams later in life. Keohane, who was a staunch republican, stood for Kevin Boland's short-lived party Aontacht Éireann in the Kerry North constituency in the 1973 general election. His 695 votes (2.5% of the vote) were not enough to elect him.

Johnny Walsh (Kerry – Clann na Poblachta)

From Ballylongford, Johnny Walsh played his first championship game for Kerry at midfield in the 1932 All-Ireland final win over Mayo. Kerry's win completed the county's first ever four-in-a-row and Walsh went on to win a further four All-Ireland medals in 1937, 1939, 1940 and 1941. Walsh claimed that he was dropped from the Kerry team 'because of my politics' in 1933 and he vowed never to play Gaelic football again. He played rugby for the Garryowen club in Limerick for two years, in which he was capped for Munster in 1935 before he returned to play for Kerry. Walsh unsuccessfully stood for Clann na Poblachta in the Kerry North constituency at the 1948 general election.

Tom 'Gega' O'Connor (Kerry – Fianna Fáil)

Tom O'Connor's nickname 'Gega' was derived from the Greek word 'Gigas', meaning giant. The Dingle clubman captained Kerry to the 1939 All-Ireland football title. Remembered as one of the greatest half-forwards to ever wear the Kerry jersey, O'Connor captained a team that included legendary Kerry figure Joe Keohane and future Labour TD Dan Spring. While Spring managed to enjoy electoral success for Labour on the back of a successful football career, Tom 'Gega' O'Connor was unsuccessful in two attempts to get elected to the Dáil for Fianna Fáil in the Kerry North constituency in 1948 and 1951.

Con Brosnan (Kerry – Cumann na nGaedheal)

Reckoned by many critics to have been the best midfielder ever to play Gaelic football, Brosnan was heavily involved in the North Kerry brigade of the IRA during the War of Independence. His family home in Moyvane, then known as Newtownsandes, was burned out by the Black and Tans in 1921. He became a captain in the Free State Army after the Civil War.

Brosnan kicked the winning point in the 1924 All-Ireland final win over Dublin and won five more medals afterwards. He became the first All-Ireland winning captain to train an All-Ireland winning team when he trained Kerry in 1939.

Despite polling over 5,000 votes, Brosnan's attempt to win a Dáil seat in Kerry for Cumann na nGaedheal at the 1933 general election was unsuccessful.

Leabharlanna Poibli Chathair Bhaile Átha Cliath
Dublin City Public Libraries

Bibliography

Dunmore MacHales: A history of football in Dunmore Parish by Michael Leydon (Tuam, 1983)

The Best of the West: GAA greats of Connacht by John Scally, The Collins Press, (Cork, 2008)

The Green Above the Red: A compilation of Mayo's greatest football triumphs by Terry Reilly and Ivan Neill, *Western People* (Ballina, 1985)

Football Immortals by Raymond Smith, Creative Press Ltd. (Dublin, 1971)

The Clash of the Ash by Raymond Smith, Creative Press Ltd. (Dublin, 1972)

General O'Duffy: His Life and Battles by Liam Walsh, unpublished manuscript, courtesy of the McHugh family Castleblayney.

Kings of September by Michael Foley, O'Brien Press, (Dublin, 2007)

Stair CLG Chonnacht: History of Connacht GAA 1902-2002, edited by Tommy Moran (Connacht GAA Council, 2002)

Princes of Pigskin: A century of Kerry footballers by Joe Ó Muircheartaigh and TJ Flynn, Collins Press, (Cork, 2008)

Football Captains: The All-Ireland winners by Brian Carthy, Wolfhound Press, (Dublin, 1993)

Giants of Gaelic Football: All-time greats by Seán Óg Ó Ceallacháin, Gill and Macmillan (Dublin, 2007).

Martin Ferris: Man of Kerry by JJ Barrett, Brandon Book, (Dingle, 2005)

Rule 42 and all that by Seán Kelly, Gill and Macmillan, (Dublin, 2007)

Jack Lynch: Where he sported and played by Liam O'Tuama, Blackwater Press, (Dublin, 2000)

Yes, Taoiseach by Frank Dunlop, Penguin Ireland, (Dublin, 2004)

Election and Rejection: General elections in Co Monaghan since the foundation of the Free State by Brendan O Dufaigh (Monaghan, 2005)

Eoin O'Duffy: Self-Made Hero by Fearghal McGarry, Oxford University Press, (New York, 2007)

Roscomáin: 101 years of Gaelic Games in County Roscommon 1889-1990 by Tony Conboy, published by *The Roscommon Herald*, (Boyle, 1990)

Action Replay by Jack Mahon, (Galway, 1984)

Twelve Glorious Years by Jack Mahon (Galway, 1965)

A Year 'til Sunday, TV documentary by Pat Comer, (Galway, 1998)

The GAA: A People's History by Mike Cronin, Mark Duncan and Paul Rouse, The Collins Press, (Cork, 2009).

Austin Stack: Portrait of a separatist by J. Anthony Gaughan, Kingdom Books (Dublin, 1977)

Jack Lynch: A Biography by Dermot Keogh, Gill & Macmillan, (Dublin 2008)

The IRA: A History by Tim Pat Coogan Roberts Rinehart Publishers, 1994

www.electionsireland.org, www.gaa.ie and Oireachtas members' database at www.oireachtas.ie

The newspaper archives of *The Irish Times, Sunday Tribune, Irish Independent, Irish Press, Irish Examiner, Mayo News, Western People, Kerryman, Longford Leader, Dundalk Democrat, Tuam Herald* and *Connacht Tribune.*

Bainisteoir

The 10 Greatest GAA Managers

Finbarr McCarthy

Bainisteoir tells the individual heroic stories of the GAA's 10 most successful managers – based on personal interviews given to the author.

- **Dublin's** Kevin Heffernan – how he trained the Dubs' teams for victory.
- **Kerry's** Mick O'Dwyer – the secrets of his long run of success with the Kingdom – and **Kildare**, **Laois** and **Wicklow.**
- **Kilkenny's** Brian Cody –the 4-in-a-row, his research, 'player management' and training routines.
- **Cork's** Billy Morgan – dogged by controversy and his outspoken nature – yet **he** achieved great things down South.
- **Meath's** Seán Boylan – how he combined an outstanding run of success with the 'royal' county and his role of 'Healer'.
- **Clare's** Ger Loughnane – followed by controversy at both Clare and **Galway** but he's a great motivator and retains the will to win.
- **Tyrone's** Mickey Harte – outsmarted Kerry and motivated his players to success.
- **Kerry's** Páidí Ó Sé – straight-talking stewardship of the Kingdom, and later with **Westmeath** and then . . . **Clare**.
- **Cork's** Jimmy Barry Murphy – hurling success on Leeside with an Adidas controversy and Greyhound-racing hobby.
- **Armagh's** Joe Kernan – how he achieved three-in-a-row in the Ulster Championship.

Tunnel Vision

Behind the Scenes at Great Irish Sports Events

Tadhg de Brún

Tunnel Vision takes the reader where no Irish sports book has ever gone before – behind the scenes at great Irish sporting events – from the Irish Open to the Heineken Cup to the All-Ireland Finals. Over 30 years with RTÉ Sports as event/floor manager has given Tadhg de Brún a unique insight into the stories and secrets at all the biggest Irish sporting events.

- Memories of the Irish Open – the golfers, their egos and their problems – and some very rewarding bets placed by the RTÉ crew!
- Snooker Finals at Goffs – the tension and the chaos; how Dennis Taylor was neatly put in his 'seat' after complaining about the facilities.
- All-Ireland Final days – the craziness *not* shown on TV; how the Kilkenny captain emerged from the victorious dressing room dressed in boots and gear and rushed off to church.
- The characters you meet on the road – the managers, players, caterers, cleaners, as well as the rakes of Liberty Square and the security man at the Brandywell. The comedy and tragedy of their lives as witnessed on great sporting occasions.
- Behind the great events of the Charlton Era, including an eventful trip by Tadhg and his crew to the World Cup in America in 1994.

Working On A Dream

A year on the road with Waterford footballers

DAMIAN LAWLOR

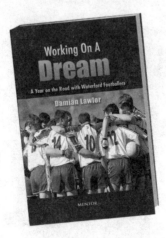

Far from the madding crowds of Croke Park, the inflated egos of star players and boardroom wrangles in the top counties, some GAA teams are fighting for their very existence....

Working On A Dream goes where no Irish sports book has ever gone before - a no holds barred, behind-the-scenes look at an intercounty GAA team struggling to survive at the lower end of the scale: Waterford senior footballers.

With access to all areas, the author, award-winning journalist Damian Lawlor, spent the 2009 season on trains, planes and in the dressing room with the Waterford players as they chase their goals for the year: climbing out of Division 4 of the national league and winning a championship game.

The tale that emerged is an honest, dramatic, sometimes tragic, sometimes comic depiction of what it's really like to be involved at the very grassroots of the GAA.

Larry Cunningham

A Showband Legend

Tom Gilmore

Despite a number of heart attacks, a cancer scare and several attempts at retirement, showband legend Larry Cunningham is still singing in his 70s. His story is a *potpourri* of humour, success, shady deals – as well as sadness, death and murder on the music scene.

Larry Cunningham was the first Irish artist to make the UK Pop Charts – long before U2, the Boomtown Rats, Boyzone or Westlife. His 'Tribute to Jim Reeves' spent over three months in the British hit parade, sold more than a quarter of a million copies and culminated in his appearance on *Top of the Pops* alongside Cliff Richard and others.

When 'Gentleman Jim' Reeves walked off the stage at a dance in Donegal, Larry's singing of Reeves' songs stopped an angry mob from burning the place down. His first No. 1 'Lovely Leitrim' sold over a quarter of a million but the song has sad links to a bloody shooting in a New York bar. The gunfight and deaths, as well as two forgotten song verses, are recalled in this book.

Fascinating reading for those interested in Showbands and Sixties nostalgia, Country 'n' Irish music, the rise and decline of the Ballroom dances and Jimmy Magee GAA All-Stars Football charity.

The Dark Side of Celebrity

Irish Courtroom Scandals of the Rich and Famous
LIAM COLLINS

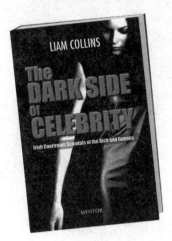

A journey to the other side of fame – telling the story of Ireland's rich and famous fighting each other across the courtroom floor. The stories of the sexual affairs, the alcohol abuse, the dirty tricks and the greed that ruined relationships and tore friendships apart.

- The beauty queen Michelle Rocca's bitter courtroom battle with Ryanair heir Cathal Ryan over a brawl at a socialite's birthday party.
- Solicitor-to-the-stars Elio Malocco and his dodgy dealings – leading to a falling out with Twink, the de Valera familly and the entire Law Society!
- How Manchester United boss Sir Alex Ferguson fell out with his Irish friend John Magnier over the wonder horse Rock of Gibraltar.
- How the sex of Bono's baby became a central issue in a court case that had absolutely nothing to do with him or U2.
- The Illusionist Paul Goldin disappears from a theatre stage and turns up in Hawaii with 'the other woman'.

Irish Family Feuds

Battles over Money, Sex and Power

LIAM COLLINS

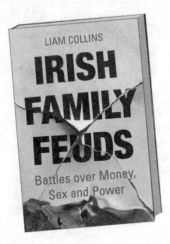

When families fall out, the bitterness that emerges is matched only by the ferocity of their attacks on each other. Family feuds are far more vicious than disputes between strangers, as family members compete to crush each other completely and without mercy.

Cases include many rich and famous Irish families:

- Ben v Margaret – Duel at Dunnes
- The PV Doyle family 'hotel' war
- Comans and the 'Pub brawl'
- Enya, Clannad and the Brennan family feud
- 'Volkswagon vendetta' – the O'Flahertys' family secret

and many more family feuds over money, power and sex.

Irish Crimes of Passion

Killing for Love, Lust and Desire

LIAM COLLINS

Liam Collins investigates the tragic cases where love, lust, desire and jealousy twist and contort in a spiral of madness.

- Picture the beautiful temptress who buys her own grave, then lures her lover to a dramatic death scene in her bedroom . . .
- the husband who goes through his wife's mobile phone messages and unleashes a rage that not only leads to her murder but wipes out an entire family . . .
- or the coward brooding in a love triangle who hires a ruthless killer to murder his pregnant wife.

The are all here in the hidden Ireland, where ordinary men and women suddenly get caught up in that deadly moment when crime and passion collide.

The Great Irish Bank Robbery

The Story of Ireland's White Collar Villainy

LIAM COLLINS

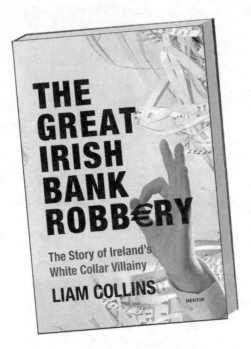

In this mesmerising book, Liam Collins weaves a fascinating tale of the biggest financial scandal ever witnessed in Ireland. Ten years after uncovering the shocking conduct of AIB Bank, Collins explains in clear, concise language the web of deceit involving some of Ireland's most prominent business figures, the banks they ran, the greed of their customers and the negligence of the tax authorities. A fast-paced saga of financial avarice that tainted almost every village and town in Ireland.

TRUE CRIME

BLOODY EVIDENCE
Michael Sheridan

Killers do not have to prove their innocence.

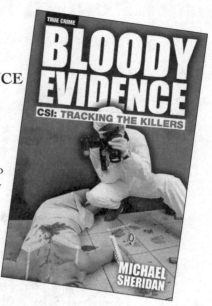

It is the burden of others to prove their guilt beyond any reasonable doubt. Detection, crime-scene investigation and forensic science have evolved hugely as killers become increasingly aware of the need to cover their tracks and destroy evidence.

Murder has become an epidemic in Ireland and the patterns, methods and motives mirror the progress of this disease in other countries. Bestselling author Michael Sheridan illustrates the complex nature of a murder investigation by exploring modern and well-established techniques of detection through a number of cases, such as the horrific Black Dahlia murder in which the victim was cut in half and drained of blood; the bizarre murder of six-year-old JonBenet Ramsey, which ten years on has hit world headlines again; or the savage West of Ireland murder of teenager Siobhán Hynes.

Foot In Mouth

Famous Irish Political Gaffes

SHANE COLEMAN

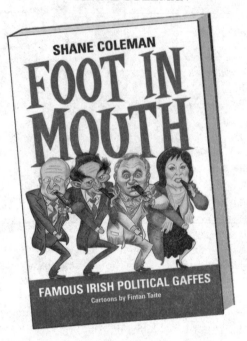

Foot In Mouth – Famous Irish Political Gaffes recounts the gaffes that rocked governments, shocked public opinion and mocked accepted uses of the English language.

Containing over 70 cringe-inducing gaffes, including:

- Pee Flynn's musings on the *Late Late Show* on life on a measly income (how will he pay for that third housekeeper?)
- Jack Lynch's memory loss concerning two British agents
- *That* Fine Gael Ard Fheis
- The PDs' excessive housekeeping (let's dump these sensitive financial records in this skip!)
- De Valera's notorious response to the death of Hitler

. . . and many more.

Up the Poll

Great Irish Election Stories

SHANE COLEMAN

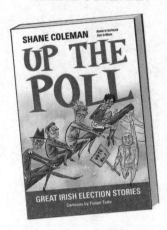

Up The Poll gathers together all the comical, tragic and farcical moments from Irish election campaigns from 1917 to 2007.

- Michael McDowell's shimmy up a poll in 2002, which kick-started the PDs' campaign and landed them in government. Surely the most profitable poll-dance in Irish history?
- The senior Fianna Fáil politician seen assembling a machine gun in a phone booth in Dáil Éireann after the 1932 election.
- The clash of the titans – Charlie v Garret in three RTÉ television debates. Would Garret's hair get any wilder? Would Charlie postpone dinner at Mirabeau's?
- Bertie's run-in with Vincent Browne about spending *his* money how *he* wants. So there.

. . . and many more.

Beyond the Pale

The best of Ireland's local news stories

DONAL HICKEY

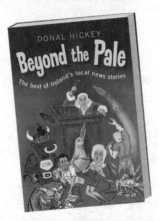

The stories you <u>won't</u> hear on the 6 o'clock news!

We've all read articles in local newspapers that make the mind boggle – the type of story that when repeated to family and friends is greeted with outright disbelief. Stories so outlandish, so strange, so downright weird that you have to re-read them just to check you didn't imagine them in the first place. Well, they're all in Beyond the Pale. A collection of stories from regional newspapers that proves beyond any doubt that the 'characters', the chancers, the rogues, the naïve, the gullible and the just plain insane are still out there causing havoc in all parts of Ireland.

From checking with an undercover cop to see if he'd be on for murdering your wife to the Casanova bull whose passing was mourned by thousands of cows in Ireland to the tongue-tied councillors who were too shy to list how many of them took part in a 'fact-finding' mission to New York for St Patrick's Day – as the fella says – read all about it!